GAMIFICATION TOOLS

for Social and Emotional Learning

Jaime Dombrowski

RESEARCH PRESS
PUBLISHERS

Champaign, Illinois ▪ [800] 519-2707 ▪ www.researchpress.com

RESEARCH PRESS
PUBLISHERS

PDF versions of forms, illustrations, and checklists included
in this book are available for download on the book webpage at
www.researchpress.com/downloads

Copies of this book may be ordered from Research Press at www.researchpress.com.

Composition by Jeff Helgesen
Cover design and illustrations by Matthew Dombrowski
Printed by Martin One Source

ISBN 978-0-87822-730-3
Library of Congress Catalog Number 2020946654

*To Nick, Hazel, and Matt, who inspire me
to do the things I once thought impossible.*

Contents

Acknowledgments

I have been drawn to all aspects of education and mental wellness for as long as I can remember. I started my career providing mental health services at a community mental health agency, but it wasn't long before I felt the pull into the world of education. I had the great honor of starting my educational journey in the public school system as a school counselor at a Title I elementary school.

My principal knew of my love of social and emotional learning. He was a strong principal and played to the strengths of his employees. Knowing that teaching social and emotional skills was a passion of mine, he asked me to provide social and emotional learning lessons to some of the classrooms that had some challenges in this area. I promptly (and excitedly) went home and started researching curricula. I quickly became overwhelmed with all the options available. While there were many wonderful curricula, they either required a lot of preparation or didn't fully meet the needs of all my classes.

I had many other responsibilities that year, and taking the time to prepare for multiple classes and multiple curriculums felt overwhelming. I remember imagining that this is how many teachers must feel when asked to do social and emotional learning lessons. While I knew the value in teaching these skills, had a passion for it, and wanted to do it well, I worried that I would fall short and let down my kids. Through my frustrations and doubts, I started to create my own curriculum that I could easily and effectively implement. While it has evolved over time, the premise has remained the same.

My hope is that by providing easy-to-follow and engaging curriculum, *Power Up* will help educators effectively implement these evidence-based strategies while maybe even having a little fun!

I'd like to thank my husband, Matt, for supporting me throughout the creation of this curriculum and the many late nights I spent putting it together. I would also like to thank him for the fun and engaging icons he lovingly created. I would also like to thank my son, Nicholas, for all the love, laughter, and joy he has brought to my life. Last, I would like to thank my daughter, Hazel, who reminds me daily how wonderful and fulfilling life can be.

Thank you for choosing *Power Up*. I can't wait to see all the wonderful things your class will do!

Sincerely,
Jaime Dombrowski, PhD, LMHC, RPT, CSC, CST

Introduction and Program Overview

Power Up uses game elements to engage and motivate students as they learn vital social and emotional skills. The Power Up board allows students to have fun while learning, and the visually appealing icons represent and reinforce each skill learned. This curriculum is intended for students ages 8 to 11 years but can be used for any students for whom it is developmentally appropriate. *Power Up* addresses all five domains of social and emotional learning (SEL): self-awareness, self-management, social awareness, relationship skills, and responsible decision-making (CASEL, 2018). The curriculum includes five lessons per domain and a total of 30 lessons in all. As students move through the lessons, they will focus on practicing specific skills that support each of the five domains. The goal is for students to demonstrate the skill and earn the icon and "power up." By the end of the curriculum, they will have built strong foundational skills in all five domains of SEL.

The curriculum includes a game board and icons, worksheets, lesson outlines with scripts, sample permission slips and letters to parents and guardians along with tips on implementation. *Power Up* is a flexible curriculum. Instructors have the option of teaching it in daily or weekly lessons, within classrooms or in small groups. Guidance on teaching the program through virtual lessons is also provided. Information on the Small Group program format along with supporting materials appears on page 12.

Background

Many students do not have the social and emotional skills they need to reach their full potential at school or in the home. As a result, we see talented students whose behaviors lead them to receive suspensions, expulsions, and other disciplinary referrals. As these students mature and move through the school system, their behaviors are less and less tolerated. Poor behavior is met with more discipline referrals or, in some cases, legal action. Many believe that by the time students are teenagers, they should know social and emotional skills and appropriate behaviors. The problem is that these students might have never been taught these skills. We are doing a disservice to them by thinking they should know better.

Compounding the difficulties in managing emotions and responsible decision-making for these students is the rapid development teenagers' brains and bodies are experiencing. The brain during adolescence still has up to 10 years to continue to grow. It has not fully developed many of the regions needed to think through and navigate adult situations. The teenage brain is typically focused on rewards, such as social status and pleasure seeking, causing them to take more risks and not think through their actions.

Students who lack social and emotional skills may also experience negative feelings about school. When asked to describe the emotions they felt the most at school, students named "tired," "bored," and "stressed" as their top three, although they wanted to feel "happy," "excited," and "energized" (Brackett, 2016). Because emotions have such an impact on learning, behavior, relationship building, and overall satisfaction levels, it is important that we help students feel positive emotions while at school.

The importance of students' building appropriate social and emotional skills has become widely recognized. Many states either have or are considering making SEL in the classroom mandatory. Through the introduction of SEL curricula, elementary schools are working to provide students with foundational skills that will support their personal and academic success. Learning social and emotional skills helps students create neural networks that help them learn how to cope with adversity, adapt to changes, and utilize critical thinking and problem-solving skills. The earlier we start helping students make these connections, the easier it will be for them.

Research shows that learning and using social and emotional skills have many benefits for students. Durlak et al. (2011) found that SEL programs increase academic performance, decrease behavioral issues, and produce more positive views of self and others for at least 6 months following the intervention. Furthermore, exposure to SEL was also shown to improve academic performance by as much as an 11 percentile academic gain (Durlak et al., 2011). As a separate study found, students who were exposed to SEL in kindergarten showed academic benefits up to 18 years after exposure (Taylor et al., 2017).

Not only can SEL curriculum provide academic, behavioral, and social benefits but it may also be good for the economy. A cost-benefit analysis revealed that on average, every dollar invested in SEL resulted in an $11 return (Belfield et al., 2015). In an analysis collected through multiple studies of randomized populations, students who learned SEL skills were found to be less likely to incur or create economic costs through criminal activity, drug use, unemployment, health care services, or government assistance (Jones et al., 2015). It is important to note that this study recognized that improving SEL skills in at-risk students might enhance SEL outcomes even more than it does in students who are not considered at risk. The findings further highlight the importance of SEL for short-term and long-term outcomes in both the school and community setting.

While very few studies have examined the impact of SEL programs on teachers, there are some indications that teachers who had strong beliefs about SEL and integrated it into their curriculum showed stronger commitment to their teaching and their school (Collie et al., 2011). All in all, SEL has shown benefits for students, teachers, school climate, and the community. Giving students social and emotional tools early in life will help them become caring and responsible students who grow up to become caring and productive adults.

The Five Domains of Social and Emotional Learning

The Power Up curriculum includes lessons on each of the domains of SEL. The following outlines the importance of each of the five domains in the development of SEL skills.

Self-Awareness

Self-awareness focuses on the ability to accurately label emotions, relate feelings to thoughts and behaviors, identify strengths and weaknesses, and demonstrate self-efficacy and optimism (CASEL, 2018).

Mindsets have been found to play a significant role in student success. As defined by Boylan, Barblett, and Knaus (2018), mindsets are "beliefs that people hold about their most basic qualities, such intelligence, talents, and personality" (p.16). Dweck (1999) postulated that there are two types of mindsets: fixed and growth. With a growth mindset, children understand that they can improve upon certain abilities if they put the time and energy into it. With a fixed mindset, students feel that their abilities are set and unchangeable. Part of having a growth mindset is having awareness of individual strengths, weaknesses, and deficits. If students have an understanding of themselves and their abilities, they can work to increase their abilities over time, thus fostering a growth mindset.

The term *emotional intelligence* describes the processes related to recognition, use, understanding, and management of the emotional states of oneself and others (Salovey & Mayer, 1990). Goleman (1995) postulated that emotional intelligence is one of multiple intelligences and estimated that it accounts for up to 80% of success. While there has been conflicting research on whether emotional intelligence impacts academic success, Barchard (2013), Iannucci (2013), and Libbrecht et al. (2014) found a significant relationship between academic success and emotional intelligence. Furthermore, studies by Adeyemo (2007) and Kiss et al. (2014) found a connection between emotional intelligence and grade point average.

Self-awareness can impact the other four domains of SEL. Students who are able to effectively identify their feelings are more likely to have more positive relationships with their peers (the relationship domain) (Han & Johnson, 2012; Denham, 2006). They show an increase in self-concept, which allows them to see the perspective of others (the social awareness domain) (Schulze & Roberts, 2005). They are more likely to demonstrate self-regulation (the self-management domain) (Arguedas et al., 2016). Lastly, they are less likely to engage in conflict with others when working in teams (responsible decision-making domain) (Dierdorff et al., 2019).

Self-Management

Self-management is one's ability to regulate emotions, manage stress, demonstrate self-control, exhibit self-motivation, engage in stress management techniques, and set and achieve specific goals (CASEL, 2018). By having students gain the ability to utilize self-management techniques to regulate emotions, we are giving them the opportunity to learn and grow from obstacles rather than be frustrated by them and met with punitive and disciplinary measures. Students can learn from experience that conflict is a growth opportunity. The term *self-management* will be used interchangeably with the word *self-regulation* throughout this curriculum.

The development of self-regulation skills has been identified as vital to successful adaptation into adolescence (King et al., 2013). Thought to be a feature of temperament; self-regulation is considered to be part of one's biological makeup and capable of being impacted by external influences (Rothbart et al., 2000). Lack of self-regulation can lead to both behavioral and emotional problems (King et al. 2013). Consequently, mastery of self-regulation skills is generally associated with better social functioning (Moffitt et al., 2011). Children who can effectively manage their thoughts, feelings, and actions do better in social and academic environments (Blair & Diamond, 2008; McClelland et al., 2010).

While self-regulation is an important predictor of school success, there are students who are more at risk of having poor self-management skills. Students from disadvantaged ethnic and socioeconomic backgrounds are at higher risk due partly to being exposed to low family income and poverty-related issues (e.g., unhealthy living conditions, poor social support, parenting style) (Evans & Rosenbaum, 2008).

Part of self-management is the ability to motivate oneself. Social determination theory identifies five major kinds of motivations: external, introjected, identified, integrated, and intrinsic (Hardy et al., 2015). These five motivations range from controlled to autonomous. Autonomous motivations are driven by the individual's wants, desires, and interests (Hagger et al., 2014). The behavior is self-determined because the individual has a choice. Due to this personal investment, interest, and choice, the individual is more likely to use self-regulation skills to continue with the behavior without the need for intervention.

On the other hand, controlled motivation occurs when students engage in behaviors for external reasons (Hagger et al., 2014). With controlled motivation, students feel pressure to engage in specific behaviors and generally only do so either to receive a reward or avoid punishment. Since this behavior is not self-motivated, it is likely to stop when the external rewards are removed. Therefore, individuals who are control motivated are less likely to show strong self-regulation skills because they are not as personally invested or motivated.

Social Awareness

Social awareness is one's ability to see multiple sides of an issue, demonstrate empathy, respect diversity, understand social and ethical norms of behavior, and recognize social supports (CASEL, 2018). Social awareness sets the foundation for our interactions with others and the quality of the social connections we will make.

Empathy, considered a fundamental human characteristic, has influence over prosocial and antisocial behavior (Damon et al., 2006). Prosocial behavior is behavior that is positive and beneficial for all involved. Antisocial behavior is disruptive or aggressive toward others. One example of antisocial behavior is bullying. In most studies, empathy and bullying have been found to be inversely related (Walters & Espelage, 2018). Jolliffe and Farrington (2006) found a negative relationship between empathy and offending behaviors (as instances of offending went up, levels of empathy went down). Variables such as socioeconomic status and intelligence were thought to be predictors of empathy levels.

Perspective taking is another aspect of social awareness. Perspective taking is when we try to see a situation from someone else's point of view. The use of perspective taking can promote decision-making that takes others into consideration and weighs the benefit of the outcome for all involved (Galinsky et al., 2008). Perspective taking can also help prevent the formation of negative group stereotypes and lead to more positive evaluations of individual members of a specific group (Galinsky & Moskowitz, 2000; Shih et al., 2009).

Social learning theory postulates that all learning is social and that we learn by watching what is modeled by others (Bandura, 1977). Students look to teachers, adults, and peers to model appropriate social awareness skills. Their behaviors are further reinforced when they receive positive praise or rewards for demonstrating what they have learned. Behaviors also increase when observers see them being reinforced in others, an effect Bandura called "vicarious reinforcement" (1977). Instructors' use of pivotal praise is a good example of this. When teachers want to see a specific behavior in a student, they praise others who are demonstrating that behavior. Students can also reinforce desired behaviors in themselves. With self-reinforcing behaviors, students support behaviors on their own by giving themselves rewards for making progress toward their goals. Students develop personal standards by which to judge if their performance should be rewarded or punished (Bandura, 1977). These concepts inform instructional approaches to social and emotional learning.

Relationship Skills

Relationship skills focus on building diverse relationships with individuals and groups, communicating clearly, working together in a cooperative manner, resolving conflict, and seeking help when needed (CASEL, 2018). This domain revisits the idea that humans are social creatures who seek connections and relationships with others. By having the appropriate relationship skills, students will be able to develop positive relationships and connections with others, thus helping them grow in a positive manner.

The development of peer relationships is considered an important component for positive adaptation (Erdley & Nangle, 2001). Students who are subject to negative peer interactions (rejection, isolation, victimization, bullying) are more likely to experience loneliness, depression, negative self-image, and social difficulties (Hawker & Boulton, 2000). On the other hand, positive peer interactions (social support, acceptance by peers) can promote adaptive development, self-esteem, prosocial behaviors, and a sense of belonging with increased engagement in school (Wentzel, 2009; Liem & Martin, 2011). When students feel accepted by their peers, they do better academically and feel a stronger connection to their school, especially when their peers are academically engaged (Gallardo et al., 2016; Boulton et al., 2011; Newman Kingery et al., 2011; Veronneau & Dishion, 2011; DeRosier & Lloyd, 2011). Adolescents who are accepted by their peers are more likely to appropriately express their emotions (Kim & Cicchetti, 2010).

When talking about peer connections and interactions, it is important to make a distinction between social prominence and social preference. Social prominence is perceived popularity whereas social preference is when peers are actually liked. Hawley et al. (2007) used resource control and social dominance theory to explain that students with aggressive *and* prosocial behaviors can become prominent socially because they use their aggressive and coercive strategies to exert control. Just because someone is socially prominent, it does not mean they are well liked (Hawley et al., 2007). Students who are actually liked (social preference) are more likely to be helpful to peers, cooperative with others, and to utilize social skills (Gifford-Smith & Brownell, 2003). Throughout *Power Up*, students will be exposed to strategies that will help them gain social preference over social prominence through promoting these key prosocial skills.

Responsible Decision-Making

The responsible decision-making domain includes making good decisions based on the well-being of oneself and others, recognizing one's responsibility to behave ethically, making decisions based on safety and social and ethical considerations, being able to evaluate consequences of actions and making safe and constructive choices for oneself and others (CASEL, 2018). Being able to actively think through all the possible solutions helps individuals make the best decision for themselves and others.

After conducting a literature review, Modecki et al. (2017) identified a positive link between emotion regulation and decision-making. In other words, if individuals can't regulate their emotions, they aren't likely to make good decisions. Good decision-making requires the ability to regulate negative emotions because negative emotions can cause us to think and behave in ways that don't promote responsible decision-making.

During adolescence, the brain undergoes both neural and physical changes as it grows. The prefrontal cortex is one of the last brain regions to mature (Casey et al., 2000). Neurodevelopmental models of adolescent behaviors postulate that problem behaviors are a result of the prefrontal cortex not being fully developed (Luciana, 2013). Because their prefrontal cortex is not yet fully developed, adolescents seek out novel situations that can be risky and that require them to make decisions quickly, overloading the still developing prefrontal cortex (Ernst et al., 2006). The prefrontal cortex is at even more risk of being overloaded in adolescents who have poor emotion-regulation skills because the prefrontal cortex is trying to process both social and emotional cues to make decisions (Luciana, 2013). As a result, adolescents who struggle with emotion regulation are less likely to be able to effectively cope with stress, which leads them to make bad decisions.

The polyvagal theory also helps describe how adolescent brain development can impact responsible decision-making. Developed by Stephen Porges, the polyvagal theory focuses on the three different branches of the autonomic nervous system and describes what is happening in the brain when decisions are being made (Porges, 2019). Each branch can trigger a different response to a threat: immobilization, fight or flight, or social engagement (the latter being specific to mammals). In decision-making, these branches can influence young people to either self-regulate, fight, or run away. Since adolescent brains are still developing, it can be difficult for our students to manage the signals being sent by these branches. Student brains might also perceive a nonthreatening situation to be threatening and respond accordingly with a "fight" response.

In the Power Up curriculum, students will learn about the brain and how brain development can impact their ability to make decisions. Students will also be given concrete ways to make decisions and foster the use of their prefrontal cortex. The Power Up curriculum as a whole incorporates aspects of these theories in its lesson design and its game model. The curriculum also draws on Bandura's postulate that learning is a social experience and his focus on the impact of environmental factors on learning and behavior (1977).

His insights also inform the concept of the domains of SEL. Bandura's construct of self-efficacy, defined as "the conviction that one can successfully execute the behavior required to produce the outcomes," (1977, p. 79), also plays an important role in SEL. As students learn more skills and implement them, they become more confident in their abilities to execute the skill and get their desired outcome. The ability to meet goals and expectations, according to Bandura, is heavily influenced by one's level of self-efficacy (Bandura, 1989). For example, Bandura and Wood (1989) found that when students believed strongly in their problem-solving skills, they were more able to effectively work through a problem.

The Power Up curriculum's emphasis on goals and expectations is designed to help students build a sense of self-efficacy and reinforce positive SEL skills. Drawn from information processing theory, the curriculum's use of visuals and acronyms present another way for students to learn and retain the material. The acronyms of CREATE and MAGIC that appear respectively in Lessons 21 and 22 and 25 and 26 help in the development of relationship and decision-making skills.

Gamification of Learning

Power Up utilizes elements of games to enhance student learning. Students practice and master SEL skills by earning icons and advancing across the game board. The board, icons, and controller are visual reminders of the SEL skills taught in each lesson, and they present familiar images from video games. Gamification has been defined as the "use of game attributes ... with the purpose of affecting learning-related behaviors or attitudes" (Landers, 2014, p. 768). Gamification helps motivate and engage students in learning the lesson information, while reinforcing skills such as problem-solving, collaboration, and communication (Dicheva et al., 2015).

Gamification has been described as an approach that can help bridge the generational gap between students and teachers (Kapp, 2007; Oblinger, 2004). According to Apostol et al. (2013), specific elements are key to the effective use of gamification in learning: rules, goals and outcomes, feedback and rewards, problem-solving tasks, a story and player(s), a safe environment, and activities that create a sense of mastery.

Power Up uses rules to govern how students can master skills, earn power bars, and accomplish "powering up." The goal is for students to use each skill at least four times in order to earn the skill icon. By requiring students to use each skill at least four times on four different occasions to "power up," the outcome is that students will learn and practice using each one.

In receiving feedback from their teacher and other adults, students will better master the skill they are practicing and will analyze its effectiveness, while also identifying which skills work best for them. Rewards for icons earned, even if they are, at the very least, the reward of being allowed to color in the icon, gives students a sense of pride, accomplishment, and mastery.

Students also need to use their problem-solving skills throughout the curriculum in order to appropriately implement each skill. To be successful and achieve all of the icons, students will need to navigate and overcome their unique challenges. They will be the player and responsible for telling their own story. *Power Up* should also allow facilitators to create a safe environment where students can practice the skills and receive support, positive reinforcement, and constructive feedback.

While games on their own aren't enough to enhance learning or to allow students to overcome learning difficulties (Apostol et al., 2013), the literature suggests that, when used appropriately, game elements can positively impact motivation, engagement, and performance. These environments have positive impacts in cognitive, social, and emotional areas (Faiella & Ricciardi, 2015). As Perrotta et al. (2013) postulate, game-based learning is intrinsically motivating, fun, authentic, and experiential, and it allows learner autonomy. Through the gamification elements in *Power Up,* students are able to find learning social and emotional skills to be intrinsically rewarding and fun. As discussed previously, when students are intrinsically rewarded, they are more likely to repeat the behavior.

The Power Up Program

The Power Up board includes icons that represent each skill learned. Each student will have his or her own game board. (Students should be given a copy of the game board in Lesson 4.) Each Power Up icon is enclosed in a circle that is divided into four segments, or "power bars." The bars are colored in when the student is observed using each skill. A guide for the skills each icon represents can be found in the Support Materials (Icon Cheat Sheet). Large images of each icon are to be used for display during the lesson. Reproducible 8½ × 11" versions of each icon are included in the download available at the web address listed on the copyright page.

In order to play the game, teachers will throughout the day observe their students to identify when they put the learned skills into action. When the teacher, or administrator, counselor, or school adult sees the student using the skill, that student will get one power bar in the skill icon colored in. When all four power bars are colored in for a specific skill (or when a student has demonstrated using the skill on four separate occasions), the student will have "powered up" and be given the opportunity to color in that icon to show it has been mastered. Students will have all year to practice using the skills in order to "power up." Teachers can opt to offer additional rewards for powering up.

The section Rewards and Tallying Up Power Bars in the manual offers ideas on rewards and ways to record student achievements.

On the right-hand side of the Power Up board is an image of a game controller, which is used to represent emotional states and the control students have over them. The controller is divided into the three "modes" of rewind, home, and fast-forward that describe different feeling states students might experience. Students will be introduced to the controller and learn more about the importance of being able to identify what mode their feelings fall into in Lesson 4.

Curriculum and Lessons

Power Up lessons include an introduction to the skill and an activity with accompanying worksheet. In most cases, it is beneficial for teachers, as an example, to complete the worksheets along with the class as they are teaching the lesson. Teachers will be role modeling the skills and showing that they are just as useful for adults. The lessons use the verbiage of "we" not "you" because it demonstrates unity and that you, the teacher, and the students are in it together.

Each lesson ends with a commitment circle. In this exercise, students stand in a circle and make a commitment related to the lesson. They will have the remainder of the lesson week to complete their commitment. For example, if the lesson is on kindness, students will make a commitment to being kind that week. Having students stand in a circle gives them a chance to face each other and hold each other accountable.

The commitment circle will work differently, depending on whether lessons are held on a weekly or daily basis. With daily lessons, students will make their commitment after the last session of the lesson, likely at the end of the week on a Friday. Because they will have less time before the next lesson begins, their commitment should be smaller in scope (e.g., they might use the learned strategy once that day). In weekly lessons, students' commitments can be bigger in scope because they will have the remainder of the week to practice. (For example, they might commit to using the learned strategy four times in the coming week.) At the beginning of the week following the lesson, teachers should check in with students to see how they did with their commitments.

Lessons in the curriculum include objectives, success criteria, information on materials needed, and sample scripts. Each lesson includes what you can say when introducing activities. As the facilitator, you can use the script or modify it to meet your unique classroom needs and your level of comfort. In addition to sample scripts, lessons also include instructions for teachers. The lessons are broken up into five sessions. It is recommended that you do one session per day (e.g., Session 1 on Monday, Session 2 on Tuesday, etc.), but you can complete the sessions as best fits your classroom's unique needs.

Each lesson includes instructor support materials. After the instruction of each lesson, a letter to parents and guardians should be sent home with the kids to further reinforce the lessons at home All 30 lessons have a sample letter for adaptation at the end of each lesson. General support materials also include an Icon Cheat Sheet and sample tallying sheet for recording students' practice of the skills. Reproducible versions of all instructor support materials are available as part of the download at the web address listed on the copyright page.

Those conducting Power Up for Small Groups will find sample parent/guardian permission slips and lesson summaries for use in communications to school staff. The Small Group Lesson Summary in Appendix D provides brief descriptions of each lesson's purpose and goals.

This is a flexible curriculum! While it is scripted, instructors can alter the script to make it fit their needs. Instructors who aren't comfortable deviating from the script, can also use it word for word!

Additional Materials

Teachers or program facilitators or, in some instances, students will have to provide some Power Up session materials. The following is a list of additional materials used in the curriculum:

- Ring binder, spiral notebook, or folder to serve as the student's workbook for keeping worksheets and papers (one per student)
- Coloring utensils
- Notebook paper
- Optional prizes
- Scissors
- Tape
- 1 piece of poster board (1 per class)
- One basket or bucket (for teacher use in lesson 1 and 15)
- One paper clip (for teacher use in Lesson 8)
- One wooden pencil (for teacher use in Lesson 8)

Implementations of *Power Up*

Daily versus Weekly Lessons

This curriculum is designed so that it can easily be taught in either a weekly or daily format. If taught in daily lessons, instructors should teach one lesson session a day and simply follow the prompts. Daily lessons should take between 10-15 minutes to conduct. If teachers choose to run the program as weekly lessons, they should teach all lesson sessions in one longer once-a-week lesson period. They will use the same curriculum materials and script, but should cover all sessions included in the lesson. Weekly lessons should take between 30-60 minutes. If you are conducting weekly lessons, session 4's lesson is optional.

Small Groups

This curriculum can also be taught as small group lessons. Small group programs focus on one of the five SEL domains: self-awareness, self-management, social awareness, relationship skills, and responsible decision-making. Small group programs can run from 6 to 8 weeks, depending on the group's needs. All small group programs start with Small Group Lesson 1, which can be found in the section Power Up for Small Groups, and then proceed through the five lessons identified for the domain. For example, if you are focusing on self-awareness, you would begin with Small Group Lesson 1 and then proceed through Lessons 4 through 8, the five lessons in the self-awareness domain. Each domain has its own Power Up game board that can be used with the small group. See Power Up for Small Groups to find the game board and more details on how to run small groups.

Virtual Lessons

There are times when a virtual environment might be the necessary or preferred platform on which to teach SEL skills. With this in mind, an adapted version of the curriculum for a virtual setting has been included. The lessons are set up in a manner so that instructors can post the directions into a module, announcement, or assignment or can email them to students. The virtual lessons address the students directly so that instructors don't have to change or modify anything unless directed to. Teachers can also edit the lesson to meet their students' specific needs.

Most of the virtual lessons include a discussion post, some responses to student discussion posts to encourage engagement, and assignments that are to be submitted directly to the teacher. In the first lesson, students will research and learn about digital citizenship. It is important to make sure that instructors hold students to the standards that they set for their classroom (e.g., maintaining an inclusive environment, student confidentiality, and use of appropriate language). As instructors set up their virtual courses, they might want to consider screening the discussion posts before they appear to the group in order to ensure that what the students share is appropriate and not too personal. If teachers read anything concerning, they should always discuss it with the appropriate personnel or follow their state's rules and regulations on reporting abuse.

While the Power Up board and icons will not be used in the virtual lessons, the Power Up controller will be discussed, and some of the virtual lesson activities require support materials. The following student workbook worksheets will need to be made available to students taking virtual lessons:

- Handout 10.1: Power Up Controller
- Handout 10.2: Mandala
- Handout 10.4: Finger Mazes
- Handout 11.2: Progressive Muscle Relaxation
- Handout 12.4: Stretching
- Handout 13.1: Goal Setting
- Handout 17.1: Group Roles
- Handout 17.2: Group Role Assessment
- Handout 19.1: Qualities in a Friend

Most importantly, this should be a fun program in which students can share ideas, and work on building skills together. This promotes engagement and a sense of community.

Preparations

The large icons can be used for display to introduce the skills being covered in the lesson. They will give students a visual reminder of the skills they should be using, and teachers may find it helpful to refer to them throughout the day. Facilitators will need to identify a place in their classroom where they can post the large image of the icons.

They will also need to consider where each student should keep their individual Power Up boards. The boards can remain on student desks, or teachers can find a place to post them in the room. Wherever the boards are placed, teachers should keep in mind that it should be easy for them to color in the Power Up bars. Bars should be colored in each time students demonstrate a skill, or skills can be tracked and recorded on a clipboard worksheet and the bars colored in at the end of the day. (A sample tallying sheet can be found in the Support Materials.)

It is important to use positive reinforcement and praise students when they are caught using the skills. Do not call students out who do not have bars colored in. Shame should not be used as a tool for teaching SEL skills. While students might feel shame for their actions on their own, it shouldn't be fostered by this curriculum.

Each student will be responsible for a keeping a workbook with all the lesson worksheets. Workbooks can be in the form of spiral notebooks, binders, or folders where papers are kept. Notebooks should be private, and only information the student wants to be shared with the class should be divulged.

Instructors can print out the curriculum worksheets and distribute them to students for them to add them to their workbooks. Some Power Up worksheets can be projected so that students can copy the content and write down their responses in their own individual workbooks or on a blank piece of paper to be added to their workbooks. Several lesson worksheets, however, would be difficult for students to copy from a projected image. It is recommended that teachers make copies of the following worksheets for students:

- Handout 1.1: Table of Contents
- Handout 1.3: Things We Have in Common
- Handout 10.2: Mandalas
- Handout 10.3: Finger Mazes
- Handout 12.2: Worry Box Outline
- Handout 12.4: Stretching
- Handout 17.1: Group Roles
- Handout 24.1: The Brain

Tips on Implementation

SEL programs that are implemented well show more positive outcomes than those that are not implemented well (Durlak et al., 2015). Students who were part of well-implemented programs showed academic gains that were twice as high as those among their peers in not well-implemented programs. Not only that, they showed almost twice the reduction in conduct problems and emotional distress. The following can help make your program implementation successful.

Before You Set Up the Program

Carefully review the material. While this is a ready-to-go curriculum, instructors should review the material carefully before teaching it. They can also analyze the worksheets and complete sample worksheets with their class.

Build administrator support. As the instructor, you should talk to your administrators about why you think implementing SEL is critical for your classroom. Let them know what you envision and ask their thoughts. When your administrators are on board with the training, and they usually are, it can help alleviate feelings of concern that you are teaching skills not related to reading or math (although a lot of the worksheets encourage critical thinking and reading skills). Tip: Administrators love data! Show them some of the statistical benefits of SEL if you are worried about gaining their support.

Dedicate a block of time for the program. Time set aside on the master schedule for Power Up lessons helps create consistency and structure to the students' day. Students also feel that the lesson time is important and not an "initiative of the week" that will fall to the wayside. Having dedicated time in the school day for lessons will also help you be consistent in implementing the program and give administrators a clear indication of when you are working on SEL skills.

During the Program

Build relationships. Relationship building is critical for this (or any) curriculum to be as effective as it can be. Identify two to three students each day that you, as instructor, are going to make the commitment to build a relationship with. At some point throughout the day, make an effort to ask them a question to get to know them better. Be sure to give them information about yourself in return (your interests, hobbies, etc). Make sure you have a system to rotate students, so you get to speak to all of the students frequently!

Strive for consistency. Consistency is critical in curriculum implementation. Lessons should be taught consistently and reinforced frequently. This demonstrates to students that learning these skills is a priority and the program isn't going away.

Use positive reinforcement. Giving students consistent praise and positive reinforcement when they use the skills (or at least try to use the skills) is very important. Just recognizing that the student is trying and giving them praise for their efforts can make a world of difference. Who doesn't like to be recognized for doing a good job?

Avoid telling students their responses are incorrect when they are brave enough to participate. Instead, redirect them to the correct answer by asking open-ended questions or thanking them for their response.

Follow up. It is imperative that you follow up with the students after the lesson. If you don't reinforce the skills that the students are learning, then they are less likely to demonstrate them. The skills are taught when students are calm and ready to learn but reinforced when students are in the thick of needing to use them (e.g., when they are fighting or making poor decisions etc.). Help students practice these skills when they are calm *and* when they are activated. These are learned skills. Just like any other skill, they require practice and hard work to grow and flourish.

Involve parents and guardians. Once you have your administrators and your class on board with SEL, having the parents' buy-in is important. If parents reinforce the behaviors at home, then it increases the amount of real-world experience and skill practice the students are getting. The more they use the skills at home, the more likely they are to use them in other settings.

Reflect on your work as instructor. Consistently reflecting on the progress your class is making is important and how you might adjust program implementation. There is always room for improvement. Consider what ways you can help your students be even more successful in this program. Pick one goal at a time. Think about what piece of implementation is most important to you and focus on that. Once you've reached that goal, you can move onto another. For example, you might decide to focus on getting the letters out to parents more consistently, or you might decide to dedicate more time to tallying up the students' use of the skills.

Use self-care. Implementing something new always comes with its challenges and its insecurities. You might doubt if you are making a difference or doing it right. Take a deep breath. Remind yourself what you *have* done and the progress your students *have* made. Be compassionate toward yourself. Take some time for yourself as well. It's important to not only model self-care but to also practice it to the degree that you have the energy and drive to dedicate to yourself and your classroom.

Rewards and Tallying of Power Up Bars

You will need to make sure you are consistent in observing and recording when students use skills so that they can get rewarded and have their power bars colored in. Skill practice should be positively reinforced with consistent recording of earned power bars and icons so that students can feel a sense of satisfaction and accomplishment. Without this consistent practice, students will not fully commit to using the skills.

It might be helpful to carry a clipboard and checklist with you to help record the students' names and skills they practiced. As you see the skills being used, you can write down the skill and color in the power bars at the end of the day. The program includes a sample tallying sheet. (See the curriculum Support Materials.)

Rewards for mastery of SEL skills do not have to be monetary in value. Examples of rewards include:

- Extra time at recess
- A special job in the class
- Treasure box
- Lunch Bunch group
- Getting to help in another class
- Lunch with an adult of choice
- Time to color
- Homework pass
- Extra credit on a test

Instructors might want to incorporate rewards that the student can earn for the entire class. This creates cohesion and camaraderie among students. For example, after a student earns four different icons to color in, the entire class might earn extra time at recess. You could also give rewards in stages. For example, one icon could get the student a homework pass. Four icons could earn the student lunch with the teacher. Six might give the entire class extra time at recess. If you are going to offer rewards, you should have them posted in a visible place in class so students can see what they are working toward.

Be creative and have fun! You can always ask the students what they would like their rewards to be as well. They might surprise you with their responses!

Further Thoughts

Sensitive Topics and Phrases

Sometimes students will share something personal that makes you (and possibly the other students) uncomfortable. It is important to thank them for sharing and move on from the discussion. Do not embarrass the student or tell them they over-shared in front of their peers. After the incident, it is important to check in with the student as soon as possible. If you are concerned for the student's safety or the safety of someone else, it must be addressed *immediately*. Some students might not understand that what they shared is alarming or worrisome. You should approach them with an open and interested attitude and be careful not to make judgments about what was shared.

If the student is aware that they are sharing something sensitive in a group discussion or in front of peers, you can say things like, "Thank you for sharing. That sounds like a difficult situation," or "Thank you for bravery in sharing that information." If the student does not appear to be aware that what they are sharing is sensitive (e.g., stories about abuse or trauma), you can simply thank them for sharing. When you are one-on-one with the student, and trying to gain insight into what they shared, you can ask things like, "What you shared sounded like it was really upsetting for you. Have you talked to (insert school counselor name) before? She's really nice and has helped other students with similar things." or "Can you tell me more about what you shared this morning?"

As with any sensitive topic, if you feel uncomfortable about the issue, you should get the school counselor or administrators involved. Follow your school's policies and procedures. Depending on your relationships with the student or the intensity of the information shared, you can involve others after the information is shared or after you have gathered more information on your own. You know your comfort levels best. Don't be afraid to ask for help.

Culture and Climate

Students have a right to feel safe on their school campus both physically and emotionally. By building strong SEL skills and a classroom environment of support and authenticity, students can feel safe exploring their environment and experimenting with using the learned skills. Students should feel safe enough to be curious, learn from their mistakes, increase grit, seize growth opportunities, and ask for help when they need it.

Taking time to develop meaningful relationships with students is a critical component to SEL. When teachers take the time to build strong relationships, students want to work harder because they know that their teacher cares about them (Wentel, 1997). In studies on the impact of classroom relationships, students reported that the teachers they found most impactful were those who put time and effort into building a relationship with them (Newberry, 2010). Not only were students willing to put in more work but they also were more willing to accept rules and consequences (Marzano et al., 2003). Students who perceive school personnel as "unfriendly, unfair, and unsupportive," reported that they were less likely to comply with school rules (Gendron et al., 2011).

Students and teachers should dedicate time to get to know one another. Students should know that their teacher is a person with strengths, weaknesses, interests, and family and friends they care about. Teachers should also take the time to get to know their students. They should find out what motivates their students and what their interests are, and they should learn about their students' backgrounds and culture. Teachers should have authentic interactions with students and give them voice by listening to them (Elliot-Johns et al., 2012). When teachers and students take the time to build relationships, they humanize one another (Cammorta & Romero, 2006).

The following actions are some simple ways you, the teacher, can build a positive classroom environment by getting to know your students:

- Ask students questions about them
- Reinforce positive behaviors
- Model SEL skills
- Promote peer connections and interactions
- Give lots of praise
- Demonstrate patience

Implicit Bias

The Power Up program asks students to consider stereotyping and discriminatory behavior, both as something they may have experienced or acted upon. As we ask students to consider and assess this, we also ask teachers to reflect on implicit biases they might hold. Implicit bias refers to the stereotypes and attitudes that we unconsciously hold (Sarine, 2012). It can refer to bias or stereotypes formed on the basis of race, gender, age or other traits. Oftentimes one's unconscious biases do not align with one's values and attitudes (Gullo et al., 2019).

Implicit bias is more likely to impact us when we are stressed and overloaded, because at these times, we start to rely on our automatic responses and behaviors (Gullo et al., 2019). Implicit bias can impact our actions, perceptions, and decisions. Interestingly, our behaviors tend to be more influenced by implicit bias when we feel that our self-image is being threatened by negative feedback (Wilder & Shapiro, 1989). For example, one study (Sinclair & Kunda, 1999) found that people showed higher levels of race stereotyping when they got negative feedback from a Black professional.

While everyone has implicit bias, there are ways to manage it to ensure that our behaviors and decisions align with our values and attitudes. One way to address implicit bias is by improving our decision-making supports to make sure that we are in the best place possible to think through the decisions we are making (Gullo et al., 2019). When we are stressed, overloaded, or overworked, we are less likely to make clear decisions and more likely to be impacted by implicit bias. Other measures that help manage implicit bias and decrease cognitive load include using self-management techniques (e.g., talk to someone, go for a walk, take a break), making connections with diverse groups of people, practicing mindfulness, and using the technique of replacing negative stereotypes with positive messages (Gullo et al., 2019).

While implicit bias is unconscious and unintentional, it is important for us to be aware that it exists for everyone. As we become more aware of the biases we hold, we are able to start countering them. By following these strategies, we can help ensure that we aren't unintentionally hurting others through our decisions and behaviors.

Introductory Lessons

Icebreaker

This lesson aims to create the foundation for a strong classroom community. Students will work with their peers to find things they have in common with each other.

Introduction

Icebreakers are a popular way to build a sense of community and are used in many settings. Miller et al. (2017) found that students who participated a relationship-building program had more positive relationships with their peers, enjoyed school more, had fewer behavioral issues, and achieved a better academic performance. Starting the curriculum off with an icebreaker activity will allow students the chance to get to know another, increase feelings of connectedness, and set a positive tone for the class. This activity will also allow the students the opportunity to get to know you better and start the process of building trust and rapport that you will be building on throughout the year.

Objectives

Students will be able to

- find at least one thing they have in common with at least four peers
- identify the purpose of the program

Success Criteria

Students are able to

- identify one new thing about at least four of their peers
- understand why it is important for them to get to know their peers
- feel comfortable learning more information about their peers on their own
- understand the purpose of the group

Materials

- One copy of the Numbers worksheet for the teacher and a container to hold collected numbers cut out from the worksheet
- One copy per student of the Things We Have in Common worksheet
- One copy per student of the Table of Contents
- Optional prize
- Workbook folder or binder, one per student

Things to Note

Students might be hesitant or shy about initiating conversation with other students. Take note of the student dynamics as participants move through the classroom to complete the icebreaker activity. Which students are engaged and eager to make connections with others? Which students hold back? Encourage students who appear nervous to approach their peers. You might need to walk them up to someone and start the conversation in order to support them (e.g., "Jane, let's look at John's list. Which of these is of interest to you?")

Session 1.1: Icebreaker and Introduction to *Power Up*

You will start the lesson with an icebreaker activity and brief introduction to the Power Up curriculum. Students will also learn about the five domains of social and emotional learning and will be given a brief overview of each domain. You can use the following script as a sample, or alter as needed:

> *Throughout the year, we are going to be participating in a program called Power Up. This program focuses on building up our social and emotional skills. Social and emotional skills are helpful for everyone—adults and kids! These skills help us become more successful in school and can even help us outside of school. Adults use social and emotional skills all the time.*
>
> *These skills fall into the five domains of social and emotional learning. The first domain is **self-awareness.** Self-awareness is when we are able to tell what we are feeling. We also have insight into who we are. For example, I know my strengths and weaknesses, my morals and my values. We are going to gain insight into our feelings and ourselves. The second domain is **self-management.** Self-management is when we are able to manage our big emotions. We are able to demonstrate impulse control and utilize skills to keep ourselves calm so we are able to make good decisions. We are also able to set and manage goals that are important to us. We are going to learn*

how we can control our emotions when they feel out of control and learn how to set and achieve goals.

*The third domain is **social awareness.** Social awareness is when we are able to think about others' thoughts and feelings. We might be able to see a problem from their point of view, or we might demonstrate empathy. We are going to learn how we can demonstrate empathy and kindness to others. Social awareness also addresses diversity and inclusion. We will talk about how we can learn from our differences and ensure that we are including everyone. The fourth domain is **relationship skills.** We use relationship skills to not only make new friends but also to maintain friends that we already have. Relationship skills also help us start and maintain conversations and to work in group settings. We are going to learn relationship skills so that we can put ourselves in a good position to have positive interactions with others.*

*The last domain is responsible **decision-making**. Responsible decision-making skills help us make decisions that are best for ourselves and others. We will learn how we can think through our options, weigh the pros and cons of possible outcomes, and make the best decision for ourselves while also considering others. Learning skills in the five domains of social and emotional learning will help you now, and prepare you for middle school, high school, college, and the workforce.*

Introduce Power Up Workbook and Table of Contents

Teachers should make sure that students have their workbooks and understand how they will be used. The workbook will hold the worksheets that show the skills they are learning. In this first session, you will introduce the Student Workbook Table of Contents. Students will keep the table of contents in their folders and use it as a guide. Sample script:

Throughout our lessons, we are going to keep a workbook where we can store all of the worksheets and skills we will be completing. I'm going to pass out a table of contents for you to keep in your workbook. The table of contents will help you locate specific worksheets as you need them. It should be the first two pages of your workbook.

Lesson Activity: Things We Have in Common

Explain the purpose of the activity before starting the icebreaker activity in which students learn more about one another. You could introduce the activity as follows:

Before we dive into learning all of these skills, we are going to take some time to learn about each other and the things we have in common. Since we will be spending so much time together, it will be important for us to get to know each other. It can be both wonderful and challenging to see the same people every day. Getting to know a little bit about each other will help us build a positive classroom community.

Using the Things We Have in Common Worksheet

Students should use the Things We Have in Common worksheet when meeting their classmates and identifying what they have in common. They should talk to as many people and identify as many interests as possible, but they should use one person's name no more than twice on the worksheet.

Each student will use the worksheet and add it to their workbook after the lesson. Worksheets can also be projected, and students can copy down the listed interests on a blank piece of paper in or to be added to their workbook. To explain the activity, teachers could say the following:

We are going to do an activity where you use the Things We Have in Common worksheet to learn about your classmates' interests and see what you have in common. Your goal is to find someone who is interested in each item listed. When you find someone, write that person's name next to that item. Talk to as many people as possible, filling in as many blanks as possible. You can only use one person for up to two interests, so you should not have the same name listed more than twice.

Give students a set amount of time to work on this activity. Walk around the room as students talk and make sure they are on task. Try to discourage them from copying answers down from peers' worksheets. Reiterate that it is important that they get to know each other on their own, instead of trying to find out about others through copying responses.

After students are done, they can add this worksheet to their workbooks. As the table of contents indicates, the Things We Have in Common worksheet should be placed immediately after the table of contents. It will be page three of the workbook. As students add worksheets to their workbooks, they can use this table of contents as a guide throughout the year.

Session 1.2: Things We Have in Common Worksheet Review

This session will focus on having students review what they discovered about their classmates. Using the worksheet, you should read aloud each interest item and have the students stand for each thing they are interested in. You could explain the activity as follows:

We are going to read through the Things We Have in Common worksheet as a class. When I read the interest, if it is something that interests you, please stand. You can stand more than once, so please stand up for anything that interests you. As we do this, I want you to pay attention to who else is standing for the things that interest you. This is someone you have something in common with and could talk to later about your common interest(s).

Summarize the Activity

Encourage students to think about who had similar interests as them. Students might be pleasantly surprised to find they have more in common with their peers than they originally thought. Sample script:

I want you to think about who stood up and had the same interest you had. I bet you were surprised to find that you have something in common with almost everyone in our class! Being able to talk about what you have in common is a good way to start a conversation with someone new!

Session 1.3: Icebreakers with Teams

You can prepare for this session by cutting out each number on the Numbers worksheet, or you can have a student cut out the numbers out while you prepare the class to start the lesson. In this activity, each student will pick a number and find another classmate who shares the same number. Using the Things We Have in Common worksheet, the paired students will try to identify as many shared interests as they can. They will have five minutes to complete the activity.

Introduce the Activity

Place the cut-out numbers in a hat, cup, bucket, or other container. Have each student pick a number and find a partner with the same number. You can explain the activity as follows:

I'm going to give you some time in class to find some things you have in common with a classmate. Each of these slips of paper has a number on it, and I want you to pick one. You will be matched with the person that has that same number as you. For example, both students who have the number one will be partners.

After each student picks their number and pairs up with a student with a matching number, let them know that they will have five minutes to see how many things they have in common with their partner. Have the paired students write down each thing they find in common on the bottom of their Things We Have in Common worksheet. The team that identifies the most interests in common wins. At the end of the five minutes, see which team comes up with the most. As an option, you can award the winners a prize.

Review the Activity

After students have completed the activity, you will wrap up with an overview of the purpose of the activity. Students should come to realize that they have a lot of things in common with their peers that they might not know about. This should open up a discussion about how we have a lot of things in common, but differences are good too because they allow us to learn from each other. Sample script:

> While we have talked a lot about finding out things we have in common with other people, it is important to remember that while commonalities might bring us together, our differences also enhance the relationships we have with those around us. We learn new things from others when we have differences, and we are able to appreciate the differences of others.

Session 1.4: Icebreakers with Teams, Part II

Have each student pair with a new partner and repeat Session 3's activity.

Session 1.5: The Commitment Circle

Each lesson will conclude with a commitment circle as a way to wrap up the lesson. The commitment circle gives students a chance to think about what they have learned in the lesson and to pick a follow-up activity that will help them practice their new skill. Commitments should follow the prompt offered by the teacher and be related to the lesson topic. Students will have the rest of the week to practice and apply their learned skill. Instructors should check in with students on their progress and address barriers to using the skill or meeting their commitment.

To introduce the commitment circle, have students stand and form a circle. Facilitators can explain the activity by asking students what the word *commitment* means to them: "We are going to do our first commitment circle today. Who can tell me what a commitment is?"

After students respond, you can explain that a commitment is a promise or obligation. If we commit to something, we are saying that we will do it. Let students know that at the end of the week's lessons, they will get to choose how they will practice the skill. You will provide a prompt, or question, that they will use to create their commitment. Commitments should be specific and something the student can carry out in the allotted time (the rest of the week). You might use the following script to introduce commitment circles:

A commitment is an obligation or promise that we will do what we say we are going to do. As we learn about and practice the skills in each lesson, we will end with a commitment circle. At each commitment circle, I will ask a question for you to answer. The question will be about what we've learned, and your answer will be your commitment for the coming week. I want you to think about everything you have learned when you respond. Be realistic about your commitments. Think about how much time you have left in the week and how much you can reasonably accomplish. For example, today our prompt is going to be, "How many other people are you going to find out new things about?" For example, for your commitment, you might say, "I'm going to try to get to know two new things about at least two other people this week." We will check in during next week's lesson on our progress with our commitments.

Moving from student to student around the circle, have students share how many other peers or adults they plan to find out new things about. Encourage them to use the students' names. Note any students who aren't called on and encourage others to connect with them throughout the week.

Reinforcing the Lesson

Throughout the week, encourage students to have conversations with each other about things they have in common. Try to set aside some time for students to be able to talk to each other about their shared interests. While it is difficult to find time for this, the relationships that are built as a result will help build a positive classroom community and save you a lot of time and energy later.

You can also take time this week to talk to students about things you have in common with them. This helps students feel comfortable talking to adults while also giving you a chance to build a relationship with them. Many students find they are surprised to have something in common with an adult.

Sample Letter to Parents and Guardians—Lesson 1

Dear Parent/Guardian,

[Introduce self and Power Up group or classroom.] In this lesson our class was introduced to the social and emotional learning curriculum *Power Up*. We will be using this curriculum throughout the year to learn social and emotional skills in the five domains of social and emotional learning: self-awareness, self-management, social awareness, relationship skills, and responsible decision-making. After each lesson, you will receive a short letter with a summary of what we learned as class.

This week we focused on building a classroom community and making positive connections with our peers. In a shared interests activity, we learned the many things we have in common with our peers. It is important for us to learn new things about our peers so we can work toward building a positive classroom environment.

You can ask your child the following questions about the lesson:

- What did most of your class have in common?
- What were you surprised to find you had in common with someone else?
- Why is it important to know that you have things in common with others?

Regards,

Student Workbook Table of Contents

Numbers Worksheet

1	1	2	2
3	3	4	4
5	5	6	6
7	7	8	8
9	9	10	10
11	11	12	12
13	13	14	14
15	15	16	16

Things We Have in Common

Item	Name	Item	Name
I have a pet.		I like history.	
I liked to read.		I like to play outside.	
I like math.		I like to draw.	
I like science.		I like to paint.	
I like to dance.		I like to tell jokes.	
I like to sing.		I like to hear jokes.	
I like to play sports.		I like P.E.	
I like to run.		I like lunch.	
I like to watch movies.		I like to swim.	
I like animals.		I like ice cream.	
I like pizza.		I like making new friends.	
I like candy.		I like to jump rope.	
I like to play board games.		I like to run.	
I like to play video games.		I like football.	
I like to stay up late.		I like to listen to music.	
I like to get up early.		I like funny movies.	
I like to play cards.		I like to sleep in.	
I like computer games.		I like art.	

Getting To Know Me

In this lesson, students will create a character that is representative of them. Their strengths and weaknesses will be conveyed through their character, giving them and the class insight into who they are.

Introduction

See the Lesson 1 for more information on icebreakers and the importance of students getting to know one another and building strong relationships with peers and teachers.

Objectives

Students will be able to

- identify at least two of their strengths.
- identify at least two of their weaknesses

Success Criteria

Students are able to

- identify their strengths and weaknesses
- understand the importance of knowing what their strengths and weaknesses are
- feel comfortable building on their weaknesses

Materials

Preferred coloring utensils

Things to Note

When completing a sample character for the lesson activity, be sure that students know to include one or two weaknesses that represent their own weaknesses. For instance, to provide an example, you could say that you struggle to be on time or you struggle with math and so your character does too. Do not dwell on the negative aspects when you present your character to the class. The idea is to acknowledge that everyone has weaknesses without letting them define the character. Take note of students who only present the weaknesses of their character or who seem stuck on the negative aspects of themselves. Use your judgment as to whether you or the school counselor should conduct a follow-up conversation with the student.

If students do present a mostly negative view of their character, this might be a reflection of how they view themselves. Throughout the week, be sure to point out things they are good at while they are doing them. This will call attention to their strengths and hopefully give them a self-esteem boost!

Session 2.1: Introduction and Creating a Character

Check in on the students' commitments from the last lesson. Ask the class who would like to volunteer to share how they did in getting to know others last week. Allow students a chance to share how they did on their commitments. If you find that the same students respond each week, encourage new students to participate. If you have some students who never speak up, try to check in with them individually. You can say, "Let's do a check in. Who would like to volunteer to share how they did with their commitment in getting to know their classmates better?"

Introduce the Lesson Activity

In this lesson, students will create a game character representation of themselves in a drawing. Students can draw this character on the cover of their workbooks or they can draw it on a piece of paper that they attach to the cover. If students prefer to create a character in writing, they can do so. Once students have created their character, they will share it with the class. To begin the activity, teachers can say,

> *Since we spent the first lesson learning a little bit about our classmates, we are going to spend the second lesson creating representations of ourselves so our peers can get to know us even more. Get out your workbook and keep it closed. On the cover, I want you to create a character that best represents you. You can draw this right on the cover or you can draw it on a blank piece of paper and attach it to the cover. We will be using game boards later in this program to support our learning, so if it is helpful, you can think of your character as a video or board game character. Just remember to make sure it represents you! If you feel more comfortable with writing, you can write down your character's traits. I want you to include the strengths and weaknesses of the character. As you grow and change and learn new skills, your character might*

too. You can update your character as often as you would like throughout the year. We will be presenting this character to the class.

Give students some time to work on the creation of their character. If you haven't already, create your own character while students work.

Session 2.2: Creating a Character

Allow students time to continue to work on their characters. Remind students to include the character's strengths and weaknesses.

Session 2.3: Sharing the Character with the Class

In this activity, you will ask students to tell the class about the character they created. Remind students that learning about the characters is a way for them to learn about each other. To begin the activity, teachers can model the activity by going first and describing the character they created. You can use the following script as an introduction:

Since we have worked so hard on our characters, we are going to share them with the class. This is a great way for us to continue learning about each other. You do not have to share everything about your character, only the things you want others to know about them. Remember if you don't want to share the picture you can just verbally tell us your characters traits. I will go first. [Present your character.]

Have students present their characters to the class. If needed, you can give them a specific amount of time to describe their character. If a student is hesitant to present, you can have them describe it to you at another time. If you are conducting daily lessons, split the presentations up between Sessions 3 and 4.

Session 2.4: Sharing the Character with the Class, Cont.

Have students continue to present their characters until all students who want to speak have had a chance.

Session 2.5: The Commitment Circle

Have students gather in a circle and remind them that this is the time to make their commitment to practice the lesson activities on their own. Introduce the prompt:

Today, we are going to create our second commitment circle. The prompt is, "Who are you going to talk to in more detail about your character?" For example, I'm going to tell my sister about my character and see if she has any ideas for her that I didn't think about.

Go around the circle and have students make their commitments. Encourage them to make these commitments for both the home and school setting so they can see how these skills translate to the home setting.

Reinforcing the Lesson

Throughout the week, check in with students to see if they have talked to their identified person about their character. If students have already spoken to their person, encourage them to talk to other peers in the classroom about their character.

Sample Letter to Parents and Guardians—Lesson 2

Dear Parent/Guardian,

In this lesson our class continued to focus on building a positive classroom community. Students created a character that is representative of them. This character might evolve and change over the year, as the students evolve and change. Students focused on identifying their character's strengths and weaknesses and then presented the character to the class.

Creating and sharing these characters is a way for us to learn more about one another. It is important for us to learn new things about our classmates so we can work toward building a positive classroom environment.

You can ask your child the following questions about the lesson:

- What did your character look like?
- What were your character's strengths?
- What were your character's weaknesses?
- What other characters in your class had the same strengths as yours?
- What other characters in your class had the same weaknesses as yours?

Regards,

Getting to Know You

Students will learn what stereotyping and discrimination is in this lesson. They will learn the harm that stereotyping and discrimination can cause, and they will combat it in the classroom by including classmates in activities and by treating each other equally. Students will also create a class pledge to treat each other with respect.

Introduction

Bias is part of everyday life, and it is important that students, teachers, and staff make the effort to be aware of their own attitudes and behaviors toward others so that they don't unintentionally cause harm. Implicit bias, or the stereotypes and attitudes we unconsciously hold, can impact our behaviors and the decisions we make in ways we aren't always aware of.

One way that we can see the impact of bias, whether implicit or explicit, is in the disparities in the enforcement of disciplinary measures across ethnic and demographic groupings. Students of color experience higher levels of suspension or expulsion rates than do their white peers (Fabelo et al., 2011). Students in special education and lesbian, gay, bisexual, and transgender students are also at a higher risk of receiving discipline referrals and out-of-school suspensions than are their nondisabled and heterosexual peers (Losen & Gillespie, 2012; Himmelstein & Bruckner, 2011; Poteat et al., 2015).

In the school setting, it is most often the case that disparate treatment does not happen consciously or intentionally. Nevertheless, it is important for all of us to be aware of these disparities and our own attitudes and behaviors so that we can move towards ensuring that all students have an equal opportunity for success. It is also important for us to understand implicit biases so that we can work towards overcoming our own. For more information on implicit bias, including strategies to overcome it, see the section Further Thoughts.

Objectives

Students will be able to

- define stereotyping and discrimination

- give two examples of how stereotyping and discrimination are harmful
- identify at least one way they can combat discrimination
- create a community pledge that describes how students will show respect to one another

Success Criteria

Students are able to

- identify the negative impact stereotyping and discrimination can have on an individual
- understand the importance of inclusive thinking
- feel comfortable practicing inclusion and equality

Materials

- One piece of poster board paper per class
- One blank piece of paper per student (optional lesson)

Things to Note

This can be a difficult topic to discuss with students. Giving students voice is important while also keeping the conversation appropriate. Encourage students to check in with you or the school counselor if something comes up during discussion that they would like to talk about further. If you notice something concerning about a student (ex., they are uncomfortable while discussing stereotypes or make insensitive comments), you should follow your school procedures about making referrals to the counselor. Encourage students to report instances of stereotyping, discrimination, and racism to trusted adults.

Session 3.1: Learning about Stereotyping

Before the lesson, check in with students about the commitment they made last week. Ask, "Who would like to volunteer to share how they did talking to others about the character they created?" Allow students a chance to share how they did on their commitments. If you find that the same students speak each week encourage new students to contribute. If you have some students who never share, try to check in with them individually.

Discuss What It Means to Place Things or People into Categories

Begin the lesson on stereotypes with a discussion on what it means to categorize things. It is best to begin with a familiar example, like food groups, to help students understand. You can use the script below for the discussion:

What does it mean to categorize things? [Allow time for responses.] When we group similar things together we are placing them in categories. We often can categorize many different things. For example, we can place food into categories, such as vegetables, meat, dairy, and fruits. What foods might fall into each of these categories?

Have students name foods in each category (vegetables, meat, dairy, and fruits). For example, vegetables might be spinach, kale, cabbage, etc. Once you are done, look at the list and find foods that might fit into two different categories. For example, fried rice might be grains and vegetables because it has both items. Pizza might be grains, dairy, and meat. Ask students which *one* category these items belong in. Students should come to the conclusion that you can't categorize them into *one* category. You can say,

Sometimes there are things that don't fit nicely into one specific category. For example, pizza can have dairy, grains, meat, and vegetables. This is one of the barriers of trying to categorize items. What other things can you think of that might be categorized?

Have a discussion regarding other things that might be categorized. Examples might include: clothes, animals, transportation, people etc.

Define Stereotyping

Use the discussion of categories and categorizing to introduce the concept of stereotyping. Start by asking students what problems they can think of when trying to categorize things. Once students have identified problems, expand on the problems with a discussion of stereotyping. You can say,

Creating categories isn't a bad thing, but the items we put in a category might not tell us everything we need to know about that item. This is especially true when we try to categorize people. People don't fit into nice little boxes. When we try to put someone in a category we lose important information about who they are and what they like.

When we categorize a person, we are saying that the person can be understood by their grouping. We are saying that the person will act and think and be like what we think is true of the group. We call these kinds of categories stereotypes. Stereotypes are widely accepted and fixed beliefs about a group of people. Stereotypes can be based on your gender, skin color, culture, and many other factors.

When we try to categorize and stereotype people, we fall into the trap of seeing them for what we think they should

be—not who they actually are. We can miss out on some great opportunities to get to know people when we stereotype them. We also make people feel unimportant because we didn't even take the time to get to know them.

Everyone is unique and special, and when people try to box you into a category it can make you feel angry and alone. We wouldn't like to be put into a box, so we shouldn't do it to others.

Session 3.2: Focusing on Inclusion

This session will continue to focus on creating a classroom of inclusivity where every student is welcomed, included, and accepted. Students will learn about discrimination and the dangers discrimination poses.

Begin the discussion by asking students if they know what the word *discrimination* means. Ask them, "What is discrimination?" After students respond, define discrimination and explain why it's a problem. You can say,

Discrimination is the unfair treatment of someone based on the color of their skin, their gender, their age, their family background or culture. Discrimination is dangerous because it assumes that one group of people is better than another. Discrimination can lead to arguments, anger, frustration, and people being left out based on some part of who they are. In this classroom, we will include everyone and treat everyone equally. We will practice inclusion and equality. Inclusion is when we make sure that everyone is involved, and no one is left out. Remember, everyone belongs in our classroom community.

Have Class Discuss How to Help Everyone in the Class Feel Included

To begin the discussion, you can ask the students what it feels like to be excluded: "Raise your hand if you have ever been left out before. [Pause for responses.] How did it feel? We would not want to make someone feel that way. What are some ways that we, as a class, can make sure that everyone feels like they are included?"

Brainstorm some concrete steps your class can take to make sure everyone feels included. Some examples include making sure everyone has someone to play with at recess, making sure everyone has someone to sit with at lunch, etc. End the discussion by placing the focus on treating people fairly and equally. You can say, "When we are interacting with others, we should remember that we are all equal. We all matter, and we are all important."

Session 3.3: Creating a Class Pledge

In this session, students will create a class pledge to be inclusive and treat class members fairly and equally. The pledge should present a plan on how to be inclusive and what behaviors are expected from all students. Write student ideas on a poster board for them to sign in agreement at the end of the lesson. Sample script for the discussion:

> *We are going to make a pledge for our class. Our pledge will explain how we will treat others so that everyone in class feels included and is treated equally.* [On your poster board write, "In this class we…"] *What would you like to include in our pledge? For example, we could say we treat everyone with respect.*

Allow students a chance to come up with ideas for the pledge. It should directly address how they plan to make sure everyone feels included and is treated equally. Write their ideas on the poster board and give praise for the students' ideas and commitment to inclusivity.

Items written down on the pledge should be framed in a positive rather than negative manner. For example, instead of saying, "No leaving anyone out at lunch," you could say, "Make sure everyone has someone to sit with at lunch." Be prepared to reframe some of the ideas suggested or make a new (related) suggestion. It is important all students have a voice in the activity. If the student makes a well-meaning suggestion that isn't appropriate or is misguided, thank them for their idea and change the wording to be more appropriate. If the idea warrants it, you can have an individual conversation with that student later to let them know why you altered their idea. Be careful to approach it with positivity and unconditional positive regard rather than from a corrective and punitive place. If students purposely suggest something inappropriate, a follow-up conversation is also needed. You can ask questions like "What made you think of this suggestion? How would you feel if this was done to you? Do you think this is an appropriate suggestion? Why do you think I left this out? What would a better suggestion be?"

Once you have compiled the students' ideas and written them on the poster board, ask them to sign the pledge: "Now that we have created our pledge, I would like for everyone to sign it. By signing it you are committing to upholding our pledge and taking it seriously."

Have students each sign the pledge. Refer to the pledge as needed throughout the year.

Session 3.4: Writing a Journal Entry about Experiences of Stereotyping

Ask students to write a journal entry about their experiences with stereotyping. Students will not be sharing what they write with the class. Let students know this and let them know that they will be writing their journal entry on a separate piece of paper so that others can't read it unless they choose to share it with someone. You can say,

> Today we are going to write about our experiences with ste-reotyping. You are going to write a journal entry on a sepa-rate piece of paper that will not be included in your binder or shared with others, unless you choose to share it. Write about a time when you were stereotyped against. What was the ste-reotype? How did it make you feel? Was the stereotype accu-rate? Why or why not? In your second paragraph, write about how you plan to make sure you do not stereotype others.

Allow students time to write. Students should write their entry on a separate piece of paper so they can discard it later or take it home for safekeeping. This way, no one else will see what they wrote by finding it in their workbook, as this is a sensitive topic.

Session 3.5: The Commitment Circle

Have students form a circle and present the commitment prompt. You can say,

> Our prompt for our commitment circle this week is, How are you going to help everyone feel included in the classroom? For example, I'm going to make sure I take the time to talk to everyone in the class and get to know them. The more I know about someone the less I will make assumptions about them.

Go around the circle and have students make their commitments. Encourage them to make these commitments for both the home and school setting so they can see how these skills translate to the home setting.

Reinforcing the Lesson

It is important that students understand that discrimination and stereotyping will not be tolerated in your class. You should handle instances of stereotyping and discrimination in your classroom in a consistent manner. You might want to discuss your plan with administrators so that everyone is on the same page. You can review with the class your school's policies and procedures in regard to discrimination.

Sample Letter to Parents and Guardians—Lesson 3

Dear Parent/Guardian,

In this lesson our class learned about stereotyping and discrimination and created a class pledge on how we will treat one another. Students learned it is important not to judge others based on their gender, race, ethnicity, age, disability or other factors. By believing stereotypes, we miss out on the opportunity to get to know other people. Students learned that being inclusive and treating everyone equally are positive ways we can support each other in our homes, schools, and communities.

Our class is committed to including all students and making sure that everyone feels safe and cared for in our classroom.

You can ask your child the following questions about the lesson:

- What is stereotyping?
- What are the dangers of stereotyping and discrimination?
- How can you combat stereotyping and discrimination?
- What did your class include its pledge?

Regards,

Self-Awareness

The Power Up Board and Building a Feelings Vocabulary

Home Mode Icon

In this lesson, students will be introduced to the Power Up board and the various skills, represented by the board icons, that they are going to learn throughout the year. This board will be used to track their progress in using the learned skills. This lesson also introduces students to the home icon on their controller. This will also be referred to as the home mode. The home mode represents our resting state. This is the state we enter into when starting a game. We have good health and energy levels, and no boosters or ways to boost our energy or abilities. In the home mode we have positive feelings and feel good about taking on the challenges that might be presented to us, resulting in us being productive. Last, in home mode students are in control of their thoughts, feelings, and behaviors. Feelings in the home mode include happy, confident, calm, grateful, peaceful, proud, relaxed, content, loved, pleased, cheerful, and joyful.

Introduction

The Power Up board and icons serve as visual reminders for students of the skills they are learning. Images and symbols are all around us in billboards, videos, phones, and video games. Since visuals are such a large part of our culture, it is helpful to incorporate what students know and are familiar with as a means to reinforce learning. Visuals in the classroom give students the chance to experience information in a form other than auditory, while also aiding with the processing of more abstract thought processes (Pezzino, 2018).

Feelings Vocabulary

The majority of communication is through nonverbal cues (e.g. eye contact, facial expressions, gestures). When working with students, it is important to support them in their being able to express themselves both verbally and nonverbally. Many times, we can see students expressing their emotions with undesired behaviors. By increasing students' vocabulary for feelings, we are giving them the building blocks to express their wants and needs through verbal means.

Affect labeling is naming the emotion you are feeling at the time. Lieberman et al. (2011) found that distress decreases with affect labeling. Fan et al. (2018) found that while negative emotions are not felt for a longer period of time than positive emotions, negative emotions do decrease in intensity more quickly after they have been expressed. Payer et al. (2012) found that affect labeling was associated with increasing activity in the prefrontal cortex, resulting in a decrease in activity in the amygdala. This indicates that when people are able to affect label, they are tapping into the part of their brain that helps them think critically and problem solve.

Objectives

Students will be able to

- identify the purpose of the Power Up board
- identify at least three feelings that represent being in home mode
- use at least three of their senses to describe home mode feelings

Success Criteria

Students are able to

- identify at least three feelings that represent the home mode
- understand what the home mode looks, sounds, and feels like
- feel comfortable talking to others about their home mode experiences

Materials

- Dry erase board or chalkboard
- One copy per student of the Power Up board
- One copy per student of the My Home Mode worksheet
- Preferred coloring utensils
- Scissors
- Photocopy or printout of the Feelings Words worksheet. Feelings words will be cut out from this worksheet for Session 3's activity.
- Stapler (for Session 4's optional activity)
- Three blank pieces of loose paper per student (for Session 4's optional activity)

Things to Note

Prior to the lesson, teachers should review the components of the Power Up board and determine if they would like to offer rewards when students "power up." Examples of rewards can be found in the section Rewards and Tallying of Power Up Bars in the introduction. There are also many ways to reward students with something they value but that represents no monetary expense.

Teachers should designate an accessible, visible place for each student's Power Up board. The recommended place for the boards is on the students' desks so they can easily see their progress and have a quick visual reminder of the skills they are working on. As the instructor, you will want to consider how to attach printouts of the boards to students' desks so that the board doesn't become loose and create a distraction. You will also need a designated place to hang up a larger version of the Power Up board icons, also referred to as skill cutouts. These can be displayed on a bulletin board or a designated wall. The skill cutouts should be easily visible to students.

This curriculum features game elements, but it is important to note that *Power Up* should not be construed as a contest between students. Student progress should not be compared, and shaming should not be used to motivate a student to comply. Instead, you should focus on positive reinforcement, acting as if each student is in a single player game. Give plenty of praise when students *do* practice the skills. You can also give pivotal praise when you see other students using the desired skill. This will hopefully help motivate the student in whom you want to see the desired behavior, without calling that student out for not yet showing the behavior.

Avoid telling students that they are incorrect in their affect labeling. You can ask students to expand on why they feel or identify feeling a certain way. For example, if they tell you they are feeling sad, you can ask them how they know they are feeling sad. By asking open-ended questions, you allow them the chance to explore the feeling they identified and determine if what they named as the feeling was correct. What elicits one feeling in a student, might elicit a totally different feeling in another.

In Session 4's optional activity and in Lessons 5 and 6, students will be making flip-books. Students can make their own flip-books, but if you have parent volunteers, you could task them to make these flip-books in advance to save time.

In Lessons 4, 5, and 6, students will begin to learn how to categorize their feelings into three modes: home, rewind, and fast-forward. The purpose of these lessons is to help them become aware of their feelings and the impact that they might have on productivity levels. They will learn what to do with those feelings in the self-management lessons.

Session 4.1: Introducing the Power Board and Controller

Begin the session by checking in on the students' commitments from last week. Ask students, "Who would like to volunteer to share how they did with their plan to include everyone?" Allow students a chance to share how they did on their commitments. If you find that the same students speak up, encourage new students to share. If you have some students who never share, try to check in with them individually.

At this time, distribute one Power Up board to each student. When introducing elements (the controller, icons, and power bars) of the Power Up board, you will want to have a photocopy of them to reference for the class. Let students know that they will each have a board, and let them know where they will be kept in the classroom. Draw from the sample script below when presenting:

> *In this lesson, we are going to learn about our Power Up boards and start working on building up our feelings vocabulary. We are going to be using our boards for the rest of the year. On the top right of your board, you will see a controller. It is divided into sections called home, rewind, and fast-forward modes. We will talk more about the controller in the next few lessons.*

Describe the Icons

Introduce the Power Up icons and explain how students can practice skills and "power up":

> *On the rest of the page you will see circles with black-and-white pictures in the middle. These are called icons, and each one of these represents a skill that we will be learning about. Each skill icon is enclosed in a circle that is divided into four parts called bars. Each time you are seen using the skill, I will color in one of your bars. Once you have all four bars colored in, I will let you color in the icon to show that you have mastered that particular skill. The goal is to demonstrate each skill at least four times to "power up."*
>
> *You have the entire year to demonstrate these skills, not just the week we are talking about the specific skill. Each time we learn a new skill I will add a large printout of it to our classroom board where each skill will be displayed so you can refer back to it and start earning power bars.* [Point to the place you will be displaying the skill cutouts.]

Note on rewards: If you are offering incentive for students powering up, mention that at this point.

Show Where Students Can Display Their Boards

Mention the designated area for the student boards and let students know they will be taking care of their own Power Up boards: "You are going to keep your own board. We are going to be using them all year so keep your Power Up boards safe and clean."

If students destroy their board when angry or frustrated, you should give them a new one when they are calmer. If you are able to see how many bars they previously had colored in, recolor the bars to make sure students don't lose the progress they made. You can ask them to take the time to piece their board back together to show that it is important to both teacher and student that progress is not lost. If the board can't be pieced back together (or if it is so destroyed you can't see the previous progress), explain in a calm and gentle tone that you tried very hard to get them credit, but the board was so destroyed the information was lost. (You don't need to remind them that they had destroyed the board. This could cause them to become defensive.) You can ask them if they remember three skills they had received bars in. This limits the progress they have made but does not make them feel as if they have to start over. If students feel as if all progress is lost, they might not feel motivated to continue trying the skills. Brainstorm ways they can avoid ruining their board in the future.

Introduce Home Mode

Let students know that you are going to talk about the home mode icon first. Students should connect the home mode icon with feelings of being at rest, safety, contentedness and productivity. Use the large skill cutout when explaining the home mode and the feelings associated with it. You can use the following script for the introduction:

> *We are going to start by focusing on the home mode' section of your controller. It stands for one of the three game categories that our feelings can fall into. These three categories are called home mode, rewind mode, and the fast-forward mode. These modes help us determine how productive our behaviors might be. When I say the word home, what feelings come up?*

Ask students what feelings come up when they think about the home mode. Allow students a chance to respond. Students should generally respond with pleasant feelings, such as happiness, contentedness, or feelings of love. If students respond in a concerning manner (e.g., by using words like *scared* or *angry* when describing home mode), you should bring this to the attention of the school counselor or follow your school protocols.

Record Student Descriptions of Home Mode Feelings

Write down the feeling words that students name on a poster board or white board. List all feelings noted whether they reflect this mode or not. To begin the exercise, you can say,

> *Our home mode houses feelings that make us feel peaceful, relaxed, and most importantly at rest. When we start a game we usually have full health, normal energy levels, and our character is in good shape to start playing. We are able to be productive and use our critical thinking and problem-solving*

skills on missions. What are some other feelings that you think
might fall into the home mode? [Let the students call out sen-
sations and emotions.]

We named a lot of great feelings. Let's go through these feel-
ings and see if they all fall into the home mode. The first feel-
ing is [read out from the list, e.g., happy]. Do we feel relaxed
and at rest when we are [name listed feeling]?

When students respond correctly, you can say, "Correct, we feel relaxed and
at rest when we feel [name identified feeling]."

Go through the list until you have named all of the feelings and correctly
identified whether they reflect the home mode or not. If a feeling listed on
the poster board is not part of home mode, have a discussion about why that
feeling is not present in that mode. For example, *frustrated* is not a home
mode feeling. When we are frustrated, our muscles might get tense. We might
scrunch up our faces or feel like moving around (e.g., by making fists or slam-
ming our feet on ground). These emotions, feelings, and actions don't reflect
the home mode's relaxed or resting state.

Work on the My Home Mode Worksheet

Congratulate the class on their work on the home mode feelings list and ask
them to complete the first section of the My Home Mode worksheet detailing
what the home mode looks like. You can introduce the exercise as follows:

Great job class. I want you to open to the My Home Mode
worksheet in your workbook. At the top of the page, it says
Looks Like. I want you to write down home mode feelings in
this section and then draw an emoji to match that feeling.

Present an example on your own worksheet so students can see what you are
asking them to do. Walk around the room to check on students' work and
make sure they are copying down the correct feeling words.

Session 4.2: What Home Mode Sounds and Feels Like

Introduce the lesson by explaining that the class has covered what the home
mode looks like. This time they are going to think about what the home mode
sounds like. They will be working with a partner to identify and practice what
home mode sounds like. Explain the activity to the class:

I want you to meet up with your partner and practice making
noises you might hear when someone is in the home mode. For
example, I might laugh when I'm in the home mode because I
laugh when I'm happy. [You can demonstrate with a laugh.]

Have students work with partners to make home mode noises. Walk around the room while students are practicing and give praise for noises made. Ask students to explain the noises they are making if you feel they don't reflect the home mode. It is recommended that students change partners when working on each new section in the worksheet, but if time is an issue, you can keep them with the same partners.

Complete the Sounds Like Section in the Worksheet

Ask students to retrieve their My Home Mode worksheet. They will work with their partner and write down the sounds of home mode in the worksheet section Sounds Like. Provide an example to guide students with the worksheet. You can introduce the exercise as follows:

> *I heard some great home mode sounds out there! On the My Home Mode worksheet in your workbook, I want you to write down some sounds that you might hear, or did hear, when you or someone else is in the home mode. For example, I wrote laughter. See how many words you can come up with.*

As students work, praise them for their work on the sounds. Gently correct them when the students identify an incorrect noise. If students write down a sound that you think is incorrect, ask them why they think that it might represent a home mode feeling. This will help determine whether students understand the concept or are simply identifying an ambiguous expression. For example, a student might write "sighing," and when asked to explain, might say they let out a contented sigh when they are in the home mode. Give students a chance to share their responses with the class. Be prepared to give some suggestions.

Identify What Home Mode Feels Like

Have students work with a partner to identify what home mode feels like. Have students think about physical sensations they associate with home mode. Students can explain or use gestures and expressions to identify these feelings:

> *We have talked about what the home mode looks and sounds like. Now, we are going to talk about what the home mode feels like. I want you to discuss with your partner where you feel the home mode in your body. For example, when I feel happy, my shoulders feel light,* [point to shoulders] *and my cheeks hurt a little bit from smiling* [point to cheeks]. *People experience home mode feelings in different places in their bodies, so it is OK if your answer is different than your partner's.*

Walk around the room and observe while students work with partners to identify where in their body they feel the home mode.

Complete the Section Feels Like in the Worksheet

Color in the figure. Have students use the figure in the My Home Mode worksheet to identify where they feel home mode sensations. They will color in these areas in the outline figure. You can demonstrate how use the worksheet and introduce the exercise as follows:

> *Great job! It looks like we know where we feel the home mode in our bodies! In your workbook in the outline of the body, I want you to color in where you feel the home mode. For example, I would color the cheeks and my shoulders.*

As students are working, walk around and give praise for their coloring. Ask questions about what they colored. For example, you might say, "I see you colored the feet. Do your feet feel heavy or light when you are in the home mode?" or "I noticed you colored the stomach. Does your stomach feel like it is tied in knots or relaxed when you are in the home mode?"

Write down these home-mode feelings. Once students have colored where in their bodies they feel the home mode, have them write one or two sentences about how it feels to experience home mode. They should use the lines underneath the worksheet figure to write out their responses. To get the class started with the exercise, you can say,

> *Now that you have colored in your body where you feel the home mode, I want you to write one to two sentences about how it feels to experience this mode in the lines below the figure. For example, I wrote, "When I am in the home mode, my shoulders feel light and bouncy. My cheeks also hurt from smiling and laughing."*

Walk around the room and observe while students work and inquire about what they are writing.

Explain How to Practice the Skill and Earn Power Up Bars

Conclude the lesson by displaying the skill cutout and reminding students that they can earn Power Up bars each time they practice the skill of identifying home mode feelings. In order to earn Power Up bars, students need to let the teacher know when they have a home-mode feeling or see someone else who looks like they are in this mode. Teachers will fill in power bars. You can say,

> *I am going to hang our home mode skill cutout on the wall so we can refer back to it as needed. Remember, you can earn power bars each time you practice identifying a home mode feeling. To get a power bar, you just need to let me know when you or someone else is experiencing a home mode feeling, and what home mode feeling is being experienced.*

Earning power bars: Students earn a power bar for each occasion or day in which they are found demonstrating the skill. Sample script:

> *Remember, four bars surround the skill icon. When I see you using this skill of identifying home mode feelings, I will color in one of your power bars. You get one power bar for each separate occasion. For example, if you tell me that you are experiencing the home mode three times in one day, you will only get one power bar. You can only earn one bar per day.*

Earning the skill icon. Let students know that when they have four bars filled in they have powered up and have earned the icon. You can use the sample script to explain the rules:

> *When you have all four bars colored in, I will give you some time to color in your icon to indicate that you have powered up and have unlocked that achievement.*

If you are offering rewards to earned icons, you can mention that incentive at this time.

While students won't get more than one bar per day, encourage students to use the skill more than once a day. Let students know that the idea is for them to practice the skill over time to develop a habit of using it, which is why they can only earn one power bar per day.

Session 4.3: Feelings Charades

In this exercise, you will have students act out feelings in a game of charades. Use the Feelings Words worksheet to provide prompts for the game. To prepare for the activity, cut out the home-mode feeling words from the worksheet and place the slips of paper in a hat or bucket. The student acting out the feeling word will select one of these slips of paper to begin the activity. To reduce prep work, you can have a student cut out the feeling words while you are giving directions. Explain the rules of charades when introducing the activity:

> *We are going to play feelings charades. I will ask for volunteers to pick a feeling word from the container and then act it out. The volunteer can't use words but they can use facial expressions and bodily cues to help us figure out what emotion they are acting out. Each volunteer will have 1 minute to act out the emotion. The class will call out what feeling they think is being presented. When the correct feeling is called out, a new volunteer can come up and act out another feeling. Who would like to volunteer first?*

Set a timer for 1 minute and have students select a word and act out the feeling. The rest of the class will try to guess what feeling the student is acting out.

After students have acted out all of the emotions, ask students which mode is represented by these emotions. Students should come to the conclusion that the home mode was represented in all of these emotions.

Session 4.4: The Feelings Flip-book

In this activity, students will create a flip-book as a way for them to visualize different emotions. Flip-books present one image per page so that when they are flipped through rapidly, the image appears to move or change. To create the flip-book, students will draw faces that change from a neutral expression to a home mode expression. Each page should have a small change from the previous page to give the illusion of movement. If the changes are too large from page to page the illusion of movement will be disrupted.

How To Make a Flip-book

Introduce the exercise: "We are going to have some more fun with our feeling words! We are going to make a feelings flip-book. Let's start by putting our flip-book together."

Instructors should create a flip-book with the class to show students how it is done. (You can also choose to make the flip-books in advance and skip this part.) To start, take out three pieces of notebook paper. Fold the paper in half, folding left side to right side and then in half again, folding from top to bottom. Unfold the paper and then cut along the fold lines to make even rectangles. Repeat this for your other two pieces of paper. Next, stack the pages on top of each other. These will be the pages in your book.

Create a Home Mode Feeling Flip-book

The students will select a home mode feeling to draw in their flip-book. They can use the Home Mode Feelings Words worksheet as a guide. Their flip-books will show drawings of faces that go from a neutral expression to their chosen home mode feeling. You can use the following script to introduce the activity:

> For this next part, I want you to pick a home mode feeling. In your flip-book, you will draw a person or face showing this emotion. On the first page of the flip-book, the figure will show no expression (or a neutral expression) and the last page will show the home mode feeling you picked. To make the flip-book, you will start with a drawing of the neutral face. Each following page will have a new face that looks a little bit closer to the face you ultimately want. For the best effect, each picture should only be slightly different than the one before it.
>
> For example, if you are starting with an emoji with a straight line for a mouth and want your last face to show a smile, each

> *new page will show the mouth slowly turning up into a smile.*
> *If your emoji is going from gray to yellow, each new emoji will*
> *get a shade closer to the yellow you want. Hang on to your*
> *book because we will be adding to it over the next two lessons!*

Once the students have finished with their drawings, staple the flip-book pages together and encourage the students to flip through the pages to see the face change.

Session 4.5: The Commitment Circle

Have students gather in a circle to make their commitment. Let them know it is time to identify a commitment and provide them with the prompt:

> *Our prompt for our commitment circle this week is, Who are*
> *you going to tell when you find yourself in the home mode?*
> *For example, when I'm experiencing a feeling in the home*
> *mode I'm going to tell* [name a student]. *Make sure you*
> *follow through on your commitment and tell the individual*
> *when you are experiencing a home mode feeling. It is import-*
> *ant to tell others when you are in a specific mode because it*
> *helps them understand what you are feeling and what would*
> *be appropriate to do and say around you.*

Go around the circle and have students make their commitments. Encourage them to make these commitments for both the home and school setting so they can see how these skills translate to the home setting.

Reinforcing the Lesson

You can demonstrate the skills you'd like the students to practice. Point out to students when you see someone in the home mode. Encourage them to tell you or their class partners, when they see someone in the home mode. When they tell you they see someone in the home mode, ask them how they know this. Encourage them to respond with examples that uses "looks like," "sounds like," and "feels like." Give praise for correct answers and ask open-ended questions when students present a feeling that is not congruent with the senses they are describing. Make sure to color in power bars when students identify that they or someone else is in the home mode.

Sample Letter to Parents and Guardians—Lesson 4

Dear Parent/Guardian,

In this lesson students learned about home mode feelings and practiced identifying and naming feelings that represent the home mode. In the home mode, students feel relaxed and at rest resulting in them being productive and accomplishing their daily tasks. Emotions in the home mode include: happy, content, loved, joyful, and relaxed.

Students were also introduced to the Power Up boards and icons. This board will be used to track students' progress in practicing the learned skills. Students earn power bars each time they are seen using a learned skill. When they are seen using the skill, a power bar is colored in. The goal is to complete all four power bars and earn the skill icon.

It is important for students to be able to identify when they are in the home mode so they can effectively communicate what they are feeling.

You can ask your child the following questions about the lesson:

- How does the Power Up board work?
- What is the home mode?
- What feelings represent the home mode?
- When are you in the home mode?
- When have you seen others in the home mode?

Regards,

Power Up Board

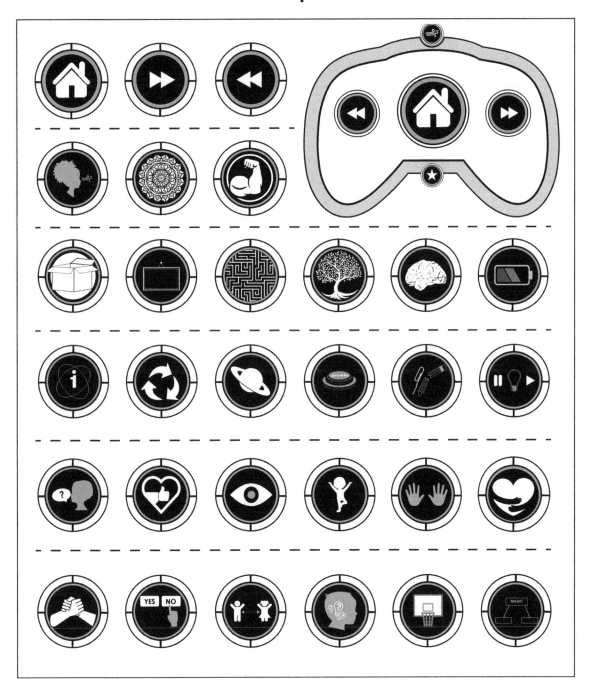

Feeling Words

Home Mode Feeling Words		
happy	confident	calm
peaceful	proud	relaxed
grateful	content	joyful
loved	pleased	cheerful

Rewind Mode Feeling Words		
sad	worried	hopeless
tired	guilty	embarrassed
disappointed	lonely	discouraged
bored	depressed	exhausted

Fast-Forward Mode Feeling Words		
frustrated	angry	enraged
jealous	nervous	surprised
anxious	excited	exuberant

My Home Mode

Looks like:

Sounds like:

Feels like:

_____

_____

_____

_____

_____

Rewind Mode: Building a Feelings Vocabulary

Rewind Mode Icon

This lesson introduces students to the rewind mode icon on the Power Up board controller. This will also be referred to as the rewind mode. The rewind mode represents experiences that cause us to feel as if we are trying to do everything in reverse, causing us to feel low energy levels. These low levels of energy cause us to feel unmotivated and contribute to us being unproductive. The rewind mode includes feelings such as sadness, worry, discouragement, disappointment, embarrassment, guilt, loneliness, tiredness, hopelessness, depression, and boredom.

Introduction

Depression can lead to an array of physical and emotional ramifications. Physical impacts include changes in weight or appetite; sleep disturbances; aches and pains; heart problems; thyroid issues; joint, limb, and back pain; gastrointestinal problems; and psychomotor activity changes (Trivedi, 2004; Harvard Health Publishing, 2017). Depression decreases the production of the neurotransmitters that make us feel good (e.g., norepinephrine, serotonin, and dopamine) (Harvard Health Publishing, 2017).

Depression is often overlooked, even though its symptoms are widespread. As reported in an analysis of World Health Organization findings (Trivedi, 2004), 69% of patients who fit diagnostic criteria for depression reported only somatic symptoms. While everyone experiences sadness at times, it is important to notice if students continuously report feelings of sadness, hopelessness, or lethargy.

Objectives

Students will be able to

- identify at least three feelings that represent the rewind mode
- use at least three of their senses to describe the rewind mode

Success Criteria

Students are able to

- identify at least three feelings that represent the rewind mode
- understand what the rewind mode looks, sounds, and feels like
- feel comfortable talking to others about their rewind mode experiences

Materials

- Dry erase board or chalkboard
- One copy per student of My Rewind Mode worksheet
- Preferred coloring utensils
- Scissors
- Stapler (for Session 4's optional activity)
- Three blank pieces of loose paper (for Session 4's optional activity)
- Cut-out feelings words for the rewind mode

Things to Note

Avoid telling students what situations would or wouldn't cause rewind mode feelings. Everyone experiences situations differently. Instead, ask them open-ended, guiding questions to help them fully determine if in a specific situation, they truly felt themselves to be in rewind mode. For example, you can ask students, "Did you feel like you were moving in reverse or slow motion in that situation? Did you feel unmotivated? Did you feel low energy levels? Were you productive? What emotion were you experiencing?"

Session 5.1: Learning about Rewind Mode

Begin the lesson by checking in on the students' commitment from last week. Ask students, "Who would like to volunteer to share how they did checking in and letting their person know they were in the home mode?"

Allow students a chance to share how they did on their commitments. If you find that the same students speak up each week, encourage new students to contribute. If you have some students who never share, try to check in with them individually.

Introduce Rewind Mode

Let students know that this lesson will focus on the rewind mode on their controller. Students should connect the rewind mode icon with feelings related to low energy levels, poor concentration, and low productivity. Feelings in the rewind mode include sad, bored, disappointed, and lonely. Use the skill cutout when explaining the rewind mode and the feelings and experiences associated with it. You can use the following script for the introduction:

> *In this lesson, we are going to talk about the rewind mode on your controller. In the rewind mode your game character might be struggling. They might be going through motions or combos that drain their energy, decrease concentration, and cause them to be unproductive. They might not finish missions, they might take longer to finish them, or they might not even start them. The rewind mode includes experiences and feelings that make it seem like we are going through our daily motions in reverse, causing us to feel low energy levels, low motivation, and low productivity. When we are in the rewind mode, it might be hard to stay awake, or we might experience feelings of sadness. When we feel like this, it might be hard to get up out of bed, be social, eat, or stay interested in school or hobbies.*

Ask students what feelings they think might be in the rewind mode. Write down student responses on a dry-erase white board or chalkboard. Write down all feelings whether they fall into this mode or not.

Review Student Descriptions of Rewind Mode Feelings

To continue the exercise, you can say,

> *You named a lot of great feelings. Let's go through these feelings and see if they all represent being in rewind mode. The first feeling is* [read aloud a feeling on the list]. *Do we feel low energy levels and/or unproductive when we are feeling* [name listed feeling]?

After students respond accurately, you can say, "Correct, we might feel like we don't have a lot of energy, and are unproductive when we are feeling [name identified feeling]."

Continue to go through the list until you have named all of the feelings and correctly identified whether they are rewind mode feelings (e.g., feeling sad, tired, hopeless, bored, depressed, exhausted). If there is a feeling listed on the board that doesn't reflect the rewind mode, have a discussion about why that feeling does not fit into the rewind mode. For example, the feeling mad would not be representative of the rewind mode because we likely experience high energy levels rather than low energy levels. These reactions and experiences are the opposite of feeling low energy levels, poor concentration and decreased productivity.

Work on the My Rewind Mode Worksheet

Congratulate the class on their work on the rewind mode feelings list and ask them to complete the first section of the My Rewind Mode worksheet where they identify what the rewind mode looks like. You can introduce the exercise as follows:

> Great job class. Now, I want you to open to the My Rewind Mode worksheet in your workbook. At the top [point to the section], it says Looks Like. I want you to write down rewind mode feelings in this section and then draw an emoji to match the feeling word.

Walk around the room to check on students' work and assist as needed.

Session 5.2: What Rewind Mode Sounds and Feels Like

Introduce the session by explaining that the class has covered what the rewind mode looks like. This time they are going to think about what the rewind mode sounds like. Have students work with partners to make rewind mode noises. It is recommended that students change partners when working on a new section in this worksheet, but if time is an issue, you can keep them with the same partners. To begin the exercise, you can say,

> Now that we have talked about what the rewind mode looks like, I want you to meet up with your partner and practice making noises you might hear when someone is in the rewind mode. For example, I might cry in the rewind mode [Make a sob sound].

Walk around the room and give praise for noises made. Ask students to explain the noises they are making if you feel they don't belong in the rewind mode.

Complete the Sounds Like Section in the Worksheet

Ask students to retrieve their My Rewind Mode worksheet. They will work with their partner and write down the sounds of rewind mode in the worksheet section Sounds Like. Provide an example to guide students with the worksheet. You can introduce the exercise as follows:

> I heard some great rewind mode sounds out there! On the My Rewind Mode worksheet in your workbook, write down some sounds that you might hear when you or someone else is in the rewind mode. You can write down the sounds you and your partner made and any others you can think of. For

> *example, I wrote "crying." See how many words you can come up with.*

As students are working, walk around the room and give them praise for their work on the sounds. Gently redirect when students identify or write down an incorrect sound. You can ask them why they think that sound represents the rewind mode. Be prepared to give some suggestions.

Identify What Rewind Mode Feels Like

Have students work with a partner to identify what rewind mode feels like. This can be a new partner, or they can continue with their current partner. Have students think about physical sensations they associate with rewind mode:

> *We have talked about what the rewind mode looks like and sounds like. Now, we are going to talk about what the rewind mode feels like. I want you to tell your partner where in your body you feel the rewind mode. For example, when I feel sad my chest feels heavy* [point to your chest] *and my back hurts* [point to your back]. *Everyone experiences these modes in different places in their body, so it's OK if your answer is different than your partners.*

Walk around the room while students work, observing responses. Assist as needed.

Complete the Feels Like Section in the Worksheet

Color in the figure. Have students use the figure in the My Rewind Mode worksheet to identify where they feel rewind mode sensations. They will color in these areas in the outline figure. You can demonstrate how use the worksheet and introduce the exercise as follows:

> *Great job! It looks like we know where we feel the rewind mode! In your worksheet in the picture of the person, color where you feel the rewind mode in your body. For example, I colored the chest and the back* [point to the worksheet figure].

As students are working, walk around the room and praise their coloring work. Ask questions about what they colored. For example, you might say, "I see you colored the feet. Do your feet feel heavy or light when in rewind mode?" or "I noticed you colored in the stomach. Does your stomach feel settled or unsettled when you are in rewind mode?"

Write down rewind mode feelings. Once students have colored in where they feel the rewind mode, have them write one to two sentences about how it feels to experience rewind mode. They should use the lines underneath the worksheet figure to write out their responses. To get the class started with the exercise, you can say,

> *For example, I wrote "When I am in the rewind mode, my chest feels heavy, as if a weight has been placed on it. My back also hurts from slouching over." You can use the lines underneath the figure to write out your responses.*

Walk around the room and inquire about what the students are writing. Offer assistance as needed.

Explain How to Practice the Skill and Earn Power Up Bars

Let students know that they can earn a Power Up bar each time they practice the skill and let you know when they or someone else is in rewind mode. You, the teacher, can then color in a power bar for them. Conclude the session by displaying the skill cutout. Sample script:

> *I'm going to add the rewind mode skill to our board. When you have a feeling in the rewind mode, or see someone else who looks like they are in the rewind mode, let me know so that I can give you a power bar. Remember, you can earn one power bar per day.*

Session 5.3: Feelings Charades

In this session, you will have students act out rewind mode feelings through a game of charades. To set up the game, photocopy or printout the Feelings Words worksheet and cut out the rewind feeling words for use as prompts. Place the slips of paper in a hat, bucket, or container for the volunteer student to pick from. To reduce prep work, you can have a student cut out the feeling words while you are giving directions. Remind students of the rules of charades when beginning the activity:

> *Who would like to volunteer to pick a feeling word from the hat and act it out in front of the entire class? Remember, if you are the volunteer, you can't use words to describe the feeling, but you can use facial expressions and bodily cues to help us figure out what emotion you are acting out. You will have 1 minute to act out the emotion. The class will call out what feeling they think you are acting out. When you hear the correct feeling, you let the class know. We will then ask for a new volunteer to act out another feeling.*

Set a timer for 1 minute and have students act out the feeling. At the end, ask students what mode they thought all of the feelings fell into. Students should conclude all of the feelings were rewind mode feelings.

Session 5.4: The Feelings Flip-book

In this session, students will add drawings of a rewind mode feeling to their flip-book. This time the drawings will start with an image of the home mode face and move gradually to show the rewind mode expression they want. Have them first create the pages and then add the new pages to their flip-book so the images go from the neutral face to the home mode face to the rewind mode face. To introduce the lesson, you can say,

> *We are going to have some more fun with our feeling words! I want you to pick a rewind mode feeling from the worksheet. We are going to add to our flip-books. In this section of the flip-book, you will draw someone in the rewind mode. The first drawing will show the home mode face that you ended with in the last lesson. Each page will show expressions a little bit closer to the rewind mode face you want. When you add the pages to your flip-book, the figure will go from the neutral face you started with to the home mode face you finished with in the last lesson to the rewind mode face you picked to draw today.*
>
> *You can make flip-book pages out of your notebook paper. Once you are done, we will staple the new pages behind the pages you made in the last lesson. Hang onto your book because we will add our final pages next week!*

Staple the flip-book pages together and encourage the students to flip through the pages to see the face change.

Session 5.5: The Commitment Circle

Have students gather in a circle to make the lesson commitment and provide them with the prompt:

> *Our prompt for our commitment circle this week is Who are you going to tell when you find yourself in rewind mode? For example, when I'm experiencing a feeling in the rewind mode I'm going to tell [name a student]. Throughout the week, make sure you follow through on your commitment and tell this person when you are experiencing a rewind mode feeling. It is important to tell others when you are in a specific mode because it helps them understand what you are feeling and what would be appropriate to do and say around you.*

Go around the circle and have students make their commitments. Encourage them to make these commitments for both the home and school setting so they can see how these skills translate to the home setting.

Reinforcing the Lesson

Model the skills you'd like students to practice. Point out to students when you see someone in the rewind mode. Encourage them to tell you or their class partner when they see someone in the rewind mode. When they tell you they see someone in the rewind mode, ask them how they know this. Encourage them to respond with examples that use "looks like," "sounds like," and "feels like." Give praise for correct answers, and ask open-ended questions when students name a feeling is not congruent with the sensations they are describing. Make sure to color in power bars when students identify that they or someone else is in rewind mode.

Sample Letter to Parents and Guardians—Lesson 5

Dear Parent/Guardian,

In this lesson, our class continued to focus on self-awareness, a skill covered in social and emotional learning. In this lesson, we learned to identify emotions that make us feel like we are moving in reverse. These emotions cause us to have low energy levels and poor concentration and cause us to be unproductive. They include being sad, tired, worried, or embarrassed. We call these feelings being in "rewind mode," and we learned what this mode looks, sounds, and feels like.

It is important for us to be able to identify what we are feeling so we can effectively communicate those feelings to others.

You can ask your child the following questions about the lesson:

- What is the rewind mode?
- What feelings represent being in rewind mode?
- When do you find yourself in rewind mode?
- When might others find themselves in rewind mode?

Regards,

Feeling Words

Home Mode Feeling Words		
happy	confident	calm
peaceful	proud	relaxed
grateful	content	joyful
loved	pleased	cheerful

Rewind Mode Feeling Words		
sad	worried	hopeless
tired	guilty	embarrassed
disappointed	lonely	discouraged
bored	depressed	exhausted

Fast-Forward Mode Feeling Words		
frustrated	angry	enraged
jealous	nervous	surprised
anxious	excited	exuberant

My Rewind Mode

Looks like:

Sounds like:

Feels like:

_____

_____

_____

_____

_____

Fast-Forward Mode: Building a Feelings Vocabulary

**Fast Forward
Mode Icon**

This lesson introduces students to fast-forward mode and the icon on the Power Up controller. The fast-forward mode represents emotions that cause us to feel as if we are trying to do everything in fast-forward motion or very quickly. The fast-forward mode (like the rewind mode) causes us to be unproductive. The main difference is that in the fast-forward mode our high energy levels are what get in the way of us completing a task. Higher energy levels might cause our hearts to race, our palms to sweat, or our fidgeting to increase. The fast-forward mode includes feelings, such as being frustrated, angry, enraged, anxious, jealous, nervous, surprised, or excited. In an online game, energy boosters or special abilities might make game characters move faster, which decreases the amount of control the player has over them. This can lead to missions not being completed or being missed all together.

Introduction

If students are anxious, angry, or overexcited for too long, they can face long-term physical consequences due to their heightened state of emotions. When we experience anger, the body releases the stress hormones of cortisol, adrenaline, and noradrenaline (Alvarez et al., 2018). Adrenaline causes an increase in blood pressure and heart rate. The increase forces the heart to work harder in bringing oxygenated blood to the body (Harvard Health Publishing, 2006) and causes strain on the body. Prolonged feelings of anger are linked to increased risk of heart disease and stroke (Harvard Health Publishing, 2006) due to the body's release of adrenaline.

Elevated cortisol levels impact decision-making because they cause a loss of neurons in the prefrontal cortex. Increased cortisol levels also kill neurons in the hippocampus, which interferes with the formation of new neurons (Alvarez et al., 2018). Because the hippocampus stores memories, this loss interferes also with short-term memory.

Strong, unmanageable emotions can impact students' ability to function in the classroom without accommodations. Adolescents who experience anger or frustration to the point that it interferes with their ability to function in the home or school setting might merit screening to determine whether they meet diagnostic criteria for the following conditions: intermittent explosive disorder, conduct disorders, impulse control disorders, oppositional defiant disorder, and disruptive behavior disorder (American Psychological Association, 2017).

Learning to identify and name emotional states, also called affect labeling, can decrease the intensity of the emotion being experienced, which in turn, can provide emotional and physical benefits. See the manual for more information.

Objectives

Students will be able to

- identify at least three feelings that represent the fast-forward mode
- use at least three senses to describe fast-forward mode feelings

Success Criteria

Students are able to

- identify at least three feelings that represent the fast-forward mode
- understand what the fast-forward mode looks, sounds, and feels like
- feel comfortable talking to others about their fast-forward mode experiences

Materials

- Dry erase board or chalkboard
- One copy per student of My Fast-forward Mode worksheet
- Preferred coloring utensils
- Scissors
- Stapler (for Session 4's optional activity)
- Three blank pieces of loose paper (for Session 4's optional lesson)
- Photocopy or printout of the Feelings Words worksheet. Feelings words will be cut out from this worksheet for use in Session 3's activity
- Hat or container for feeling word cutouts

Things to Note

Avoid telling students what situations would or wouldn't cause them to feel that they are in fast-forward mode. Everyone experiences situations differently. Instead, ask them guiding questions to help them determine whether they truly felt they were in fast-forward mode in a specific situation. For example, you can ask students, "Did you feel as if your body was moving in fast-forward motion? Were you fidgeting? What were your energy levels? What emotion were you experiencing?"

Session 6.1: Introduction to Fast-forward Mode

Begin the lesson by checking in on the students' commitment from last week. Ask students, "Who would like to volunteer to share how they did checking in and letting their person know when they were in rewind mode?"

Allow students a chance to share how they did on their commitments. If you find that the same students speak each week, encourage new students to participate. If some students never share, try to check in with them individually.

Introduce Fast-forward Mode

Let students know you will be discussing the fast-forward mode on their controller. Students should connect the fast-forward mode with feelings of high energy and low productivity. Use the skill cutout when explaining the fast-forward mode and the feelings associated with it. You can use the following script for the introduction:

> *In this lesson, we are going to talk about the fast-forward mode on your controller. The fast-forward mode is when we experience high energy levels that cause us to become unproductive. The difference between the fast-forward mode and the rewind mode are the energy levels. Think of a video game character that uses a booster to attempt to defeat a boss. Using the booster causes high energy levels that can be difficult to control, resulting in the character making a mistake and not defeating the boss or failing the mission. For example, if you are playing a racing game, the booster of added speed makes the car difficult to control.*

Ask students what are some of the feelings they think would fall into the fast-forward mode. Let the students call out feelings. Write down the feelings they name on a dry erase board or chalkboard. Record all feelings that the students name, whether they are correct or incorrect.

Review Student Descriptions of Fast-forward Mode Feelings

Read through the students' list and ask students if they fit the fast-forward mode:

> *We came up with a lot of great feelings. Let's go through the list and see which ones fit into the fast-forward mode. The first feeling is [state the listed feeling]. Do we feel like we have*

*high energy levels that cause us to be unproductive when we
feel [identified feeling]?*

If students respond correctly, you can say, "Correct, we might have high
levels with low levels of productivity when we feel [identified feeling]." Continue to go through the list until you have named all the listed feelings and
correctly identified whether they are fast-forward mode feelings. If there are
feelings on the board that are not part of this mode, have a discussion about
why the identified feeling is not an appropriate fit. For example, the feeling
sadness would not be a fast-forward mode emotion because when we are sad,
we experience decreased, not increased, energy levels.

Work on the My Fast-forward Mode Worksheet

Congratulate the class on their work on fast-forward mode feelings list and
ask them to complete the first section of the My Fast-forward Mode worksheet where they identify what the fast-forward mode looks like. You can
introduce the exercise as follows:

> *Great job class. Now, I want you to open to the My Fast-forward Mode worksheet in your workbook. At the top of the
> worksheet [point to section], it says, Looks Like. I want you
> to write down fast-forward mode feelings and then draw an
> emoji face to match each feeling word."*

Walk around while students work and offer assistance as needed.

Session 6.2: What Fast-forward Mode Sounds and Feels Like

Introduce the session by explaining that now that the class has covered what
fast-forward mode looks like, they will consider what fast-forward mode
sounds like. Have students work with partners to make fast-forward mode
noises. If time permits, you can have them work with new partners for the
exercise. To begin the exercise you can say,

> *Now that you have identified what the fast-forward mode
> looks like I want you to work with your partner and practice
> making noises that you might hear when someone is in the
> fast-forward mode. For example, I might grunt when I'm frustrated and in the fast-forward mode [make a grunt sound].*

Walk around the room and interact with students while they work. Guess
what feeling goes with the sound they are making. If the feeling and sound
don't appear to match, ask them to elaborate on why they would make that
sound when experiencing that feeling.

Complete the Sounds Like Section in the Worksheet

Ask students to retrieve their My Fast-forward Mode worksheet. They will work with their partner and write down the sounds of fast-forward mode in the worksheet section Sounds Like. Provide an example to guide students with the worksheet:

> *I heard some great fast-forward mode sounds out there! I'm going to ask you to write down on the My Fast-forward Mode worksheet sounds that you might hear when you or someone else are in the fast-forward mode. For example, I wrote "grunting." See how many words you can come up with.*

As students are working, walk around the room and praise them for their work on the sounds. Gently correct when the students write down an incorrect sound. You can ask them why they think that sound represents the fast-forward mode. Be prepared to give some suggestions.

Identify What Fast-forward Mode Feels Like

Have students work with a partner to identify what fast-forward mode feels like. This can be a new partner, or they can continue with their current partner. Have students think about physical sensations they associate with fast-forward mode:

> *We have talked about what fast-forward mode looks and sounds like. Now, we are going to talk about what fast-forward mode feels like. I want you to tell your partner where you feel the fast-forward mode in your body. For example, when I feel angry, my fists tense up* [make fists], *and I feel like steam is coming out of my ears* [point to ears].

Walk around the room while students work and ask them questions about where they report feeling the fast-forward mode in their body.

Complete the Section Feels Like in the Worksheet

Color in the figure. Have students use the figure in the My Fast-forward Mode worksheet to identify where they feel fast-forward mode sensations. They will color in these areas in the outline figure. You can demonstrate how use the worksheet and introduce the exercise as follows:

> *Great job! It looks like we know where we feel fast-forward mode in our body! In your worksheet in the picture, color in the outline where you feel the fast-forward mode in your body. For example, I colored the fists and ears* [point to example].

As students are working, walk around and praise them for their coloring work. Ask questions about what they colored. For example, you might say, "I see you colored the hands. Do your muscles feel tense or tired when you are in fast-forward mode?" or "I noticed you colored the head. Does your head feel full or light when you are in the fast-forward mode?"

Write down fast-forward mode feelings. Once students have finished coloring in the figure, have them write one or two sentences about how it feels to experience fast-forward mode. They should use the lined area of the worksheet to record their responses. You can provide an example to get them started:

> *Great job class! Last, I want you to write one to two sentences*
> *about how it feels when you experience fast-forward mode.*
> *For example, I wrote, "When I am in fast-forward mode, my*
> *fists start to clench and feel heavy. My ears also feel hot, like*
> *they have steam coming out of them."*

Walk around the room and inquire about what the students are writing. Give assistance as needed.

Explain How to Practice the Skill and Earn Power Up Bars

Let students know that they can earn a Power Up bar each time they practice the skill. Remind them of the icon for this skill:

> *I'm going to add the fast-forward mode skill to our board.*
> *When you have a feeling in this mode or see someone else*
> *who looks like they are in this mode, let me know so I can give*
> *you a power bar.*

Session 6.3: Feelings Charades

In this session, you will have students act out fast-forward feelings through a game of charades. To set up the game, photocopy or print out the Feelings Words worksheet and cut out the fast-forward mode feeling words. Place the pieces of paper in a hat, bucket, or other container for a volunteer student to pick from. They will have one minute to act out the feeling while the rest of the class tries to guess what feeling they are acting out. Remind students of the rules of charades when beginning the activity:

> *Who would like to volunteer to pick a feeling word from the*
> *hat and act it out in front of the entire class? Remember, if*
> *you are the volunteer, you can't use words, but you can use*
> *facial expressions and bodily cues to help us figure out what*
> *emotion you are acting out. You will have 1 minute to act out*
> *the emotion. The class will call out what feeling they think*
> *you are acting out. When you hear the correct feeling being*

*named, you let us know. We will then ask for a new volunteer
to act out another feeling.*

Set a timer and have students act out the feelings. When done, ask the students what mode the feelings acted out were in. Students should conclude that all of the feelings were in the fast-forward mode.

Session 6.4: The Feelings Flip-book

In this session, students will add drawings of a fast-forward mode feeling to their flip-book. You will want to remind students that the drawings should start with the image of the rewind mode feeling from the last lesson and move gradually to show the fast-forward mode expression they want. Have them first create and add pages to their flip-book. To introduce the lesson, you can say,

> *We are going to have some more fun with our feeling words! I
> want you to pick a fast-forward mode feeling from the work-
> sheet. You are going to finish your flip-book by adding one
> more section. In this section of the flip-book, the figure will go
> from the rewind mode feeling you drew in the last lesson to
> the fast-forward mode feeling you will pick today. Remember,
> the first drawing will show your person with the rewind mode
> expression, and each page will show expressions a little bit
> closer to the fast-forward expression you want.*
>
> *You can make your flip-book pages out of your notebook pa-
> per. When you are done, we will staple all the pages together
> for the final product that will go from the neutral expression
> to the rewind mode expression to the fast-forward mode
> expression!*

When students are finished, encourage them to flip through the pages to see the face change.

Session 6.5: The Commitment Circle

Have students form a circle to make the lesson commitment and provide them with the prompt:

> *Our prompt for our commitment circle this week is, Who are
> you going to tell when you find yourself in the fast-forward
> mode? For example, when I'm experiencing a fast-forward
> mode feeling, I'm going to tell [name]. Throughout the week,
> make sure you follow through on your commitment and tell
> the individual when you are experiencing a fast-forward
> mode feeling. It is important to tell others when you are in
> a specific mode because it helps them understand what you*

are feeling and what would be appropriate to do and say around you.

Go around the circle and have students make their commitments. Encourage them to make these commitments for both the home and school setting so they can see how these skills translate to the home setting.

Reinforcing the Lesson

Model the skills you'd like students to practice. Point out to students when you see someone in the fast-forward mode. Encourage them to tell you or their class partner, when they see someone in the fast-forward mode. When they tell you they see someone in the fast-forward mode, ask them how they know this. Encourage them to respond with examples that use "looks like," "sounds like," and "feels like." Give praise for correct answers, and ask open-ended questions when students name a feeling is not congruent with the senses they are describing.

Sample Letter to Parents and Guardians—Lesson 6

Dear Parent/Guardian,

In this lesson, our class continued to focus on the self-awareness domain of social and emotional learning. We learned what the "fast-forward" mode looks, sounds, and feels like. Students focused on identifying emotions in which they feel like they have high energy levels that results in low productivity. It is important for us to be able to identify what we are feeling so we can effectively communicate those feelings to others.

You can ask your child the following questions about the lesson:

- What is the fast-forward mode?
- What feelings are in the fast-forward mode?
- When do you feel the fast-forward mode?
- When have you seen others in the fast-forward mode?

Regards,

Feeling Words

Home Mode Feeling Words		
happy	confident	calm
peaceful	proud	relaxed
grateful	content	joyful
loved	pleased	cheerful

Rewind Mode Feeling Words		
sad	worried	hopeless
tired	guilty	embarrassed
disappointed	lonely	discouraged
bored	depressed	exhausted

Fast-Forward Mode Feeling Words		
frustrated	angry	enraged
jealous	nervous	surprised
anxious	excited	exuberant

My Fast-Forward Mode

Looks like:

Sounds like:

Feels like:

_____

_____

_____

_____

_____

Triggers, Feelings, Thoughts, and Behaviors

Trigger Icon

This lesson focuses on students being able to identify what triggers specific feelings for them and to understand the connection between their feelings, thoughts, and behaviors. Students might be triggered by people, places, situations, or things. Once students identify their triggers, they will then make connections between their feelings, thoughts, and behaviors.

Introduction

Emotional triggers are unique to each person because they bring up memories of what the individual was experiencing in that moment. Triggers can include people, places, things, colors, sensations, smells, or anything that can be related to a memory. Because our triggers are related to our memories, our memories influence how we feel and consequently how we react to a specific trigger (Hunter, 2011).

Trigger identification is considered a proactive coping technique because it allows individuals to identify and avoid situations that might cause them distress (Aspinwall, 2011). While not all triggers can be avoided, knowing their triggers can help students respond to the situation in a manner that is beneficial to them. It can also help them find the words to express to others why a particular situation might be upsetting for them. For triggers that can't be avoided, students can use the self-management strategies they will learn in Lessons 9–12.

Feelings, thoughts, and behaviors. Feelings, thoughts, and behaviors are linked. When someone experiences a feeling, it leads to a thought, and that thought leads to a behavior. Since everyone is unique, it can be difficult to predict what emotion will be elicited from specific experiences and what thoughts and behaviors will follow. As previously discussed, what emotions are triggered will depend on the individual's previous experiences and the memories the person associates with those experiences.

Objectives

Students will be able to

- identify at least three of their triggers
- articulate the connections across their feelings, thoughts, and behaviors

Success Criteria

Students are able to

- identify three of their triggers for each mode
- understand why it is important to know their triggers
- feel comfortable analyzing how their feelings, thoughts, and behaviors are connected

Materials

- Preferred coloring utensils
- One copy per student of the Triggers List worksheet
- One copy per student of the Home Mode Triggers worksheet
- One copy per student of the Rewind Mode Triggers worksheet
- One copy per student of the Fast-forward Mode worksheet
- One copy per student of the Feelings, Thoughts, Behaviors worksheet

Things to Note

Don't push the students if they appear triggered by this lesson. This can be a difficult activity, and some students might struggle with it. Be on the lookout for students who are struggling to complete the activity, acting out, or withdrawing. Let the students know they can choose to not complete the activity if they appear distressed. Give them the option to sit quietly at their desk. Ensure that you check in with these students as soon as possible.

Be aware of what you are comfortable discussing with the students and when you need to refer them to the school counselor. Even if you are comfortable handling the situation, you might still want to make sure a school counselor or administrator is informed if a particularly difficult situation arises or is discussed.

Avoid telling a student what mode an event would trigger them into. Triggers for students vary and are unique to them. For example, homework might trigger some students into home mode if they enjoy homework, into fast-forward mode if they get frustrated with homework, or into rewind mode if they get bored with homework. Instead, focus on making sure that the students are aware of how an event triggers them. For example, if students report that homework makes them feel happy, make sure that they identify it is a home mode trigger.

Session 7.1: Learning about Triggers

Check in on students' commitment from last week. Ask, "Who would like to volunteer to share how they did checking in and telling their person that they were in the fast-forward mode?"

Allow students a chance to share how they did on their commitments. If you find that the same students are speaking up each week, encourage new students to participate. If you have some students who never share, try to check in with them individually.

Introduce the Concept of Triggers

Open the lesson by defining what triggers are before presenting students with example scenarios for them to respond to:

> *Today we are going to talk about our triggers, or our "hot" buttons. Triggers are people, places, situations, or things that cause us to go into a specific mode. For example, math homework puts me in fast-forward mode because I get frustrated when I don't understand the problems. Arguing with friends puts me in the rewind mode because it makes me sad.*

Read the list of triggering scenarios below and ask students to raise their hands to be called on to tell the class which mode the situation would trigger them into. Let them know that there is no right or wrong answer. A situation can trigger each of us differently. As students respond, ask if the scenario might trigger people into any other modes.

Trigger Scenarios

- You are at recess and a student comes up to you and calls you a name. What mode might this trigger you into? Are there any other modes this might trigger someone into?

- You are reading your book during silent reading time, and you keep coming upon difficult words. You try to sound them out, but you spend so much time trying to figure out the words that you forget what the story is about. What mode might this trigger you into? Are there any other modes this might trigger someone into?

- Another student in your class calls you a name, so you push them. The teacher catches you pushing the student and you get in trouble. What mode might this trigger you into? Are there any other modes this might trigger someone into?

- You got two questions wrong on your math test. What mode might this trigger you into? Are there any other modes this might trigger someone into?

- You didn't get a lot of sleep last night, and it's difficult to stay awake this morning. What mode might this trigger you into? Are there any other modes this might trigger someone into?

- Your friend told you this morning that you can't be friends with one of your other friends anymore if you want to keep being friends with them. What mode might this trigger you into? Are there any other modes this might trigger someone into?

- You think another group of students is talking about you at lunch because they keep looking down the table at you and laughing. What mode might this trigger you into? Are there any other modes this might trigger someone into?

- A new student started school and you became friends with this person. What mode might this trigger you into? Are there any other modes this might trigger someone into?

- Your friends moved away and you can't see them every day anymore. What mode might this trigger you into? Are there any other modes this might trigger someone into?

- You finished a book that you really liked. What mode might this trigger you into? Are there any other modes this might trigger someone into?

Work on the Trigger List Worksheet

Once the students have talked about some of the triggering scenarios as a class, have them look at a list of triggers in the Triggers List worksheet in their workbook and identify which ones apply to them. Explain the worksheet to students by pointing out that in the far left column, various scenarios appear. In the columns to the right, all three modes are listed. Have students circle the mode that scenario puts them in. Let students know that any of the answers can be correct: "Remember, everyone is a little different so your answers won't match everyone else's in the class and that's OK." Walk around the room while students work and take note of their specific triggers.

Display the Triggers Skill Cutout

Conclude the lesson by pointing out the importance of understanding our triggers and reminding students to practice their skills to earn Power Up bars:

> *Great job class! I want you to continue to be aware throughout the day of how different situations can trigger you into different modes. It's important for us to understand our triggers so that we can create a plan for when we are triggered*

> *into each mode. This week, when you figure out what triggers*
> *you into a specific mode, tell me so I can give you a power bar.*

Add the triggers skill cutout to your wall.

Session 7.2: How We React to Triggers

In the first session, students had a chance to talk about triggers in general. In this session, students will learn about situations, people, and things that can trigger home mode, rewind mode, or fast-forward feelings. In the course of the discussion, teachers should take opportunities to remind students of what the modes represent and provide examples. Begin the session with a discussion of home mode triggers: "Today we are going to talk about our home mode triggers. Remember, a trigger is a person, place, situation, or thing that puts us into a specific mode."

Ask students what feelings might come up if they are triggered into the home mode. Allow students to share their thoughts. After students respond, be sure to remind them of what emotions and reactions are represented by home mode. You could say,

> *Remember, the home mode is when we are feeling happy,*
> *confident, calm, grateful, loving, peaceful, proud, relaxed*
> *and content. Our energy levels are good and we are able to*
> *be productive. When we talk about what triggers us for the*
> *home mode, we are talking about people, places, situations,*
> *and things that make us experience any of those feelings. For*
> *example, I am triggered into the home mode when I am given*
> *candy or when someone wants to go out to dinner with me.*
> *At home, I might be triggered into the home mode when my*
> *family surprises me with my favorite dessert.*

Complete the My Home Mode Triggers Worksheet

Have students turn to the My Home Mode Triggers worksheet in their workbook. Ask students to write down their home mode triggers on this worksheet. If they have time, students can draw some pictures to go with their written list of triggers. Students should try to **identify at least four triggers** for the home mode. To begin the exercise, you should provide an example:

> *We are going to write down our triggers for the home mode.*
> *For example, I wrote eating candy, playing with my friends,*
> *reading, eating my favorite dinner, playing on my phone,*
> *playing games, and eating cheesecake.* [Teachers can write
> down their responses on an example worksheet].

Walk around the room and ask students questions about their triggers and engage them in conversation.

Discuss Rewind Mode Triggers

Once students have had a chance to record home mode triggers on their worksheets, teachers should introduce the concept of triggers for rewind mode feelings. To begin, review what is meant by being in rewind mode. You can say, "What feelings might come up if you are triggered into the rewind mode?" After students respond, explain rewind mode and provide examples of what might trigger someone into rewind mode. You could say,

> *The rewind mode is when we have low levels of energy that make it hard for us to concentrate and be productive. When we talk about something that triggers us into rewind mode, we are talking about events and things that make us feel sad, bored, worried, discouraged, disappointed, embarrassed, exhausted, guilty, and lonely. For example, I am triggered into the rewind mode when no one will play with me or when someone says something mean to me. At home, I might be triggered into the rewind mode when my family doesn't want to eat dinner with me.*

Complete the My Rewind Mode Triggers Worksheet

Have students turn to the My Rewind Mode Triggers worksheet in their workbook and ask them to write down their triggers on this worksheet. Students can draw pictures to go with their list of triggers if time permits. Students should try to **identify at least four triggers** for the rewind mode. To begin the exercise, you should provide an example. You might say, "We are going to write down our triggers for the rewind mode. For example, I wrote down being left alone, no one wanting to talk to me, having nothing to do, and someone calling me names." Write down your responses on an example worksheet. Walk around the room and ask students questions about their triggers and engage them in conversation.

Discuss Fast-forward Triggers

Once students have had a chance to talk about their triggers for the home and rewind modes, turn to a discussion about triggers for the fast-forward mode. You can ask, "What feelings might come up if we are triggered into fast-forward mode?"

After students respond, take time to remind them what feelings and sensations represent fast-forward mode. Provide an example of triggers that might cause people to fall into fast-forward mode feelings. For this part of the discussion, you could say,

> *Fast-forward mode is when we have high levels of energy that cause us to be unproductive. We might feel angry, anxious,*

excited, frustrated, jealous, nervous, or surprised. Our heart might race, our breathing might quicken, and we might be fidgety. For example, I am triggered into fast-forward mode when I'm behind on my lesson planning or when we have a fire drill. At home, I might be triggered into the fast-forward mode when my family doesn't clean up after themselves.

Complete the My Fast-forward Mode Triggers Worksheet

Have students turn to the My Fast-forward Mode Triggers worksheet in their workbook. Ask them to write down their triggers for the fast-forward mode on this worksheet. If there is time, they can draw pictures for these triggers or feelings, too. Students should try to **identify at least four triggers**. To begin the exercise, you should provide an example. You can say,

> *Use your My Fast-forward Mode worksheet to write down your triggers for the fast-forward mode. For example, I wrote down when I'm behind on my lesson planning, during fire drills, when my family doesn't clean up after themselves, and when I'm looking forward to going to the pool over the weekend.*

Write down your example in your sample worksheet. Walk around the room and ask students questions about their triggers and engage them in conversation.

Ask Students to Continue to Identify Triggers and Conclude the Session

Let students know that you want them throughout the day, to look for more triggers they might have. As they discover new triggers, they should return to these workbook pages and add them to the list.

Session 7.3: Connecting Feelings, Thoughts, and Behaviors

In the previous sessions, students should have had a chance to talk about their triggers and feelings after being triggered into either home, rewind, or fast-forward modes. In this session, the focus is on creating an understanding of how our feelings are connected to our thoughts and behaviors. As the teacher, you could introduce the session as follows:

> *We have talked a lot about our feelings and our triggers. Now that we have an understanding of what triggers us to experience specific feelings, we are going to talk about how our feelings are connected to our thoughts and behaviors.*

Let's pretend that you got a bad grade on a math test. This bad grade triggers you into the rewind mode where you feel sad. What might you be thinking when you get that math test back and see that you got a poor grade?

Allow students a chance to share what they might think or how they might react. Keep the discussion on track by providing examples of what one might think or feel when faced with the situation. At this point in the discussion, you should have students begin to think about how our thoughts and feelings can direct our behavior. The following is an example of what the instructor could say,

We might be thinking things like "I'm terrible at math," "I'm never going to get a good grade on my report card now," or "I'm done trying." Our feelings of sadness have impacted what we are thinking about ourselves, the situation, and future situations. If we are feeling sad and thinking that we are never going to get a good grade in math, what might we do as a result?

Allow students a chance to share their ideas. Using the example, you could ask students how they might behave based on the thoughts they had about the bad math grade. Continue to focus on how our feelings and thoughts reinforce and affect each other. To help the class think about how feelings are connected to our thoughts and behaviors, you could say,

If you feel sad and think you aren't ever going to get a good grade in math again, you might decide not to study. When you don't study, you won't get a good grade, and the cycle will continue. Your feelings influence your thoughts about yourself and the situation. Those thoughts then influence your behaviors.

Respond to Scenarios: What Would You Feel and Think? How Would You Act?

At this point in the session, have students discuss the two scenarios presented below and help them gain insight into how feelings, thoughts, and behaviors are connected. Have students answer the following questions: What feeling might you experience as a result of the triggering event? How might that feeling influence your thoughts? How might that feeling influence your behaviors?

Scenarios

- You find out that your friend has been talking poorly about you behind your back.

- Your siblings keep taking your things even though you have asked them repeatedly not to.

Note: If you are conducting lessons once a week and are skipping the optional Session 4 lesson, let students know they can complete the Feelings, Thoughts, Behaviors worksheet in their workbook in their free time. This will let them get some more practice in thinking about how feelings, thoughts, and behaviors are related.

Session 7.4: Describing a Triggering Event

In this session, you will ask students to think about a situation specific to them and complete the accompanying worksheet Feelings, Thoughts, Behaviors. They should complete the worksheet sections moving from the top to the bottom of the page (from Trigger to Feelings, to Thoughts, to Behaviors). You could say,

> *Think about something that has influenced you recently. It could be related to your grades, friends, family, or something here at school. Turn to the Feelings, Thoughts, Behaviors worksheet in your workbook and write about it there. Complete each section from top to bottom, considering your feelings, thoughts, and behaviors.*

Allow students a chance to work. Walk around the room while they work and offer insight and assistance as needed. Once students are done, ask for volunteers to share what they wrote. Students do not have to share. Remind them to only share what they are comfortable with the entire class knowing.

Session 7.5: The Commitment Circle

Have students form a circle to make their lesson commitments and provide them with the following prompt:

> *Our prompt for our commitment circle this week is, How many additional triggers are you going to identify for each mode? For example, I am going to identify two additional triggers for each mode and add them to my workbook pages.*

Go around the circle and have students commit to how many triggers they are going to identify for each mode. For example, if they say three triggers, they will identify three triggers for home mode, three triggers for fast-forward mode, and three triggers for rewind mode, for a total of nine. Remind students to be realistic in deciding how many triggers they will identify and encourage them to write down their triggers in their workbooks.

Reinforcing the Lesson

Throughout the week, ask students at random what mode they are in. Ask them what triggered them to be in this mode. Encourage students to add to their triggers list throughout the day and week, if there is free time. When students are triggered, ask them to identify what they are feeling, how that feeling influences their thoughts, and how those thoughts might impact their behaviors. Work to dissuade negative self-talk and give positive affirmations for them to focus on, such as "I can do this," "One bad grade doesn't define me," etc.

Sample Letter to Parents and Guardians—Lesson 7

Dear Parent/Guardian,

In this lesson, as part of our work on self-awareness and social and emotional learning skills, our class focused on identifying our triggers for the home, rewind, and fast-forward modes. Students focused on identifying the people, places, situations, or things that led them to have the feelings represented by those modes. Students also worked on understanding how their feelings, thoughts, and behaviors are connected. For example, if they get a bad grade in math they might think they are bad at math and then not study in the future.

It is important for us to be aware of our triggers and how our feelings, thoughts, and behaviors are connected so that we can potentially avoid situations that might trigger us to make poor choices.

You can ask your child the following questions about the lesson:

- What are your triggers for each mode?
- What do you think some of my triggers are?
- How are your thoughts, feelings, and behaviors connected?
- Can you give me an example?

Regards,

Triggers List

You are doing math homework.	Home	Rewind	Fast-forward
Someone calls you a name.	Home	Rewind	Fast-forward
It's your birthday.	Home	Rewind	Fast-forward
Your friend is mad at you.	Home	Rewind	Fast-forward
Someone pushes you.	Home	Rewind	Fast-forward
No one will give you a turn to talk.	Home	Rewind	Fast-forward
You are told to clean your room.	Home	Rewind	Fast-forward
You are late to school.	Home	Rewind	Fast-forward
You had trouble sleeping last night.	Home	Rewind	Fast-forward
You meet someone new.	Home	Rewind	Fast-forward
You are left out of a conversation.	Home	Rewind	Fast-forward
You disagree with your classmate.	Home	Rewind	Fast-forward
You disagree with your teacher.	Home	Rewind	Fast-forward
You get a poor grade.	Home	Rewind	Fast-forward
You are late to class.	Home	Rewind	Fast-forward
You didn't get enough sleep.	Home	Rewind	Fast-forward
You are told "no" by an adult.	Home	Rewind	Fast-forward
You get to go on a field trip.	Home	Rewind	Fast-forward
You hear a loud noise.	Home	Rewind	Fast-forward
You are confused about your schoolwork.	Home	Rewind	Fast-forward

My Home Mode Triggers

My Rewind Mode Triggers

My Fast-Forward Mode Triggers

Feelings, Thoughts, Behaviors

Trigger:

_____

_____

_____

_____

_____

Feeling(s):

_____

_____

_____

_____

_____

Thought(s):

_____

_____

_____

_____

_____

Behavior(s):

_____

_____

_____

_____

_____

Lesson 8

Resiliency

Resiliency Icon

Students will gain insight into how they approach obstacles in life. When put under pressure, do they bend like a paper clip or break like a pencil?

Introduction

Resiliency is the ability to cope with and come back from difficult situations. It helps us overcome obstacles and learn how to constructively deal with them in the future. Research suggests that resilience produces many benefits, such as a higher quality of life, better mental health, decreased rates of depression, and increases in psychological flexibility and positive affect (MacLeod et al., 2016; Goubert & Trompetter, 2017). When we teach students resiliency skills, we are giving them the tools to be successful in the home, school, and community setting. Giving them the tools now will help them be more successful later in life. Not only do students benefit from learning about resilience, but Fried et al. (2018.) found that facilitators teaching resiliency skills also showed an increase in their levels of resilience.

Objectives

Students will be able to

- identify whether they are more like the paper clip (adapts under pressure) or the pencil (breaks under pressure)
- identify two ways in which they can practice being resilient

Success Criteria

Students are able to

- identify the importance of being resilient
- understand what resilience looks like
- feel comfortable practicing resilience

Materials

- Unwound paper clip
- Wooden pencil

- One copy per student of the Resilience worksheet
- One copy per student of the My Setbacks worksheet per student
- One piece of computer printer or notebook paper

Things to Note

During the discussion, avoid telling students that their responses are incorrect. Gently redirect them to the correct answer or encourage them to ask a friend for help. Being resilient is a learned skill and does not come easily to many adults, let alone students. Gently help students build up their resiliency levels by reminding them of the activity and asking them if they want to be like the paper clip or like the pencil?

Session 8.1: Learning about Resiliency

Check in on the students' commitments from the previous lesson. Ask, "Who would like to volunteer to share how they did in identifying additional triggers?" Allow students a chance to share how they did on their commitments. If you find that the same students are speaking each week, encourage new students to participate. If you have some students who never share, try to check in with them individually.

Illustrate the Concept: The Pencil and the Paper Clip

Before you begin class discussion, make sure you have your materials -- the paper clip and wooden pencil – and that you stand in front of the class where students can see you. To start the lesson, tell the class they will be learning about resilience and ask the students if they know what resilience is. Allow students a chance to respond. Give all students praise for taking a guess, even if their answer is incorrect.

Extend the discussion by presenting the analogy of the paper clip (flexibility and durability) and the pencil (rigidity and fragility), Ask students what they think will happen if you to press the unwound paperclip against your knee. To begin, take out a paper clip, unwind it, and hold each end so that it is pulled tight. You can say,

> While we are thinking about resilience, I'm wondering if
> anyone can tell me what would happen if I were to press the
> paper clip against my knee? What's the difference between a
> paper clip and a pencil?

Bring your knee up while bringing the paper clip down over your knee. The paper clip should bend when presented with the pressure of your knee. Pick up the pencil, holding it at the tip and eraser end. Ask students what they think will happen if you press the pencil against your knee.

Bring the wooden pencil down over your knee. The wooden pencil should snap under the pressure of your knee. Put the paper clip and the wooden pencil down where students can see them. Do not say anything more about the paper clip and the pencil for now. If students ask, encourage them to think about how this demonstration is related to the topic of resilience.

Define Resilience

Continue with the discussion of resilience, providing a definition and example:

> *Resilience is the ability to bounce back or recover after a setback. For example, if you received a poor grade on a math test, you could either decide not to study again because you'll just get a bad grade anyway, or you could decide to study harder so that you can get a better grade on the next test. Deciding to study harder is showing resilience because you are identifying a way that you can bounce back after a setback.*

Ask students for some examples of resilience. Encourage them to think about how we might bounce back from a setback. Next encourage them to identify two different possible responses they could have to a situation or options they could take -- one solution showing resilience and the other one not.

Connect the Idea of Resilience to the Presentation

Bring the focus back to the paperclip and pencil. Encourage students to share what they think the link between the paper clip, pencil, and resilience is. You can ask, "Now, I want you to think about the paper clip and pencil. What do you think they have to do with a lesson on resilience?"

Allow students a chance to respond. After they have responded, explain that the paper clip adapted when faced with an obstacle (demonstrating resilience) and the pencil broke (unable to overcome the obstacle):

> *The paper clip represents resilience. When faced with an obstacle, the paper clip bent and adapted. When faced with the same difficulty, the pencil snapped. When we are faced with challenging situations, we need to decide if we are going to be the paper clip or the pencil. Are we going to bend and adapt or break and snap?*

Session 8.2: Thinking about My Resilience

Extend the discussion by having students consider how they have responded to disappointments or setbacks and how the situation might have turned out differently if they had responded with more resilience. They will complete the Resilience Worksheet in this activity. Sample script: "When faced with setbacks we have two options. We can rally our efforts and face our problem with dedication and determination, or we can retreat and give up. I want you to think about times you rallied or retreated."

Complete the Resilience Worksheet

Have the students open to the Resilience worksheet in their workbook. Explain that you want students to identify two different situations, one in which they persevered and one in which they gave up. The first situation is one in which the student rallied. They were presented with setback and worked hard to overcome it. The students will write about this situation in the first box (the top right area of the worksheet).

The other situation they are going to identify is one in which they retreated. When faced with this setback, they gave up or ignored ways to overcome the problem. Have students write about this situation in the second box (the bottom right area of the worksheet).

For both situations, be sure students identify the setback, what their options were, which option they picked, how the situation turned out, and how it might have turned out differently had they done something different, for better or worse.

While the students work, walk around the room and check on their progress. Ask open-ended questions to help them gain insight into the situation and understand how they either rallied or retreated. Help them identify how the situation could have turned out differently, for better or worse depending on how they handled it.

Session 8.3: Responding to Setbacks

In this session, a piece of paper being ripped will be used as a metaphor for building up resilience in the face of setbacks. To introduce the lesson, stand in front of the students with a blank piece of white paper. Rip the paper into eight even squares, then stack the pieces on top of one another. You shouldn't be able to rip them when piled on top of each other. Explain to students that the layers of paper represent resiliency. Use the following sample script to illustrate how resiliency helps us in the face of setbacks:

> *Achieving our goals when faced with setback isn't always easy. Sometimes it can feel as if the setback is ripping us apart."* Rip the blank piece of paper down the middle into two pieces.
>
> *"If we give up, it is harder to bounce back. When another setback comes along, it rips apart our resolve a little bit more, making it even harder to rally.*

Rip each of the pieces of paper into another set of two. (You should have four pieces now.)

> *"The more we give up, the harder it is to overcome setback."*

Rip apart each of the four pieces of paper, making eight pieces. As you say the next part, start stacking the pieces of paper on top of each other.

> *But if we take our setbacks and layer them with resilience, it is harder to rip up our ability to overcome problems.*

Try to rip all of the papers while they are stacked on top of each other. This should be difficult, and you shouldn't be able to rip them all. If you can, layer those ripped papers on top of each other until you can't rip them.

Complete the My Setbacks Worksheet Exercise

After the presentation, pass out a piece of paper to each student and ask them to divide the paper into eight sections of the same size. They can use the My Setbacks worksheet in their workbook as a reference. Have the students write down eight setbacks they have experienced. To explain the exercise, you can say,

> *In each section, I want you to write down a setback that you have faced or that you are facing now. For example, I wrote "getting a bad grade or missing a deadline."* [Insert some of your own examples here. Let the students see that adults face setbacks as well.]

After the students have written down their examples, have them tear the paper into eight even sections so that one setback appears on each piece of paper. Have them next layer the papers together and try to rip them. Let them know that if they can rip the stack in half, they should stack the two halves together and try to rip that. To remind them of the purpose of the exercise, you can say, "Remember, the stack of setbacks represents the idea that if we layer our setbacks with resilience, we can overcome them more easily."

Walk around the room and observe students while they complete this activity. Once all students are done, you can ask, "How does it feel to think about overcoming these setbacks and facing them head on without retreating or giving up?"

Allow students a chance to respond. Write some of the responses on the board. Responses should include emotions and reactions like "strong," "confident," "happy," etc.

Conclude and Display the Skill Cutout

Remind students that everyone faces setbacks and that each person gets to decide how they are going to respond to those setbacks. Remind them of their options: bending like a paperclip and adapting or breaking like a wooden pencil. You can say,

We will all face setbacks. We will all have challenges and obstacles as we work toward our goals. The cool thing about that is that we get to decide how we are going to handle them. Are we going to bend and adapt like the paper clip or retreat and rip like the pencil?

This is a rhetorical question. Students don't need to answer it. Remind students that when they face a setback or conflict, they can bend like the paper clip or break like the pencil, layer their defenses or easily rip like a single sheet of paper when pressure is applied.

At the end of the lesson, display the resiliency skill cutout on the wall.

Section 8.4: Creating a Skit about Resilience

In this session, students will create a skit in which the main character responds to a challenge in two different ways, resulting in two different outcomes. Students can work in groups of four, or you can assign groups in whatever way works best for your unique class needs. You can introduce the exercise as follows:

We have been talking a lot about how we can either be resilient or break when faced with challenges. In this activity, I want you to work in your own group to create a skit. In your skit, your main character will be faced with a challenge and respond to it in two different ways. The skit will show the two different outcomes. The first outcome will show what would happen if the character broke like the pencil when faced with a challenge. The second outcome will show what would happen if the character bent like the paper clip and adjusted to the challenge. Write your skit down on a blank piece of paper so each member can read their lines from it.

Have students create their skits and encourage them to act them out for each other. Give praise for the skits. Have students brainstorm other outcomes that weren't depicted in the play. If students don't feel comfortable acting out their skits, they can give a synopsis of what their skit was about and what two possible outcomes came about from their character's actions.

Session 8.5: The Commitment Circle

Have students form a circle and introduce this lesson's prompt for the commitment circle:

Our prompt for our commitment circle this week is, How are you going to be resilient like the paper clip? For example, this week when I am stuck in traffic, I am going to play my favorite songs so the wait doesn't seem so bad.

Go around the circle and have each student make a commitment. Encourage them to make these commitments for both the home and school setting so they can see how these skills translate to the home setting.

Reinforcing the Lesson

As students are presented with conflicts and challenges throughout the week, ask them if they want to be the paper clip or the pencil. Encourage them to think through what might happen if they approached the challenges with the brittleness of the pencil or with the resiliency of the paper clip. Which outcome is better? If they have already reacted to a situation, ask them how the outcome might have been different if they reacted as the paper clip does.

Sample Letter to Parents and Guardians—Letter 8

Dear Parent/Guardian,

This week our class learned about resilience. This trait is an important part of mental well-being and part of the self-awareness domain in social and emotional learning. To illustrate what resilience is, students were presented with the example of the paper clip and the pencil. When pressure is applied to an unwound paper clip, it bends. When pressure is applied to a wooden pencil, it snaps. The class thought about how we respond to pressure and challenges and how our different responses produce different outcomes. We learned that we can work to bounce back when faced with challenges.

It is important to have insight into how resilient we are and how resilient we want to be so we can decide how we are going to approach pressure and challenges in life.

You can ask your child the following questions about the lesson:

- What is resilience?
- What is the difference between the paper clip and the pencil?
- What did the activity with the paper being ripped represent?

Regards,

Resilience

A Time When I Rallied:	
1. What was the situation?	1.
2. What were your options?	2.
3. What option did you pick?	3.
4. What was the outcome?	4.
5. How could it have turned out differently if you had retreated?	5.
A Time When I Retreated:	
1. What was the situation?	1.
2. What were your options?	2.
3. What option did you pick?	3.
4. What was the outcome?	4.
5. How could it have turned out differently if you had rallied?	5.

My Setbacks

Getting a bad grade.	

Self-Management

Lesson 9

Pause, Think, Play

Pause, Think, Play Icon

In this lesson, students will learn their first cognitive strategy (pause, think, play), which they can use when presented with a difficult situation. With this strategy, students will stop, think through their options, and then act on the option that is best for not only themselves but also for others. Throughout the lesson, having the power to control oneself (or self-regulate) will be represented by the controller on the Power Up board.

It is important for students to build an arsenal of coping skills that they can employ when they become stressed. Aldwin (2007) defines stress as what results when the demands of the environment are more than the individual can manage. Stress has been linked to negative outcomes, such as anxiety, depression, heart disease, high blood pressure, and diabetes (The National Institute of Mental Health, n.d.).

In their review of studies of interventions that support adolescents in stressful situations, Robson and Cook (1995) found that the most successful interventions were those that focused on increasing self-awareness, self-confidence, self-esteem, and problem-solving abilities. Teaching students the pause, think, play strategy helps promote their self-awareness and gives them specific tactics and action steps for managing difficult situations. The strategy also encourages students to practice complex thinking and utilize their prefrontal cortex.

Objectives

Students will be able to

- identify where the three modes are located on their controller
- identify the three steps in the cognitive strategy pause, think, and play

Success Criteria

Students are able to

- identify the three steps to the cognitive strategy pause, think, play
- understand that they are in control of their emotions

- utilize the pause, think, play strategy to make the best decision for themselves and for others

Materials

- Preferred coloring utensils
- One copy per student of the Power Up board
- Two copies per student of the Think Sheet

Things to Note

Avoid telling students that their answers are incorrect. Instead, redirect them to the correct answer or have them ask a friend for help. You should also avoid telling students what their options are. You want them to think through their options on their own. You might be pleasantly surprised about some of the options they come up with!

When discussing their options, avoid describing them as "good" or "bad" or using similar language. You want students to think about which option would produce the best outcome without labeling certain outcomes. It will be up to them to determine which option is best for them based on their morals and values.

Session 9.1: Introduce the Pause, Think, Play Strategy

To begin the lesson, check in on students' commitments from last week. Ask, "Who would like to volunteer to share how they did being resilient like a paper clip?" Allow students a chance to share how they did on their commitments. If you find that the same students speak up each week, encourage new students to share. If you have some students who never contribute, try to check in with them individually.

Power Up Controller as a Symbol for Self-Management

In this lesson, you will review the Power Up board controller with the class and ask them to start thinking about it as figure for managing one's feeling modes. Remind students about the three modes -- home, rewind, and fast-forward -- on their controller. You can begin the discussion by asking the following question:

> Now that we understand the three modes represented on our
> controllers, we are going to talk about what the controller
> itself represents. What are controllers normally used for?

After students respond, you can provide a definition as a way to begin talking about what the Power Up controller represents. Remind students that controllers are used to change settings on a device. Controllers for video games help players and their character navigate through the various missions. Controllers for televisions can change the station or the volume. When describing the Power Up controller, you can say,

> *This controller will help remind us that we are in control of our actions. Just as we use a controller to direct a game, we can make our own decisions and direct our own actions. The Power Up controller is a reminder of this. We will learn a lot of skills throughout our Power Up lessons that can aid us in making decisions we can be proud of. These skills will help us take control of our feelings, thoughts, and actions, the way a controller can take control of the device it is linked to.*

Color in the Home, Fast Forward, and Rewind Modes

Ask students to first focus on the home mode section on the controller. The home mode appears in the center of the controller and is represented by the house icon. For this exercise, you will have students color in the home mode section with a color that they think best represents the feelings. To help students have an idea what you want, you can color in the home mode in your controller and explain your color choice. You can say, "For example, I'm going to color this mode in a light blue because that is a calming color for me. It reminds me of the ocean, which relaxes me."

After students have colored in their home modes, have them do the same for the fast-forward mode and the rewind mode. The fast-forward mode is on the right side of the controller, represented by the two arrows facing to the right, and the rewind mode is on the left side of the controller, represented by two arrows pointing left.

Walk around the room while students work and validate the color they picked for their three modes. For example, you might say, "Green is a very calming color. Great choice for the home mode!" You can also ask them why they picked a particular color to gain insight into how they describe their emotions.

Introduce the Pause, Think, Play Icon

Once students have had a chance to talk about the controller, you can present the first self-management strategy. This strategy is referred to as the pause, think, and play strategy. To begin, have students look at their Power Up boards and find the icon for this strategy. Point out to students that two rows below the controller on the right side of the board is a gray icon that shows a pause arrow, light bulb, and play arrow. This icon represents the pause, think, play strategy they are learning. You can use the following script to explain the strategy:

Pause, think, play is a strategy we can use to think through difficult situations. When we think something through we are using the part of our brain called the prefrontal cortex. This is the part of the brain where critical thinking and problem-solving occur.

Practice Pausing

Let students know that they as a class are going to practice pausing. In this activity, you will set a timer for 30 seconds and challenge students to hold their position for that period. To introduce the exercise, you can say,

We will pause, or freeze, as a class. That means we won't be talking or moving. Let's practice together. I'm going to set the timer for 30 seconds. I challenge you to stay still for that entire 30-second period.

Practice pausing as a class for 30 seconds so students get used to taking a break when they need it for a longer period of time. Repeat having the class practice freezing three-to-five times. Consider making this a game to see who can stay frozen the longest.

Connect Pausing to the Self-Management Strategy

Congratulate the class let them know they did a great job on the activity. Tell them you want them to practice pausing when they feel like they are in the rewind or fast-forward mode. Let them know that in the coming days, you will challenge them to pause and then will talk to them about what actions they think they can take to respond to the situation they're reacting to. You can say,

I want you to practice pausing when you feel like you are in the rewind or fast-forward mode. I want you to imagine that you are pressing a pause button. I'm going to challenge you to use this throughout the day, week, and even year. If you hear me say "pause" I want you to freeze for about 30 seconds. You can even count to 30 in your head if you need to. After you freeze, we will talk about our options.

Note: If you are conducting daily lessons, let students know that even though you are encouraging them to practice pausing, they won't be able to earn power bars until they have learned the entire pause, think, play strategy.

Session 9.2: Using the Strategy to Think about Our Options

Now that the class has discussed and practiced the pausing part of our pause, think, play strategy, this lesson will cover the thinking part of this strategy.

Begin the session with a discussion of this phase of the strategy and ask students, "What do you think might happen in this part?"

Let students respond. They will likely guess correctly, but if they guess incorrectly, gently redirect them or have them call on a friend for help. Once they have had a chance to share their thoughts, provide an explanation. You can say,

> *That's right. When we think we are using the prefrontal cortex. We are considering our options on how to react to a situation. We always have at least two options in responding to a problem we encounter. There are often many more options available to us, but often times, it boils down to two very different options.*

Practice Using the Think Worksheet

To practice this strategy, have students complete their first Think worksheet. Have them turn to the worksheet in their workbook. Once students have turned to the correct page in their book, you can say,

> *I am going to tell you a brief story. We call this kind of story a scenario. After I tell you it, I want you to write a summary of what happens in the scenario on the top line of your worksheet. If you have time, you can also draw a picture of it. Our scenario today is "Another student starts calling you names at recess."*

Walk around the room while students work to make sure they are writing and drawing what they are supposed to. Gently redirect them if they are off task or writing and drawing something else.

After students have finished their summaries, ask them to think of two different things they could do when someone calls them names. Have them write down one option next to the number one on the worksheet. (You can point to the section on the worksheet.) Let students record the option on the worksheet, and once they are done, congratulate them ("I saw some great options!") and then ask them to think of something else they could do. What is another reaction they could have? Have them write that option next to the number two in the worksheet. (You can point to the section in an example worksheet.) After they have written down a second option, have them come up with as many other options as they can, even if they seem silly or unrealistic. Have them write those under the Other Options heading on the worksheet.

Once students are done, congratulate them and share some of the options. You can say,

Great job! A lot of you came up with some really good options. For example, you could call the student names, or you could tell the teacher what happened. Other options might include walking away, talking to your parents, and ignoring the student. Did anyone else have any other ideas?

If students don't have any other ideas to contribute, encourage them to take a minute to think about it. Give praise for all ideas, even the ones that are obviously unrealistic.

Review the Icon

After the discussion, have students find the pause, think, play icon on their Power Up board. Point out that in the icon to the right of, or after, the pause symbol, there is a picture of a light bulb. This represents the "think" part of our strategy. Remind them that the important thing to remember is that we always have options. Sometimes we just have to "pause" and "think" about them.

Session 9.3: Using the Strategy to Make a Decision and Take Action

This session will focus on the play phase of the pause, think, and play strategy. In this session, you'll review what happens in the pause and think part of the first self-management strategy and ask students to return to the Think Sheet worksheet. To begin, explain to students that the class is going to talk about the play part of our pause, think, and play strategy. The play part is when we pick which action or option to take that would be the best for us and others. At this point, you can have the students look at the pause, think, play icon. Remind them that "pause" is represented by the pause symbol (the vertical bars), the "think" part by the light bulb, and "play" is represented by the play arrow. You can define this last phase as follows:

The "play" part of our strategy is when we make a decision and choose the action that will have the best outcome for ourselves and others.

Complete the Think Sheet Worksheet

Have students return to the Think Sheet worksheet they have been working on. Remind them of the scenario they were considering (someone was calling them names at recess). Ask them to look at all the options they listed and circle the best option for themselves and others. Once they have picked their option, they should write a sentence in the blank space at the bottom of their worksheet about why that is the best option. To help them start, you can use the following example from your worksheet:

For example, my first two options were that I can call them a name back, or I can go tell the teacher. I think telling the teacher is the best option because then I won't get in trouble, so I'm going to circle telling the teacher. [Demonstrate circling the answer.] And I'll write that this is the best option because I won't get in trouble and the other person will be asked to stop.

Walk around the room while students work and ask them questions about why they think that the option they circled is the best option for them. (They might say because by taking that action, they won't get in trouble or that it is safer for them.) Expand on their comments and ask them why what they have chosen would be the best option for others. (They might say because the other person will get in trouble and learn the importance of being kind to others.) If students pick an option that does not seem to benefit them, ask them why they made that decision. Ask them what benefits they would receive from making that choice and taking that action. Guide them to determining that they should pick the option that provides the most benefits for themselves and others in the short and the long term.

Display the Skill Cutout

Congratulate students on their work on the exercise and hang the pause, think, play skill cutout in the classroom for students to refer to and see. Let them know if they forget the skill, they can look up at it as a reminder. Let the class know that now that they have learned about the pause, think, and play strategy, you will be able to start filling their power bars when they practice it.

If you are not covering Session 4's optional lesson, give students a blank Think Sheet worksheet and encourage them to use it as needed.

Session 9.4: Using the Strategy on Their Own Story

Let students know that they are going to complete another Think Sheet and create their own pause, think, play strategy. Have them turn to a blank Think Sheet worksheet in their workbook and tell them that you're going to let them choose their own scenario to write about. In this session, students will complete the entire worksheet.

Have them write the scenario at the top of the page, list their two main options for responding to it, identify other options available, and then circle the best option. In the blank space at the bottom of the worksheet, they should write a sentence or two explaining why their choice is the best option for them and others. If they have time, you can draw pictures to go with what they have written.

Walk around the room while students work and check to make sure they are writing and drawing about what they are supposed to. Gently redirect them if they are off task or writing or drawing something else, or give suggestions as needed.

Have Students Share What They Have Written

Let students know that you saw some great scenarios and choices in their work and ask for volunteers to present their Think Sheets. When students present their scenarios, discuss the options available to them, which option they picked, and why. Give students praise for sharing their sheets and encourage other students to add to what the student presented. Let students see that there are many options available and that some are more beneficial than others.

Session 9.5: The Commitment Circle

Have students gather in a circle to identify their commitments. When providing the prompt, offer your own commitment first. You can say,

> Our prompt for our commitment circle this week is, How many times are you going to commit to using the pause, think, and play strategy? For example, I am going to utilize this strategy at least twice today.

Go around the circle and have students make their commitments. Encourage them to make these commitments for both the home and school setting so they can see how these skills translate to the home setting.

Reinforcing the Lesson

Encourage students to use the pause, think, play strategy and to talk out their options and to pick the best one in responding to a situation. If students made a choice that was not in their best interest, encourage them to voice what their other options were and what would have happened had they had chosen one of these options. Look for students using their skills and be sure to fill up their power bars.

Sample Letter to Parents and Guardians—Lesson 9

Dear Parent/Guardian,

This week we focused on our first self-management skill, called pause, think, play. With this strategy, students are encouraged to stop when presented with a difficult situation, to think about their options in how to respond, and then to choose the best option for not only themselves but for others as well. Students also learned about the Power Up icon that represents the pause, think, play strategy, and they reviewed the Power Up controller and what it represents.

It is important that we are able to use the pause, think, and play strategy so that we can make decisions that are beneficial for us and for others. Encourage your child to utilize this strategy at home by reminding your child to pause, think, and play. Talk out what options they have in responding to a situation and help them think about the consequences of each so that they can pick the best option.

You can ask your child the following questions about the lesson:

- What is the purpose of the controller?
- What does pause, think, play stand for?
- Why is it important to pause before making a decision?
- Why is it important to think before making a decision?
- Who else do your decisions impact?

Regards,

Think Sheet

Scenario:

_____

_____

I can:

1. _____

   _____

   _____

   _____

2. _____

   _____

   _____

   _____

Other options:

1. _____

2. _____

3. _____

4. _____

Lesson 10

Slowing Down Strategies

Deep Breathing Icon

Mandala Icon

Finger Maze Icon

This week students will start learning strategies on how to calm their bodies when they have increased energy. They will learn three strategies that will reduce their energy levels (deep breathing, mandalas, and finger mazes) so that they are able to pick the one that works best for them.

Introduction

There are many benefits to using strategies to reduce energy levels when dealing with difficult emotions. This lesson will present the benefits arising from the practices of using deep breathing, tracing finger mazes, and coloring mandalas.

Deep breathing. Deep breathing is a self-management strategy that helps the body better cope with stress. Deep breathing increases our oxygen levels and allows us to expel carbon dioxide from our body. When stressed, our sympathetic nervous system, which is responsible for the fight, flight, or freeze response (Patel, 2017), is activated. When this response is triggered, hormones are released that increase blood pressure and pulse rate. Deep breathing activates the parasympathetic nervous system, reversing these responses and slowing down our heart rate and lowering blood pressure (Patel, 2017). When we are able to counteract the effects of the fight, flight, or freeze response and lower our blood pressure and pulse rate, we are better able to relax our body, think through our situation, and respond in an appropriate manner.

Other health benefits of the practice of deep breathing include reducing anxiety and depression, increasing energy levels and muscle relaxation, and decreasing overall feelings of stress (Patel, 2017).

Mandalas. The word *mandala* means "sacred circle" in Sanskrit (Bi & Liu, 2019). Circles are considered powerful in many cultures and are found in nature (flowers, moon, sun, etc). Mandalas are considered symbols for many things, ranging from representations of wholeness to control in times of dysregulation (Palmer et al., 2014). Coloring can reduce stress and improve well-being (Rigby & Taubert, 2016), and coloring mandalas in specific can reduce anxiety (Van der Vennet & Serice, 2012; Mantzios & Giannou, 2018).

In Van der Vennett and Serice's study, (2012) coloring a mandala was found to be more effective in reducing anxiety than free drawing.

Finger mazes. Finger mazes are a form a labyrinth. Made up of paths that lead from a starting point to and ending point, finger mazes can be simple or elaborate. Alego (2001) asserts that there are two different types of labyrinths: the maze (made up of paths that split off with one path to the end point) and the meander (a single path leading to the end point). Using finger mazes helps us shift our focus from a stressful situation to something that is nonthreatening and unrelated to the situation.

Objective

- Students will be able to identify three new calming strategies that they can utilize when they are in fast-forward mode.

Success Criteria

Students are able to

- identify at least three new calming self-management strategies
- understand when they should utilize deep breathing, mandalas, and finger mazes
- feel comfortable trying each strategy (mandalas, finger mazes, and deep breathing) to see which ones work for them

Materials

- Preferred coloring utensils
- One copy per student of the Mandala worksheet
- One copy per student of the My Mandala worksheet (or blank piece of paper)
- One copy per student of the Finger Mazes worksheet
- One copy per student of the Controller worksheet

Things to Note

Avoid telling students which strategies work best for them. If you notice them trying a strategy and it isn't working, encourage them to try a different one.

Session 10.1: Practicing Deep Breathing

Before beginning the new lesson, check in with students on how they did in using the strategy they learned in the previous lesson. Ask students who remembers what strategy they learned last week. After students respond, extend the discussion by asking if using the pause, think, play strategy helped them. How did they feel before using it? How did they feel after using it?

If students hadn't used the pause, think, play strategy, ask how the situation might have turned out differently if they had.

During the discussion, in order to feel like they are part of the group, students might make up a time that they used the strategy. Do not correct them if you think the event didn't actually happen. The fact that they could think up a scenario in which they "used" the strategy is good, because it shows that they know when they should be using the strategy and how it could have helped them.

Introduce Calming Strategies

In this lesson, the class will discuss strategies we can use to slow our body down when we are in fast-forward mode. As the instructor, remember to remind students that when we are in fast-forward mode, we have increased energy. When we use calming strategies, we send messages to our brains that we are OK. This allows our body to calm down so we can use our critical thinking and problem-solving skills.

Learning about Deep Breathing

The first calming strategy the class will learn is deep breathing. Deep breathing offers several health benefits, including reduced anxiety and depression, lower or stabilized blood pressure, increased energy levels and muscle relaxation, and decreased feelings of stress. When you introduce the practice to students, you can say,

> *When we take a deep breath we are sending oxygen to our brain, which helps slow our body down so we can think more clearly. Deep breathing also slows down our fight, flight, or freeze response. Deep breathing sends messages to our brain that we aren't in danger and that our body can return to its normal resting state.*

Lead the Class in Practicing Deep Breathing

Have students use the controller worksheet on their Power Up board to help them in the exercise. You will have them trace the outline of the controller as a way to time their inhales and exhales. You can use the following script to help introduce the exercise:

> *Let's practice taking a good deep breath to see if this calming strategy will help us throughout the week. We are going to use our game controller worksheet on our Power Up board as a breathing guide. Start by placing your finger on the star at the bottom of the controller.* [Point to the star on the controller.]
>
> *We are going to trace our controller, and as we go around the left side, we are going to breathe in slowly through our nose as*

if we were smelling a flower. When we hit the breath symbol on the top, we are going to continue tracing and breathe slowly out of our mouths as we would if we were blowing on a pinwheel. We should breathe in and breathe out the entire time we are tracing the controller. We are going to take our time breathing in and out so it helps slow our bodies down. Let's practice.

Have the students practice slowly breathing in and out while tracing the controller. Do this while tracing the entire controller about five times.

Congratulate the Class on Their Work and Display the Skill Cutout

Encourage students when they have finished and have them begin thinking about using the strategy. You might say, "Great job class! When do you think you could use this throughout the day?"

Students will have different responses. This skill works for many situations. Give praise after each response offered. Hang the deep breathing skill cutout on the board for students to refer to see and reference.

Session 10.2: Coloring Mandalas

This session will introduce mandalas and have students use the Mandalas worksheet to learn the self-management strategy. Coloring geometric patterns has been found to decrease anxiety and relax our bodies. When you begin the session, remind students that the first calming strategy they practiced was deep breathing. Begin this session with a discussion question: "The next skill you are going to try is coloring mandalas. Who knows what a mandala is?" After students respond, you can let them know that the word mandala means "sacred circle" in Sanskrit:

Circles are considered powerful in many cultures. You can find them in nature in the shape of flowers, the moon, and the sun, for example. For many people, circles make them think of wholeness, continuity, connection, unity, harmony, and the cycle of life. Coloring a symmetrical pattern like you find in a mandala decreases anxiety and relaxes our bodies.

Coloring in the Mandala Worksheet

Once you have explained mandalas and how we can use them, have students turn to the Mandala worksheet in their workbooks. Let them know that you are going to give them some time to color in the mandala. If students would like to continue coloring when they have free time, let them know to ask you if it's an OK time to do so. Let students have a chance to practice coloring.

Introduce the My Mandala Worksheet and Display the Skill Cutout

Have students turn to the blank My Mandala worksheet in their workbook. Let them know that on this page, they can draw their own mandala in their free time at school. Remind them that mandalas are generally symmetrical, but they can draw **theirs however they would like.** Hang the mandala skill cutout for students to refer to and see.

Session 10.3: Using Finger Mazes

To start the session, let students know that the class is going to continue talking about skills to use to calm our bodies down and introduce the calming strategy of finger mazes. Finger mazes are a type of labyrinth. Labyrinths are ancient symbols and have been found in many places, including China, Ireland, India, England, Scandinavia, France, Crete, and many other places. The labyrinth has often been used as a meditation tool. Labyrinths are thought to help to provide clarity, manage stress, and help with decision-making, self-exploration, and reflection.

Use the Finger Mazes Worksheet to Practice

Have students practice by tracing with their finger the maze in the worksheet. They should try to move through the maze's passageways toward the endpoint marked by the star, avoiding walls and dead ends. To begin the exercise, you can say,

> *Finger mazes are a good way to handle stress! Let's do one of our own. Turn to your Finger Mazes worksheet in your workbook. Find the maze at the top left.* [Point to the maze in an example worksheet.] *We are going to start at the top left. Place your finger at the start of the maze where the star at top is* [demonstrate where the star is], *and see if you can find your way through the finger maze to the second star.*

Give students some time to try the maze.

When you notice that most of them have completed it, continue with the lesson and have them try the other mazes: "Great job class! There are three other finger mazes on this page. Take the next couple of minutes to work through them."

Walk around the classroom and help students if they get stuck. Remind them they can utilize other self-regulation skills if they become frustrated. Conclude the session by hanging the finger maze skill cutout on the board for students to refer to and see.

Session 10.4: Practicing a Calming Strategy

In this session, let students pick one of the calming self-management strategies they have learned and practice it. You can determine the amount of time you want them to devote to using the skill. To introduce the session, you can say,

We have learned three new calming strategies. I want to devote some time for you to practice these skills. You can take this time to color your mandala, work on your own mandala, or practice the finger mazes.

Walk around the room while students work to make sure they are on task. You can also play calming music while they work.

Session 10.5: The Commitment Circle

Have students gather into a circle and offer the prompt for this week's commitment:

Our prompt for our commitment circle this week is, Which skill are you going to commit to using [deep breathing, finger mazes, or coloring mandalas] and when might you use it? For example, I am going to use deep breathing. I might use it when I'm grading papers or when I get frustrated when my family doesn't do their chores.

Go around the circle and have students make their commitments. Encourage them to make these commitments for both the home and school setting so they can see how these skills translate to the home setting.

Reinforcing the Lesson

Remind students throughout the week to utilize all three skills. Students will have favorites and that's OK, but encourage them to use the other skills every once in a while. Ask them if using the skill helped them reduce their energy levels and return to home mode. If it didn't, reassure them that that's OK and have them try a different skill or return to a skill they are comfortable using. It's good for students to have a couple of different skills that work for them.

Sample Letter to Parents and Guardians—Lesson 10

Dear Parent/Guardian,

This week, as part of our work on self-management skills in social and emotional learning, our class learned three new strategies that we can use to reduce our energy levels. We learned about taking deep breaths, using finger mazes, and coloring mandalas to allow us to reduce our energy levels and slow down. These strategies send messages to our brain that we are OK, and they allow us to stay in control of our bodies.

You can ask your child the following questions about the lesson:

- What three new calming strategies did you learn?
- Will you teach me how to take a good deep breath?
- When can you use these strategies?

Regards,

Controller

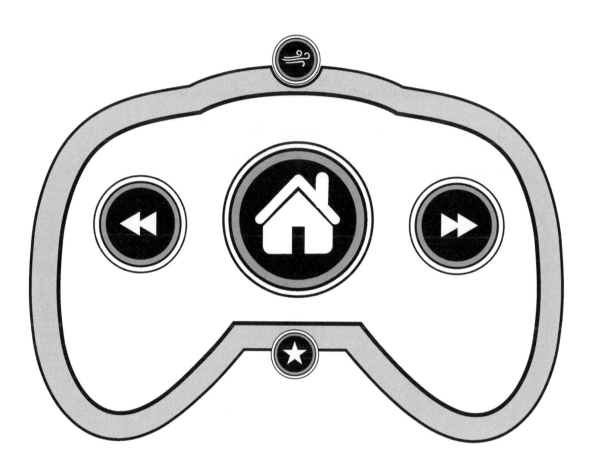

Mandala

My Mandala

Finger Mazes

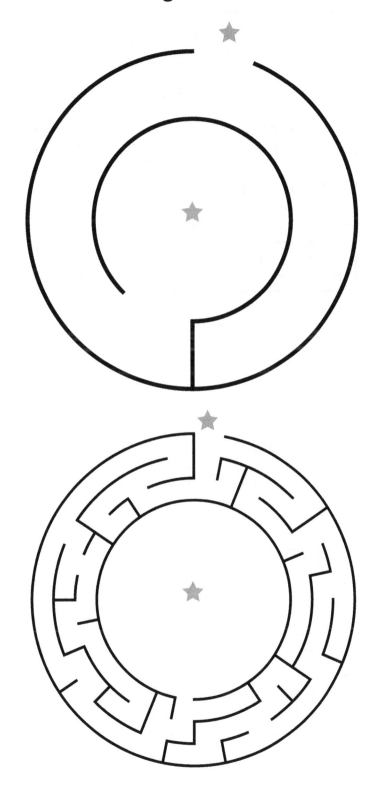

Lesson 11

Slowing Down Strategies, Continued

Progressive Muscle Relaxation Icon

Mindfulness Icon

Students will learn two new self-management strategies to reduce energy levels: progressive muscle relaxation and mindfulness. They can use these strategies when they are feeling overstimulated and in fast-forward mode.

Introduction

Progressive muscle relaxation and mindfulness are two effective self-management strategies students can use to relax their minds and bodies when they feel overstimulated.

Mindfulness. The self-management strategy mindfulness gives students the ability to focus on the present moment as a way to self-regulate. While mindfulness has its origins in religious practice, in the 1990s, it began its shift to becoming the mainstream, secular practice it is today (Cardaciotto et al., n.d.). Cardaciotto, L., et al. (2008) define mindfulness as "the tendency to be highly aware of one's internal and external experiences in the context of an accepting, nonjudgmental stance toward those experiences." Using mindfulness as a self-management strategy has many benefits. In a review of studies on mindfulness, Gallant (2016) concluded that the practice increased one's ability to cope with stress, decreased symptoms of depression and anxiety, helped reduce substance use, and led to improvements in mood and cognition (Gallant, 2016).

Progressive muscle relaxation. Progressive muscle relaxation has individuals practice breathing while and tensing and relaxing various muscles, including those in the face and neck, chest, shoulders, upper back, and abdomen, and the right and left upper legs, calves, and feet, in order to achieve a state of relaxation. (In other versions of progressive muscle relaxation, the individual is more passive and does not tense muscles groups but, instead, focuses on deeply relaxing the muscles.) By allowing individuals to systematically relax muscles in their body, progressive muscle relaxation sends messages to their brain and body that they are safe and able to handle the stressful situation at hand.

Progressive muscle relaxation was first developed by Dr. Edmund Jacobson in 1934, and the technique has undergone changes over the years (McCallie et al., 2006). In a review of the research, McCallie et al. (2006) found that the benefits of progressive muscle relaxation range from a decrease in muscle tension and headaches to its effectiveness as a pain management technique.

Objective

Students will be able to identify two new calming strategies that they can use to slow down and calm their bodies.

Success Criteria

Students are able to

- identify two calming strategies called mindfulness and progressive muscle relaxation

- understand when they can utilize mindfulness and progressive muscle relaxation

- feel comfortable trying mindfulness and progressive muscle relaxation

Materials

- Preferred coloring utensils
- Soothing song or music to play during the lesson activity
- One copy per student of the My Relaxing Place worksheet
- One copy per student of the Progressive Muscle Relaxation worksheet
- One copy per student of Other Self-Management Strategies worksheet

Things to Note

Avoid telling students which strategies work best for them. If you notice a student trying a strategy that isn't working, encourage them to try a different one. During the mindfulness activity, do not force students to close their eyes. This can be upsetting for students who have experienced trauma. Give them the option to keep their eyes open and look at their feet instead while practicing mindfulness.

Session 11.1: Learning about Mindfulness

Begin the lesson by having a discussion about their use of the previously learned self-management strategies of practicing deep breathing, using finger mazes, and coloring mandalas. In the discussion, you might find that students make up a time they used a strategy, perhaps in order to feel like they are part of the group. Do not correct them. The fact that they could think up a scenario in which they "used" a strategy is good because it shows that they know when they should be using the strategy and how it could have helped them. If they give an example of an appropriate self-management strategy that hasn't been discussed (e.g., taking a break, walking away), give them praise for mentioning another skill. Encourage them to keep using this skill and let them know that later in the curriculum the class will talk about other skills and that they can share this skill at that time.

To check in on commitments and begin this discussion, you can say,

> *Let's check in on the calming strategies we learned last week. What three strategies did we learn? Did using deep breathing, tracing finger mazes, and coloring mandalas help you? How did you feel before using these strategies? How did you feel after using these strategies? If you hadn't used a strategy how might the situation have turned out differently?*

Introduce the Practice of Mindfulness

Start the new lesson by letting students know that they are going to learn about a calming strategy called mindfulness. Ask the class whether any of them know what mindfulness is. After students respond and there is a discussion, offer an explanation and examples that draw on our five senses. Emphasize that the practice reduces stress by having us focus only on the moment. You should say that mindfulness is about being in the present moment:

> *When we are being mindful, we are engaging our senses and focusing on what is happening at the present time. We are not thinking about what happened this morning or worrying about our test later. We are focused only on the present. We use our five senses to observe what is happening around us. We take note of details.*
>
> *For example, I might notice that I have a red apple on my desk. I might notice that it is bright red. I might also notice that there are some brown spots near the stem. In mindfulness, we also use our sense of touch. I might notice that the apple feels smooth to the touch but is heavy when I pick it up. We use our sense of smell. I might notice that the apple smells fresh.*
>
> *We can also use our sense of taste. I might take a bite of the apple and notice that it tastes sweet. We also use our sense of hearing. At this point, my focus might shift from the apple to the noisy air conditioning unit. While my attention has shifted, I am still staying in the present while I focus on that noise.*
>
> *Using mindfulness can decrease our stress, decrease our anxiety, and decrease our worries because we are focusing on what*

is happening in the present. It helps us clear our mind and put us at ease.

Have Students Practice Mindfulness

Have students practice mindfulness together as a group. Some students may not feel comfortable closing their eyes for this activity, and it is not necessary for this exercise. Putting on some soft, soothing music will help. YouTube has a lot of great mindfulness music options. It doesn't matter what song or music you pick as long as it is slow and soothing. To begin, you can say,

> *Get comfortable in your chair. If you feel safe doing so, close your eyes. If you don't want to close your eyes, that is OK; just focus on the ground. I'm going to put on some quiet music while we practice mindfulness.*

Use a calm and low tone when speaking and ask students to focus on the music:

> *Listen to it. Let the lyrics flow through your ears. If you start thinking about other things, come back to noticing the music. It's OK if your mind wanders. Don't get upset with yourself if it does. Just bring your attention back to the present by focusing on the music.*

Let the students listen to the music from anywhere from 30 seconds to 2 minutes. You are the best judge of how long your students will be able to sit still. To help students stay focused, have them take three deep breaths. Tell them, "As you breathe in through your nose, I want you to focus on the temperature of the air entering your nose. As you breathe out through your mouth, I want you to notice the temperature of the air as it leaves your lips." Demonstrate taking three slow, deep breaths to pace the students.

Have students focus on sounds in the room:

> *Now I want you to listen for any sounds you might hear. I hear the music playing over everything else so I'm going to focus on that. If I find that my mind is starting to wander to other things, I'm going to bring my attention back to the music, letting the lyrics flow through my ears.*

Have students listen for anywhere from 30 seconds to 2 minutes. You know your class's attention span best.

Once students have focused on their sense of hearing, ask them to focus on their sense of touch. In a calm and soothing tone, you can say,

> *Last, I want you to feel the chair underneath you. I want you to imagine the chair is pushing up against you, while you are pushing down against it. As you feel the chair, I*

> *want you to slowly open your eyes. When you are ready,*
> *turn and look at me.*

Wait until all students have their eyes on you. Don't rush the process. It can be disorienting to come out of a mindful state.

Conclude and Display the Mindfulness Skill Cutout

Congratulate the class after the activity and let them know that mindfulness is a great calming skill that we can practice when we feel like we need to slow our body down. Hang the mindfulness skill cutout on the whiteboard or your display area for students to refer to and see.

Session 11.2: Creating a Drawing of Your Relaxing Place

To extend students' practice of mindfulness, have them practice it through drawing and describing their relaxing place. Students should use each of their five senses when writing a description of their relaxing place. Have students turn to the My Relaxing Place worksheet in their workbooks. Tell them,

> *I want you to draw a picture of a place you find relaxing and*
> *to write a few sentences about it, using your five senses to*
> *describe your relaxing place. For example, I drew a picture*
> *of the beach and wrote that when I'm at the beach I feel the*
> *waves lapping up against my feet, washing the sand away*
> *from under them. I also hear the waves crashing against the*
> *shore and seagulls overhead. If I take a deep breath I can feel*
> *the salt in the air and taste it on my tongue.*

Walk around the room while students work on their drawings and ask them about their relaxing place. If a student draws a place that doesn't look relaxing, inquire in a nonjudgmental tone what is relaxing about their place. Remember, everyone is different and different scenarios can be relaxing for different students. Do not tell a student that their place is not relaxing. If their relaxing place raises concern, be sure to contact the school counselor. Turn on some relaxing music while students work. Keep the music playing for the rest of the lesson.

Conclude the Session by Practicing Mindfulness

Once students have had a chance to work on the worksheet, congratulate them and turn their focus on practicing a moment of mindfulness. Have them focus on what each of their senses takes in:

> *Great job class! I saw a lot of relaxing places in your draw-*
> *ings. I want you to close your eyes or look at the ground and*
> *imagine you are in your relaxing place. I want you to imagine*

everything that you see. [Pause and give students some time to focus.] Imagine everything that you hear. [Pause and give students some time.] Imagine everything you smell. [Pause again.] I want you to feel your seat underneath you, pushing against you, and you pushing down against it. When you are ready, open your eyes and look at me.

Session 11.3: Practicing Progressive Muscle Relaxation

This lesson will focus on the calming self-management skill called progressive muscle relaxation, and students will try practicing this skill. Begin the activity by using the Progressive Muscle Relaxation worksheet to explain what the skill is and to guide students. Let students know that progressive muscle relaxation is an activity where we relax groups of muscles in our body, moving through each of the muscle groups until all of our muscles are relaxed. Have students find the outline of the body with a guide of the different muscle groups in the Progressive Muscle Relaxation worksheet in their workbooks. Let them know that the class will use this to guide the lesson activity. To conduct the progressive muscle relaxation exercise, you can say,

> *We are going to use this worksheet to guide our activity. We are going to start with our feet. I want you to focus all of your attention on your feet and any tension that might be in them. We are going to breathe in while we focus on the tension. When we breathe out, I want you to imagine all of the tension and stress leaving your feet as you breathe out. We are going to take three deep breaths for each muscle group. Ready? Breathe in... breathe out... breathe in... breathe out... breathe in... breathe out....*

Model breathing slowly in and out while relaxing your body. After you ask students to breathe in and out and relax their feet, repeat the process, moving up the body and focusing on each muscle group depicted in the worksheet. You can use your example worksheet to point to the group of muscles you are focusing on and relaxing.

Congratulate the Class and Display the Skill Cutout

Praise the class for their efforts ("Great job class! Our entire body should be relaxed now!") and hang the progressive muscle relaxation skill cutout on the whiteboard or display area for students to refer to and see.

If you are doing weekly lessons and plan to skip Session 4's optional lesson, encourage students to brainstorm other self-management strategies that they use and have them write down those strategies on the worksheet Other Self-Management Strategies.

Session 11.4: Identifying Other Calming Strategies

In this session, have students work with their partner to come up with as many calming self-management techniques as they can think of that the group hasn't already discussed. Give them five minutes to write down their strategies on the Other Self-Management Strategies worksheet in their workbooks. Try to vary students' partners so they are with different peers as often as possible.

Complete the Other Self-Management Strategies Worksheet

Once students have found the worksheet and gotten with their partners, set a timer for five minutes and have students begin. After five minutes, have the students share their techniques. Write the responses on the board. Let them know they can use some of the skills their classmates identified: "You came up with a lot of great ideas! If you see a skill on the board that you like, you may add it to your list."

Session 11.5: The Commitment Circle

Have students gather in a circle to identify their commitments for the lesson. Offer the following as the prompt:

> *Our prompt for our commitment circle this week is, What skill are you going to commit to using? For example, this week I am going to commit to taking a break when I feel like I need to calm myself down.*

Go around the circle and have students name their commitments. Encourage them to make these commitments for both the home and school setting so they can see how these skills translate to the home setting.

Reinforcing the Lesson

Remind students throughout the week to utilize all the skills they have learned. Have them practice the skills they mentioned as being their favorites. Students will have favorites, and that's OK, but encourage them to use other skills every once in a while. Ask them if the new skill worked. If it didn't, reassure them that that's OK and have them return to a skill they are comfortable using and that they know works. It's good for a student to have a couple of different skills that work for them.

Sample Letter to Parents and Guardians—Lesson 11

Dear Parent/Guardian,

This week, as part of our focus on self-management skills in social and emotional learning, our class learned the self-management strategies of mindfulness and progressive muscle relaxation to reduce energy levels. These strategies send messages to our brain that we are OK and allow our bodies and minds to relax so that we are able to use our problem-solving and critical thinking skills to help us make better decisions.

You can ask your child the following questions about the lesson:

- When would you use progressive muscle relaxation?
- When would you use mindfulness?
- What other self-management strategies are you going to try?
- Which strategies have worked for you before?
- Which strategies have not worked for you before?
- What other strategies do you use?

Regards,

My Relaxing Place

_____

_____

_____

_____

_____

_____

_____

_____

_____

Progressive Muscle Relaxation

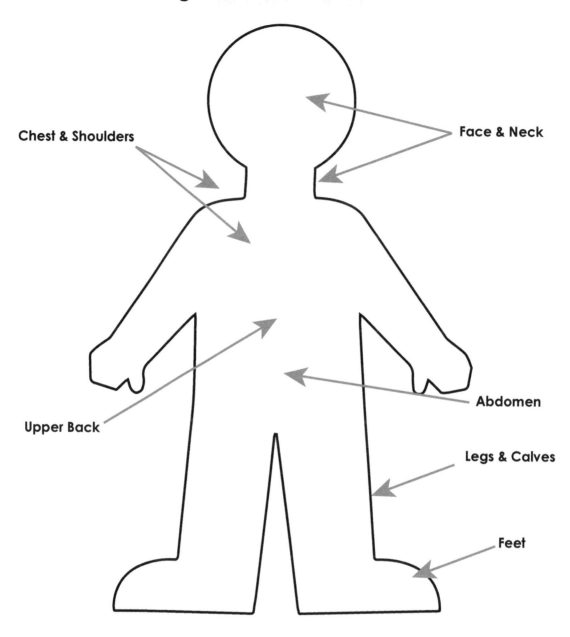

Chest & Shoulders

Face & Neck

Abdomen

Upper Back

Legs & Calves

Feet

Other Self-Management Strategies

Lesson 12

Energizing Strategies

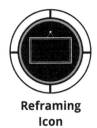

Reframing Icon

Worry Box Icon

Wall Push-Ups Icon

Stretching Icon

Students will learn four new self-management skills they can use to energize their bodies and minds. These skills are reframing, placing their worries in a worry box, performing wall push-ups, and stretching. Students can use these strategies when they find themselves in the rewind mode. These strategies can help combat anxiety and depression and help them experience a more elevated mood and move them back to the home mode.

Introduction

The four strategies in this lesson help students to shift their focus, change how they view situations, decrease anxiety and depression, and improve mental health.

Worry Box. It is important for students to be able to identify their worries so they can start to cope with them and/or resolve them. The purpose of the worry box intervention is to give students a container to "place" their worries in and to reduce stress. Students will write down their worries and leave them in the box. Getting the worries onto paper and "contained" helps them compartmentalize their feelings so they can temporarily shift their focus away from emotions that might become overwhelming. If their worries are in a box, then they aren't in their head. Students can move back to the home mode where they don't feel weighed down with feelings of sadness and anxiety.

Physical activity. Exercise poses physical, mental, and emotional health benefits. Exercise can help prevent and treat cardiovascular disease, improve cognitive functioning, and reduce the risk of stroke (Epstein, 2006; Brugniaux et al., 2014). Mental health is also positively affected by physical activity. Siqueira et al. (2016) found that exercise enabled individuals with major depressive disorder to take lower dosages of medication than those who did not exercise and achieve the same effect.

Stretching exercises can improve students' mental health and help put them in a state where they are ready to learn. If students are receptive to learning, their productivity increases and they are in a better position to achieve their educational goals. Exercise is also free, easy to implement, and can be individualized. As students move and exercise, their mood will improve, moving them from the rewind mode to the home mode.

Reframing. Defined as restating a negative statement into a more positive one, reframing can be used as an effective self-management intervention and a technique for social conversation (Koegel et al., 2016). Reframing has been shown to increase levels of gratitude, decrease depression, improve relationship satisfaction, and to treat post-traumatic stress disorder (Lambert et al., 2012; Moore et al., 2010). When students are able to see the situation from a more positive viewpoint, it can improve mood and shift the student from the rewind mode back to the home mode.

Objective

Students will be able to identify four skills they can utilize to energize their bodies and minds when they are in the rewind mode.

Success Criteria

Students are able to

- identify four new energizing self-management strategies
- understand when to utilize the self-management strategies of worry boxes, reframing, wall push-ups, and stretching
- feel comfortable practicing the use of worry boxes, reframing, wall push-ups, and stretching

Materials

- Preferred coloring utensils
- One copy per student of the My Worries worksheet
- One copy per student of the Worry Box Outline worksheet
- One copy of the Wall Push-ups worksheet per student and one for the classroom
- One copy per student of the Stretching worksheet
- One copy per student of the Reframing worksheet or two copies per student if doing Session 4's optional lesson
- Scissors
- Tape

Things to Note

Avoid telling students which strategies work best for them. If you notice students trying a strategy and it isn't working, encourage them to try another one. You will want to make sure you have a safe place for students to put their worry boxes when they are done working on them. You can have them keep their worry boxes where you can keep an eye on them or have them put them in their backpacks to take home after they have created them. If you keep them at school, it is recommended that they be in a place you can supervise access so as to ensure students don't find other students completed worry box exercises.

Don't push students to perform the movement exercises. For some students even low physical exercise can cause embarrassment and stress. If a student doesn't want to participate in a physical activity, it is OK. Let them know that all physical activities are voluntary.

Try not to reframe situations for students. Help students come up with their own reframing so they can practice seeing things from another perspective. Reframing is a skill that can take time to master, and it can be difficult for students when they first attempt it. If you are conducting *Power Up* in one weekly lesson and are skipping the optional session 4, give students an additional reframing worksheet that they can complete on their own time.

Session 12.1: Naming Our Worries

Before beginning the lesson, check in with students on how they did in using the strategies they learned in the previous lesson. Have a discussion and ask them what strategies they learned. Did using progressive muscle relaxation and mindfulness help them? How did they feel before using these strategies? How did they feel after using them? What other strategies discussed did they use? If they hadn't used one of these strategies, how might they have felt or how might the situation have turned out differently if they had?

During the discussion, in order to feel a part of the group, students might make up a time that they used the self-management strategy. Do not correct them or call them out about not having actually used a strategy. The fact that they could think up a scenario in which they "used" a strategy is good. It shows that they know when they should be using a strategy and how it could've helped them.

Understanding What Worries Are and How They Affect Us

In this lesson, students will practice an energizing self-management skill designed to help them master their worries and create a worry box. Begin by reminding students that in the last two lessons, the class talked about skills that can help slow us down when we feel like we need less energy. In this lesson, the class is going to talk about skills that can energize us when we are feeling slow-moving. Let students know that the first skill they will practice is creating worry boxes. You can describe it as follows, "A worry box is a safe place where we can temporarily put our worries that are weighing us down so that they aren't in our heads."

Begin by having the class think about what worries are. Ask, "Who can tell me what a worry is?" After the discussion, you should build on their thoughts and offer a definition and examples. You can say,

> *A worry is a negative thought about something that bothers us. A lot of times it's hard to get worries out of our heads. This*

makes it hard to concentrate. The more we try not to think about our worries, the harder it can be to get them out of our heads! The more worries we have, the more likely we are to feel bogged down and tired. Worrying is normal, and it's OK because everyone worries. I know I worry about making sure all of you know everything that you need to know to be successful next year in [the students' next grade level].

Have Students Share Their Worries

Ask who would like to share something they worry about. Remind students that they are sharing with the whole class so they should make sure that they are comfortable with everyone knowing what they share. Tell them to try to not to use names when sharing. On this point, you can illustrate what you mean by saying, "For example, instead of saying that you are worried that Jane is mad at you, you can say you worry when you argue with friends."

Allow students a chance to give some examples of things they might worry about. Remind students to only share things they are comfortable with the entire class knowing. If a student shares something concerning, thank them for sharing and check in with them as soon as possible. A referral to the counselor might be appropriate.

Use the My Worries Worksheet To List Our Worries

After the discussion, reassure students that they aren't alone in their worries. Everyone worries about something. Let them know that the goal of this lesson is to give them a way to handle those worries so that they don't become so distracted by them that they can't get other things done.

Have students open their workbooks and find the worksheet My Worries. Tell students to write down some things that worry them in the worksheet's boxes. It can be about making friends or taking tests or about anything that makes us worry. Let them know that what they write down will not be shared with the class.

Walk around the class while the students are working and inquire what they are writing. As noted before, if a student writes or shares something concerning, make sure to talk with them. Make a referral to the counselor as appropriate.

Conclude the exercise by congratulating the students on their work. ("Great job class! Now that your worries are on your paper, they aren't in your head anymore.")

Create a Worry Box

Now that students have written down their worries on the worksheet, you can have them move on to create their own worry boxes. For this exercise, the class will need coloring pencils or pens, scissors, tape, and the Worry Box Outline worksheet. When introducing the activity, you can describe the goal of the activity as follows:

> *We can put our worries in our worry box so they are temporarily out of our heads and can't bother us! If the worry is in the box, it's not in our head. While it won't get rid of the worry forever, the box is a safe place to house our worries while we get other things done.*

Have students find the worksheet Worry Box Outline in their workbook. Before they construct a box from the outline, you might want to give them a few minutes to decorate the box before cutting it out. After students have had a chance to decorate it, instruct them to use their scissors to cut along the solid dark lines on the outside edge of the box outline and then fold the paper along the dotted lines. Once students have completed these steps, they should tape the solid dark edges together and tape in the tabs to make a box. Students can also refer to the instructions on the worksheet.

Demonstrate making the box. Give students a couple of minutes to put their boxes together. Assist as needed and encourage the students ("I see some great worry boxes!").

Add Worries to the Worry Box and Display the Skill Cutout

Ask students to get out the My Worries worksheet with the worries they had written down on it. Ask them cut out each square and put the listed worry in the box they created. When they place it in the box, they can imagine the worry leaving their head and staying in the box for the time being. Finish the activity by hanging the worry box skill cutout on the board or display area for students to refer to and see. Let them know that when you see them placing a worry in the worry box, you will give you a power bar.

Session 12.2: Using Exercise to Improve Our Energy

This session will introduce wall push-ups and stretching as a way to use our bodies to energize ourselves. You can use the following to explain the goal of the lesson:

> *Our brain and body are connected. If our body is tired, our brain will also be tired. If our brain is tired, our body will follow suit. Today we are going to talk about using our body to send messages to our brain that we want to have more energy.*

Wall Push-Ups

Let students know that the class will be setting up a wall push-up station in the room. Ask them where they think the best place for this station would be. The wall push-up station should be easily accessible yet out of the way of classroom activities. Use an example Wall Push-Ups worksheet to mark the location the students identify. Pick a student to cut out the hands on the Wall Push-up worksheet and hang the hand cutouts on the wall for students to place their hands on when practicing. The cutouts should be placed at an average student's chest level.

Once the station is set up, ask students for their thoughts on why exercise gives us energy: "Why do you think moving our bodies helps wake us up?"

Allow students to respond. Give praise for correct answers and gentle redirection for incorrect answers. Once they've had a chance to share, explain how exercise enhances our energy and helps us return to home mode. Students should know that they can use the push-up station whenever they are feeling tired or sad. You can say,

> When we move our bodies, we are sending messages to our brain that we are awake and we want to learn. Pumping our muscles cause neurotransmitters to release chemicals in our brain that help us feel more awake and put us in a better mood. When we are feeling tired or sad or in the rewind mode, we can come over here, place our hands on the handprints, and do some wall push-ups. We can do between five and twenty. Do however many push-ups takes to help you feel awake and alert.

Use the Wall Push-Ups Worksheet at Home

Direct students' attention to the Wall Push-Ups worksheet in their workbook and the two handprints pictured on it. They can use these to set up their own wall push-up station at home. Even without the worksheet, they can use this skill on a flat surface.

Display The Skill Cutout

Remind students, "Don't forget to use this skill throughout the day. I'm going to add the skill cutout to our wall!" Hang up the wall push-ups skill cutout for students to refer to and see.

Introduce Stretching

Once students have learned about wall push-ups, discuss the next skill, stretching. Let students know how gentle stretching helps us:

> When we stretch, we are relieving the tension in our muscles and relaxing them while also increasing blood flow

*throughout our body. Increasing blood flow makes us feel
more alert, awake, and focused.*

Use the Stretching Worksheet to Practice

Have students locate the Stretching worksheet in their workbooks. The worksheet shows six figures demonstrating various stretches. Let students know that the class can do some of these stretches in order to get their blood flowing. Have students move carefully when trying the stretching exercises. Tell them, "When you are doing these stretches you should be cautious not to overdo it. If it hurts when you are stretching, stop. These stretches shouldn't hurt."

Have the students pick a stretch from the worksheet that they would like to try. Once they have picked a stretch, have them stand behind their desks and practice it. Students should pick a stretching activity they feel most comfortable trying. If they start a stretch and don't like it, let them try a different one. Allow students some time to practice their stretches.

Reinforce the Skill and Display the Skill Cutout

Encourage the class and remind them how exercise can help lift their energy levels and mood: "Great job class! By doing these stretches, we are sending messages to our brain that we want to speed our bodies up. The exercise helps us feel more awake and focused."

Hang the stretching skill cutout on the board for students to refer to and see. Remind students that when they practice the skill, they can earn power bars.

Session 12.3: Reframing Our Thoughts

Now that students have learned about worry boxes, wall push-ups, and stretching, in this session, you will introduce the skill of reframing. This practice represents the conscious effort to change, or reframe, a thought into a more positive perspective. Start the lesson by passing out the Reframing worksheet. Guiding students to use the worksheet as a hint, ask students, "What do you think reframing is?"

As students respond, give them praise for guessing. You can use the following to explain the concept:

> *Reframing is when we take a negative thought and make it
> into a positive one, just like taking a picture out of a broken
> frame and putting it into a nicer one. It's the same picture,
> but it looks better in the nicer frame. For example, instead
> of thinking "I have read for thirty minutes today," you can
> think "I get to read a book about baking today, which will
> help me learn how to bake delicious cookies." Either way you*

spend thirty minutes reading, but you get to decide how you look at it.

Use the Reframing Worksheet

Tell the class you will all try the reframing activity together. Have them turn to the Reframing worksheet in their workbooks. At the top of the worksheet is a picture of a broken frame. Have them draw a picture of something that they are not looking forward to in the broken frame. It can be math, lunch, reading, whatever they want. To get them started, you can give them an example of what you will draw. You can say, "For example, I'm going to draw that I have cook dinner when I get home." Point to where the drawing will go in the broken picture frame.

Walk around the room while students work and ask them about their drawings to ensure that it represents something they do not at this point view in a positive light. Redirect them as needed.

Reframe the Experience in a New Drawing

In this exercise, students will take that same thought and make it positive. They will draw the new positive thought in the whole frame that appears under the broken one in the worksheet. To guide students in the reframing exercise, you tell the students the following:

> *Instead of thinking that you have to do something, think of what good comes out of doing it. For example, instead of thinking that I have to clean the house this weekend, I'm going to think about how good it will feel to have a clean house! Draw your new positive thought in the nice frame underneath the broken frame.*

Walk around the room and assist students with reframing their thoughts. This can be difficult for students and is a skill that needs a lot of practice. Assist them in forming their ideas and give them praise when they are able to reframe their thoughts in a positive manner.

Display the Skill Cutout

Praise students for their efforts and hang the reframing skill cutout on the board for students to refer to and see. If you are not doing Session 4's optional lesson, give students a blank Reframing worksheet and encourage them to use it as needed.

Session 12.4: Practice Reframing

In this session, students will continue practicing reframing. Have them turn to the second, blank Reframing worksheet in their workbooks and introduce the activity:

I want you to draw a picture of another negative thought you might have. It might be that "no one will play with me during recess" or "I don't want to do my chores." Draw a picture of your negative thought in the broken frame.

Walk around the room while students work and ask them about the pictures they are drawing. Redirect them if they didn't draw a picture of something that they view in a negative light. Once students have had a chance to create their first picture, ask them to take that negative thought and turn it into something positive. In the unbroken frame below the first broken frame, they should draw a new picture reflecting the situation when seen in a positive manner. You can provide an example to get students started:

For example, you can reframe the negative thought and say, "If no one wants to play with me during recess, then I can read that book I've been wanting to." Or you can reframe your thought about chores and decide, "After I finish my chores, I get to play video games!"

Have students create their pictures. Walk around the room while they work and ask the students to compare their new picture to their old picture. Students might need help reframing the idea or they might need to be redirected back to the task.

Optional Activity: Have volunteers present their reframed thoughts to the class.

Session 12.5: The Commitment Circle

Have students gather in a circle to name their commitments for the lesson. You can offer the following the prompt:

Our prompt for our commitment circle this week is, Which of these four skills are you going to try? For example, I'm going to use the worry box skill. I'm going to put at least two worries a day into the box when I feel like I need a break from them.

Go around the circle and have students name their commitments. Encourage them to make these commitments for both the home and school setting so they can see how these skills translate to the home setting.

Reinforcing the Lesson

Continue to encourage students to leave their worries in their worry boxes and reframe their negative thoughts.

Sample Letter to Parents and Guardians—Lesson 12

Dear Parent/Guardian,

This week, as part of our focus on self-management skills in social and emotional learning, our class learned four new strategies that we can use to re-energize ourselves when we are feeling like we are moving slowly. The first strategy allows us to manage our worries by "transferring" them into a worry box. The second and third strategies -- stretching and wall push-ups--encourage movement. The fourth strategy allows us a chance to view situations in a positive manner.

It's important for us to be able to put our worries aside so that we can focus on accomplishing our goals. It is also important to incorporate movement and physical exercise into our routines to help us manage our feelings and energy levels. Last, it is important for us to practice seeing situations in a positive manner so that we can embrace change and difficult situations.

You can ask your child the following questions about the lesson:

- What four new energizing strategies did you learn?
- How do you reframe a negative thought?
- Can you reframe a negative thought about a situation you face?
- What is a worry box?
- What worries are you going to put into the worry box when you are home?
- Why is movement important?

Regards,

My Worries

Worry Box Outline

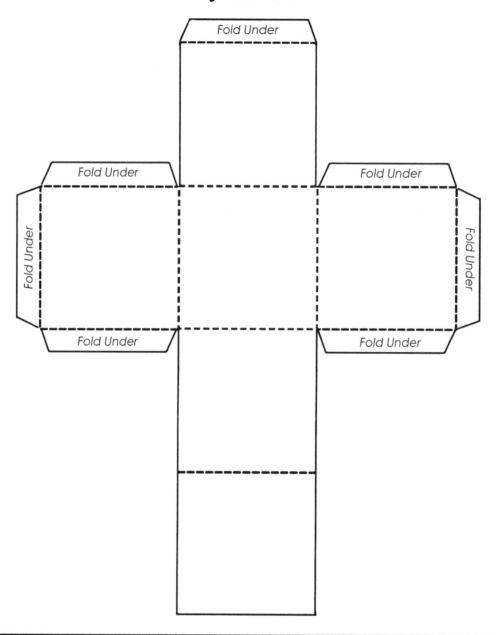

Directions:

- – – – – – – – = fold dashed lines

- ⬡ = glue tabs titled "Fold under"

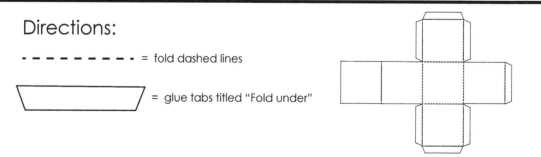

Wall Push-Ups

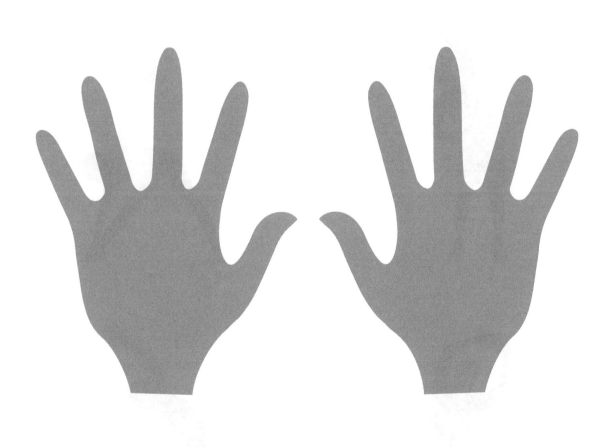

Stretching

From *Power Up: Gamification Tools for Social and Emotional Learning,* © 2022 by J. Dombrowski.
Champaign, IL: Research Press (www.researchpress.com, 800-519-2707).

Reframing

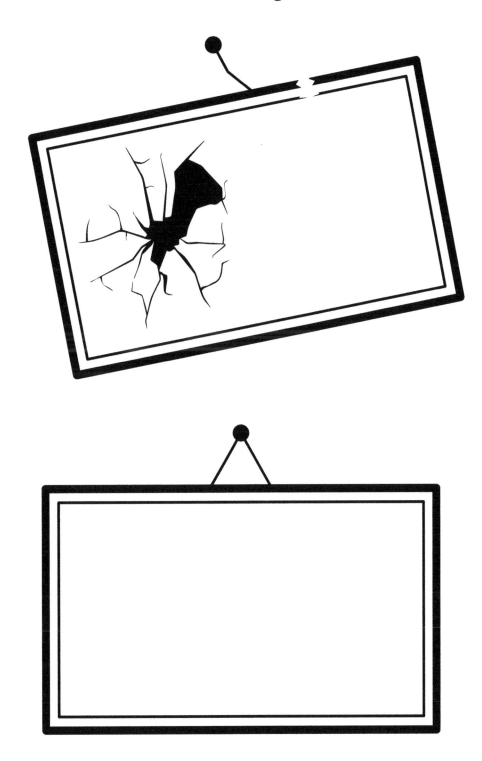

Goal Setting and Time Management

Goal Setting Icon

Students will learn how to set short- and long-term goals, how to break their larger goals into smaller goals on their way to their "big" goal, and how to manage their time effectively.

Introduction

While managing emotions is a large part of self-management, it is not the only part. Self-management also includes the ability to set and achieve goals through managing one's resources and time. Goal setting has also been linked to positive educational outcomes. Students with goal-setting skills (or specific training in goal setting) do better academically, and experience higher levels of self-efficacy (Morisano et al., 2010; Pintrich, 2000). As students experience success in reaching their goals, they are more confident in their abilities when working towards other goals.

Time management skills help in setting and achieving goals. In their review of the literature, Claessens et al. (2007) found that, in general, time management skills have a positive impact on student learning outcomes. Teaching time management skills has also been found to improve academic outcomes (Nadinloyi et al., 2013).

Objectives

Students will be able to

- identify one short-term and one-long term goal they are working toward
- break up one of their big, long-term goals into at least three smaller, short-term goals that will help them achieve their big goal
- identify the best way to manage their time in order to meet their goals

Success Criteria

Students are able to

- identify smaller goals that need to be accomplished in order to reach their big, long-term goal

- understand how to set up their time in order to give themselves the best chance to achieve their goals

- feel comfortable using time management skills to achieve smaller goals so they can reach their big goal

Materials

- One copy per student of the Goal Setting worksheet
- One copy per student of Time Management worksheet

Things to Note

Avoid giving students goals to work toward. Let them determine what goal is important to them. This creates buy-in and increases their motivation to meet the goal they set. Provide minimal help in identifying smaller goals that will help them reach their larger goal. Last, give minimal help on their time-management plan. Let the students decide what is and isn't important in their schedule and let them work through the consequences of those decisions.

While you aren't giving students answers, you can support them by asking open-ended questions that guide them to think about their responses. For example, you might ask, "Will this smaller goal help you reach your big goal?" or "Is that enough time to complete that task?"

Session 13.1: Goal Setting

Before beginning the new lesson, check in with students on how they did in using the strategies they learned in the previous lesson. Have a discussion. Ask them what four strategies they learned last week. Did using their worry box help? Were they able to reframe difficult situations? Did wall push-ups and stretching help? How did they feel before using the strategy? How did they feel after using the strategy? If they hadn't used a strategy, how might the situation have turned out differently if they had?

During the discussion, in order to feel a part of the group, students might make up a time that they used a strategy. Do not correct them about not having actually used a strategy. The fact that they could think up a scenario in which they "used" a strategy is good, because it shows that they know when they should be using a strategy and how it could've helped them.

Discuss Short- and Long-term Goals

In this lesson, you will have students begin to think about how to set goals and use the Goal Setting worksheet to identify their own goals. Begin with a discussion and ask students, "What do you think I mean by goal setting?" After students respond, you can provide a definition: "Goal setting is when we identify something that is important for us to achieve, and we decide we are going to actively work toward accomplishing it. We can have short- and long-term goals."

Ask students what they think an example of a short-term goal would be. Once they have had a chance to respond, offer an explanation with an example. You could say,

> *A short-term goal is a goal that we can reach in the near future. Deciding to study for 30 minutes tonight, reaching the next level on your video game this week, or acing a test next week are examples of setting short-term goals. What do you think an example of a long-term goal might be?*

After students respond, build on their responses by providing an explanation that emphasizes the timeline toward the goal. You can say,

> *A long-term goal is one that takes longer to reach. This might be a goal you hope to accomplish in a month, a year, or in an even longer period. Working to get a spot on the football team next year, to graduate from elementary school, or to go to college would be examples of setting long-term goals.*

Discuss the Importance of Setting Goals

Once students have had a chance to think about the types of goals we can set for ourselves, they should consider why we set goals. Ask the class, "Why do you think it is important for us to set goals?" After students respond, emphasize that it is important because it lets us know what we are working toward and what actions we need to take to achieve the things that are important to us. Encourage students to accept that goals are personal and unique to each person:

> *Each of us is different, and we will each have different goals. That is OK. What is important is that we know what is important to us and what will make us feel good about ourselves in the short- and long-term.*

Practice Using the Goal Setting Worksheet

Have students locate the Goal Setting Worksheet in their workbook. Ask them write down on the top of the worksheet one short-term goal and one long-term goal that they have right now. They should leave the section at the bottom of the worksheet ("On My Way Goals") blank for now. Remind students that a short-term goal is something that can be accomplished in the next couple of weeks. A long-term goal can take months or years to achieve. Allow students to work on the worksheet till the end of the session.

Session 13.2: Creating Steps toward a Goal

In this session, students will pick one of their short- and long-term goals they identified in their worksheet and identify smaller goals or steps they need to meet in order to reach their final goal. Let students pick whatever goal they would like to work on and provide an example of how they might identify smaller goals that will lead to their long-term goal. Be sure to emphasize how identifying these smaller goals can help us. You could say,

> *I'm going to use my own example. A long-term goal of mine is to learn how to draw. Now that I have this goal, I need to split it up into smaller, more manageable goals in order to be on my way to reaching my "big" goal of drawing. When we split goals up into smaller ones, it helps create a plan to meet our big goal. It also gives us smaller successes along the way that can motivate us to keep working!*

Ask students to help you in reaching the goal you described. Ask them, "What are some smaller goals that I can break my big, long-term goal of learning to draw into?" After students respond, you can acknowledge and mention the small goals they identified and introduce the idea of setting deadlines for reaching these small goals. For instance, using our example, you might say to students,

> *Great job! Some of the smaller goals toward reaching my big, long-term goal might be I can take a class, watch tutorial videos, ask a friend that knows how to draw, or buy a book that teaches people how to draw. Each of these is a part of my big goal of learning to draw. I'm going to take my big goal and break it up into three smaller goals. Then I'm going to give myself a deadline to complete each small goal. This will keep me working toward my big goal and help me hold myself accountable. A deadline is a specific time by which we would like to achieve our goal.*

Use your example to describe how we might identify steps toward a goal and then set deadlines for reaching those steps, or small goals:

> *In order to reach my goal of learning to draw, I'm going to set three small goals. My first small goal will be to research books that teach people how to draw. I want to read the description and the reviews to see what the book is going to teach me and to learn if others found it helpful. I'm going to give myself a deadline of next Friday to do this. My second smaller goal will be to buy the book that I think will be the best and to begin to study it. I'm going to give myself two weeks to do this. My third, and final, small goal is to start practicing drawing. The more I practice, the better I will get! I'm going to give myself three weeks to do this.*

Return to the Worksheet to Set Small Goals toward Reaching a Main Goal

Ask students to start thinking about the short- and long-term goals they identified in their Goal Setting worksheet. Have them break one of these goals into three smaller goals that will help achieve their identified goal. After they have broken up their big goal into three smaller ones, have them set a deadline to accomplish each. The deadlines should vary. Caution students: "Don't make all of your goals due at the same time! That would be overwhelming and not very much fun." Students can work on one of their short- or long-term goals for this exercise. Have them put a star next to the goal for which they are creating a plan.

While students work, walk around the room and give them encouragement. Try not to give them specific ideas for their goals. Let them think through the smaller steps on their own. You can ask guiding questions such as, "Will that help you achieve your goal of _____" or "Should that be a big goal or a small goal?"

Session 13.3: Time Management

In order to achieve our goals, whether they are big or small, we need to make sure we have time set aside for them. In this session, students will use the Time Management worksheet to help them think about how they spend their time and how planning their time can help in reaching goals. Begin with a discussion about managing our time. "Time management is a critical skill in achieving our goals. What do you think I mean by time management?"

After students respond, you should offer an explanation. You could say, "Time management is how we organize and plan our activities. Things that are more important to us tend to take up more time in the day. Sometimes we can get so wrapped up in other things that we forget to take the time we need to achieve our goals."

Complete the Time Management Worksheet

Have students turn to the Time Management worksheet in their workbooks. In this worksheet is a picture of a clock. Ask students to write down what they typically do during each hour on the clock. You can offer an example to help them begin:

> *For example, between 9:30 p.m. and 6:00 a.m. I'm usually sleeping. From 6:00 a.m. to 7:00 a.m., I am usually getting ready for work. From 7:00 a.m. to 7:30 a.m., I am usually driving to school, and so on.*

Give students some time to complete this activity. Walk around the room and observe students while they work.

Add Goal Deadlines to the Worksheet

Once students have had a chance to make notes on the worksheet, ask them for their thoughts on it. Were they surprised by how much time they spend on certain activities? After students share their thoughts, ask them to review the smaller goals they set for themselves in the Goal Setting worksheet. Have them consider the deadlines they set and the time they need to work on each small goal.

For this exercise, ask students to re-label their worksheet clock to include the time they think they will need in order to meet these goals. To guide students, you could say, "For example, from 8:00 p.m. to 9:00 p.m. I usually watch TV. I'm going to adjust this to practicing drawing from 8:00 p.m. to 8:30 p.m. and watch TV from 8:30 p.m. to 9:00 p.m."

Walk around the room while students work. Offer encouragement and validation that it is hard to fit everything into one day.

Discuss the Activity

Have a discussion about how it can be difficult to make room for achieving goals in an already busy schedule. Ask students if it was hard to give up something on their schedule in order to work towards their goals. Why or why not? At the end of the discussion, you can share that it can be difficult to make time for other goals, especially when doing so cuts into things that we do for fun like watch TV or play video games. Stress that it is important to remember the big picture when making time to reach our goals. Working toward our goals will help us be successful in the long run and give us a sense of pride. We should never get rid of all our fun activities, though. Fun is important too!

Display the Goal Setting Skill Cutout and Offer a Reminder about Power Bars

Let students know that as they achieve small and big goals in the class, you will color in a power bar for them. This might be for work on a goal the group decided on together or one that the student set. Remind students: "Make sure I know what goals you are setting for yourself so I can give you a power bar as you achieve them!"

Hang the goal setting skill cutout on the whiteboard or display area for students to refer to and see.

Session 13.4: Set a Classroom Goal

Work with the students to create a classroom goal using the process they have practiced of setting small goals toward the main, big goal. You can steer students towards choosing a goal that you have for the class but be sure to have the group identify the goal. You can begin the exercise by reminding them of the goal setting skills they have worked on: "Now that we have set our own personal goals and created a time management plan, we are going to set a classroom goal. What do you think our classroom goal should be?"

Once students have named a goal, ask them what are some smaller goals that are part of this big goal and that would help the class reach it. Have the class set three small goals and a deadline for each. Last, ask students, "When are we going to work on this goal?" Carve out time during the day to work toward the goal.

Once the class has created the plan, post it where students can see it and are reminded of the goals and deadlines. Make a point to follow through with each smaller goal and the time set aside to work on and achieve the goal. It's important to model follow through for students. Celebrate when you achieve your goals (big and small)!

Session 13.5: The Commitment Circle

Have students gather in a circle to identify their commitments. When providing the prompt, you say can:

> *Our prompt for our commitment circle this week is, What*
> *small goal are you going to work on first? For example, my big*
> *goal is that I would like to learn to draw. As I stated earli-*
> *er, for the first small goal, I am going to work toward, I will*
> *research a book that I think will help me the most.*

Go around the circle and have students identify their commitments. Encourage them to make these commitments for both the home and school setting so they can see how these skills translate to the home setting.

Reinforcing the Lesson

Remind students throughout the day to set goals for things that are important to them. Encourage them to break down their goals into smaller ones that they can work toward achieving. As they achieve goals in the classroom, color in power bars.

Note to the teacher: It's recommended that the class take a one-to-two week break at this time and practice using the skills they have learned each day during their SEL time. Have students draw pictures, write about times they used the skill, or practice using the skill as a class (e.g., mindfulness). Get creative. You know your class best and know which skills students use the most and which skills they like the best. The more they practice, the better they will get at using the skills and the more likely they will use them when needed.

Sample Letter to Parents and Guardians—Lesson 13

Dear Parent/Guardian,

This week, as part of our focus on self-management skills in social and emotional learning, we learned about setting and achieving short- and long-term goals. Students also worked to break up their big goals into smaller goals that will help them reach their big goal. Last, students created a plan to manage their time. The plan helped them dedicate time to achieving their goals.

You can ask your child the following questions about the lesson:

- What is a short-term goal you have?
- What is a long-term goal you have?
- How can you break one of these goals up into smaller goals?
- When can you dedicate time to achieving these goals?

Regards,

Goal Setting

My Short-term Goal:

_____

_____

_____

_____

My Long-term Goal:

_____

_____

_____

_____

On My Way Goals:

1. _____

_____

_____

_____

Deadline: _____

2. _____

_____

_____

_____

Deadline: _____

3. _____

_____

_____

_____

Deadline: _____

Time Management

Social Awareness

My Pillars

Students will identify the individuals in their social support system at the family, school, and community levels.

Introduction

Humans are social beings and have relied on the support of one another for survival and community. As students develop, they begin to rely not only on the social support of their families but on their friends as well, seeking social connection with others. Having a social support system is important for one's overall mental and physical health. Ozbay (2007) asserts that positive social support can improve medical outcomes and improve one's ability to handle stress and one's prognosis when dealing with trauma.

Students who feel supported have the option to reach out to others in time of crisis. When provided support, students feel heard and cared for. With support they can think through problems, gain insight into the perspective of others, and learn how to effectively cope with problems. All of this can help support students in handling stressful situations and problems in an appropriate manner. Students who don't have strong support systems are, in fact, six times more likely to demonstrate symptoms of depression (Hefner & Eisenberg, 2009).

Objectives

Students will be able to

- identify at least one family or friend support
- identify at least one school support
- identify at least one community support

Success Criteria

Students are able to

- identify support at the family, friend, school and community level
- understand the importance of having a social support system

- feel comfortable reaching out to those in their social support system when needed

Materials

One copy per student of the Social Supports worksheet

Things to Note

Avoid asking students directly about their mother, father, grandmother, grandfather, or other relatives. These questions can be triggering as not all families are made up of so-called traditional family members. In the following lesson, I would recommend giving students three to five examples of family members so that if the student is being raised by their grandparents, aunts, or uncles etc., they are not embarrassed to tell you this.

Having students identify the individuals in their social support systems allows them to think about whom they can turn to when they are having an issue. This activity can also help students identify supports they might not have thought about. For example, unless they are explicitly told, students might not realize that school counselors or teachers are options for their social support system.

Session 14.1: Our Support System

Check in with students on how they did in using the strategies they learned in the previous lesson. Have a discussion, using the following questions: What strategies have been most helpful to you? Which strategies haven't been helpful to you? Did you handle situations differently since you learned the strategies?

During the discussion, in order to feel like a part of the group, students might make up a time they used a strategy. Do not correct them on whether they actually used a strategy. The fact that they could think up a scenario in which to use a strategy is good because it shows that they know when they should be using a strategy and how it could have helped them.

Introduce the Concept of a Social Support System

In this lesson, the class will talk about our social support system. You can define a social support system as those individuals who support and help us when we are having a hard time. Our support system might include our family, friends, school, and community members. To provide examples for students, you could say,

> Our family members in our support system can be our
> parents, grandparents, aunts, uncles, cousins, foster parents,
> brothers, sisters, or anyone in our family! Our friends in our
> support system are the people we feel a connection with and

who treat us well. A person in our support system from the school can be a teacher, counselor, administrator, or any other trusted adult on campus. An individual from the community who is in our support system can include a coach, neighbor, church member, someone at our after-school program, or any trustworthy person outside of the school.

Students should understand that knowing who is in our support system is important because then we know whom we can turn to when things get hard. We might also be in someone's support system. People might turn to us when they need help and support.

Use the Social Support Worksheet to Think about Who Supports Us

Have students turn to the Social Supports worksheet. On the top of that worksheet, students will find three categories listed: friends and family, school, and community. Ask students to write the names of people that support them under each heading.

Walk around the room as students work and ask them about their support system. If they say they don't have anyone listed in a specific category, give them some suggestions. Students generally have more support than they realize.

End the session by congratulating students on their work. Let them know that as they think of more people in their support system, they should add them to their list.

Session 14.2: Family and Friends in My Support System

In this session, you will ask the class to think about the friends and family in their support system. Let students know that our friends and family can be made up of individuals who live with them or who are close to them or their family. It can include parents, grandparents, sisters, brothers, aunts, uncles, pets, cousins, someone from school, someone from their neighborhood, or any other friend or family member.

List Friends and Family Supports on the Worksheet

Have students turn to the Social Supports worksheet in their workbooks. On this worksheet, ask them to write about how their friends and family support them. Give them an example to help them get started. You might say,

For example, my mother always listens to me when I'm upset. My grandmother always gives me small gifts when I see her. My best friend always helps me study. Last, my stepfather

always tells funny jokes that make me feel better when I'm sad.

Walk around the room while students work and ask about them about the friends and family in their support system. If students have a hard time thinking of examples, give them suggestions. If a student really can't think of any support, you might consider referring them to the school counselor to determine if there is something more serious happening.

Session 14.3: My School and Community Support System

In this session, have the class think about the individuals at school in their support system. Remind them that individuals at school in their support system might include trusted adults on the school grounds. This can include teachers, bus drivers, school counselors, deans, administrators, and so on.

List School Supports on the Worksheet

On the Social Supports worksheet, have students write about how adults at school support them. For example, a teacher might help them with their work. The school counselor might listen to them when they are having a bad day. The principal might give them a high-five when he sees them.

Walk around while the students work and ask about the individuals at school in their support system. If students have a hard time thinking of examples, provide them with some suggestions.

List Community Supports on the Worksheet

Once you and the students have talked about the friends, family, and school members in their support system, talk about the individuals from the community in their support system. The individuals in the community that are part of their support system are made up of people outside of the family, friends, and school who support them. It can include a coach, people at our church, our neighbors, people at our after-school program, or other trustworthy adults who live outside of the home.

Have students write in the worksheet about how their community members support them. Offer an example to help get started. You might say, "For example, my neighbor will sometimes bring food over for me if I don't feel like cooking."

Walk around the room while the students work and ask about the individuals in the community in their support system. If students have a hard time thinking of examples, help provide them with some.

Session 14.4: Discovering How We Can Support Others

Now that your students have had a chance to think about the people who support them, in this session, have the students talk about how they can support others. Ask students to look at the list of individuals they identified as part of their support system. Begin a discussion by asking students to raise their hand to share ideas on how each of them can support these individuals. You help them start by offering an example from your list. You could say, "For example, my mother supports me by listening to me when I've had a bad day. I can support her by visiting her on the weekends."

Go around the room and have students share how they can support people in their support system. Praise them for their thoughtfulness. If some students don't want to share, that is OK. They will benefit from hearing others' ideas.

Session 14.5: The Commitment Circle

Have students form a circle to create their commitments for the lesson. To begin the activity, you can say:

> *The prompt for our commitment circle this week is, Who are you going to ask for support from this week? For example, I have a lot of cleaning to do at home so I'm going to ask my husband* [or name another member in the household] *to cook this week.*

Go around the circle and have students make their commitments. Encourage them to make these commitments in either the home or school setting so they can see how these skills translate to the home setting.

Reinforcing the Lesson

Continue to point out support the student has. If students struggle with a problem in class, you can ask them who in their support system can help them solve the problem. (It might often be the teacher.)

Sample Letter to Parents and Guardians—Lesson 14

Dear Parent/Guardian,

This week as part of our focus on social awareness skills in social and emotional learning, we created a list of individuals in our social support system. We identified people among our family and friends, at school, and in the community who can help support us.

It is important for us to identify who is in our support system so we can lean on them when we need help. It is also important to know that we might also be in their support system and can help support them when they need it too.

You can ask your child the following questions about the lesson:

- What family members are in your social support system?
- What school members are in your social support system?
- What community members are in your social support system?
- How can I support you?
- How can you support me?

Regards,

Social Supports

Friends and Family	School	Community

How my family and friends support me:

_____

_____

_____

_____

How my school supports me:

_____

_____

_____

_____

How my community supports me:

_____

_____

_____

_____

Building Empathy

Kindness Icon

Students will learn what empathy is and how to demonstrate empathy towards others.

Introduction

Understood as an emotional reaction that mirrors or is triggered by another's, empathy is caused by observing or imagining how someone else is feeling (Tone & Tully, 2014). In other words, empathy is understanding and caring about another person's feelings and experiences. Empathy plays a role in emotional development because it requires awareness of one's own feelings as well as the feelings of others (Laursen et al., 2013).

Empathy has educational benefits as well. In a study of eighth graders, students who worked to build empathy made gains in reading, were able to see different perspectives, and based on those new perspectives were able to change their own thinking (Smit, 2017). When students are able to understand and show empathy, they can make both emotional and academic gains.

Objectives

Students will be able to

- define what empathy means
- demonstrate two acts of kindness in a week

Success Criteria

Students are able to

- define empathy
- understand why empathy is important
- feel comfortable demonstrating empathy through acts of kindness

Materials

- Basket or bucket
- Cut-out stars

- Scrap pieces of paper for writing down student names (for optional Session 4 exercise)
- One copy per student of the My Kind Acts worksheet

Things to Note

Avoid telling students their answers are incorrect. Instead, ask guiding questions or redirect them back to task. Give them the option of asking a friend for help.

Session 15.1: Understanding Empathy

Begin the lesson by checking in on the students' commitments from the last lesson. Ask students who would like to volunteer to share how they did asking those in their support system for help. Allow students a chance to share how they did on their commitments. If you find that the same students speak up each week, encourage new students to participate. If you have some students who never share, try to check in with them individually.

Introduce the Concept of Empathy

In this lesson, students will learn about empathy, what it means and how it affects us. Begin the session with a discussion question: "Who can tell me what empathy is?"

As students respond, give praise for responses and gentle redirection for incorrect responses. Once they have had an opportunity to answer, offer a definition and use examples. For example, you might say,

> Empathy is when we understand what others are feeling and want to help them. It's when you feel what others seem to be feeling. For example, my friend was upset because her dog died. I sat with her and listened to her tell me about how awesome her dog was. I knew that if my dog died, I would feel sad. I felt sad that she felt sad, and I wanted to help.

Extend the discussion by asking students why empathy is important. After students respond, offer an explanation that stresses how empathy draws people together and makes them feel better. You can say,

> Empathy is important because it links us together. We feel a connection with someone else when we feel like they understand what we are going through. This connection helps us to feel better. It feels good to know someone cares. Showing empathy to others can likely also cause them to be empathetic with us when we need it.

Ask students: "When is a time that someone showed you empathy?" Have them share examples of when people showed them empathy. After they have shared, have students consider how these empathetic acts made them feel. Lead the discussion by asking the following questions:

> *How did you feel after being shown empathy? How do you think the other person felt after they showed you empathy? Did someone being empathetic with you cause you to want to be empathetic to someone else?*

Talk about a Time that You Showed Empathy

After this discussion, praise students for their responses and ask them to consider a time that they showed empathy. How do they think the other person felt after they showed empathy? How did they feel after showing empathy? Before students join the discussion, remind them not to mention any specific names when offering these examples in the class.

Give praise for students showing empathy ("Wow! I have a lot of empathetic students in this classroom!"). Conclude the session by reiterating how empathy makes everyone involved feel good.

Session 15.2: Performing Acts of Kindness

In this session, you will encourage students to show acts of kindness by rewarding them with stars. You can create the cutout stars by using the included worksheet, and you'll want a designated basket or container to hold rewarded stars. You can have students cut out the stars while you are giving the directions on rewarding stars, or you can cut them out prior to the lesson. In creating the reward stars, you will likely need several copies of the stars worksheet.

Reward Stars for Acts of Kindness

Let students know that now that we know what empathy is, we are going to start showing kindness to others. Ask students to demonstrate acts of kindness to those individuals that need a little boost. They can practice for the rest of the lesson week. For example, if they notice someone having trouble with math, they can offer to help. If they notice someone sitting alone at lunch or recess, they can ask to join that person. If someone drops their books, they can help pick them up.

Tell students that when you see someone doing an act of kindness, you are going to write the student's name on a star along with a summary of what the student did. You will then put the star in the basket. Each morning, you should pull a couple of stars out and read aloud to the class the acts of kindness. In addition, tell students that you will also fill in one power bar on a student's Power Up board when you see that student doing something kind.

At this point, you can hang the acts of kindness skill cutout on the board for students to refer to and see.

List Kind Acts at School in the Worksheet

Have students turn to the My Kind Acts worksheet in their workbooks. On the top of the worksheet in the At School section, have students list as many things as they can think of that they can do to spread kindness in the classroom and at school. Tell students that they can list nice things they have seen being done or nice things they would like to do.

In making their list, have students identify proactive as well as reactive kind acts. For example, you can explain these types of actions as follows:

> If someone falls, you can help them up. Something happened, and you reacted and demonstrated a kind act. That is reactive. Proactive acts of kindness are those where you plan or go out of your way to demonstrate kindness without something happening first. For example, I might give someone a compliment. That is proactive because I did something kind without something causing me to do so.

Give students some time to write down their ideas. Walk around the room while students work and give them suggestions of things you have seen them doing that they can add to their lists.

Have Students Share Their Ideas

Allow students a chance to share their ideas. Give them praise for their ideas. You can ask who would like to share what they wrote. Let students know that as they listen to each other, they can add ideas to their own lists if they hear one they like.

Session 15.3: Performing Acts of Kindness at Home

To begin the session, pick out some Kind Acts stars from the basket and read the acts of kindness for the class. Whether you are doing daily or once-a-week lessons, take some time to read the kind acts out loud. If you have a student that doesn't have a lot of stars in the bin, try to earmark one with his or her name on it so this student can get praise for the kindness demonstrated. This will reinforce the behavior and hopefully cause the student to go on to show more acts of kindness.

List Kind Acts You Can Do at Home

Since students have talked about how they can show kindness at school, in this session, they we will talk about how to show kindness at home. Begin the discussion with an example. You can say, "For example, at home I can cook my husband [or other member of the household] a nice meal after he has had a hard day, and I can help my son with his homework." (You can offer a scenario specific to you and your family.)

Have students turn to the My Kind Acts worksheet. In the At Home section, ask them to list as many acts of kindness they can do at home and in the community setting that they can think of.

Give students some time to write down their ideas. Walk around the room while students work and give them suggestions of things you have heard them doing to add to their list.

Have Students Share Their Ideas

Allow students a chance to share their ideas and praise them for their efforts. Ask who would like to share what they wrote. Let students know that if they hear an idea they like as they listen to each other, they can add the idea to their own lists.

Session 15.4: Writing Thank You Notes

Begin the session by picking out some stars and reading out the acts of kindness. Whether you are doing daily or once-a-week lessons, take some time to read the kind acts out loud. For this session, you will need blank pieces of paper and a container to hold these scraps of paper.

Before you start the activity, have students write their name on a scrap piece of paper. Put all of the pieces of paper with the students' names in a cup or container that students can reach into. Go around the room and have each student pick out a name. Students will write a thank you note to the person they selected. To begin the activity, you can say,

> *We have talked a lot about acts of kindness that we can do*
> *here at school and outside of school. I want you to think about*
> *a time that the student whose name you drew did something*
> *nice for you. I want you to get out a blank piece of paper and*
> *write this student a thank you note. You should include in*
> *your thank you note what that person did for you, how you*
> *felt before and how you felt after the kind act, and a thank*
> *you for the kind act.*

Let students know that if they pull a name of someone they haven't interacted with and need some help coming up with ideas, they should raise their hand so that you can help you.

Allow students a chance to write their thank you cards. Walk around the room and help students who are struggling with ideas. If students pulled the name of someone they don't interact much, encourage them to think of something that student does that is kind for the entire class (e.g., they help clean up, they follow the rules so the class doesn't get in trouble) and how that ultimately impacts the student writing the thank you note. At the end, have students give their thank you note to the other student.

Lesson 15.5: The Commitment Circle

Pick out some stars and read the acts of kindness. Whether you are doing daily lessons, or lessons once a week, take some time to read the random acts out loud.

Have students stand in a circle to pick their commitments for the lesson. Present the prompt for the commitment circle: "How are you going to demonstrate kindness proactively? For example, I am going to help my principal by [describe your activity.]" For your own example commitment, you might select an activity you can complete that week, such as helping your principal plan for an event, help pass out flyers, etc.

Go around the circle and ask students make their commitments. Encourage them to make these commitments for both the home and school setting so they can see how these skills translate to the home setting. Encourage them to identify kind acts that they can plan and carry out, rather than naming passive, reactive actions like helping someone up who has fallen or taking someone who is hurt to the clinic. Have students identify specific proactive things they can do.

Reinforcing the Lesson

Give praise for students who are showing kindness and empathy. Remind students to show empathy and ask them how they could show kindness or empathy, when presented with a learning opportunity.

Sample Letter to Parents and Guardians—Lesson 15

Dear Parent/Guardian,

This week, as part of our focus on social awareness skills in social and emotional learning, our class learned what empathy is and how to demonstrate it. Students learned that empathy is important because it helps others feel good and helps create positive connections. Students also identified acts of kindness in which they can engage.

You can ask your child the following questions about the lesson:

- What is empathy?
- Why is empathy important?
- What acts of kindness have you done?
- What is the difference between being kind proactively and being kind reactively?
- What acts of kindness do you plan to do?

Regards,

My Kind Acts

At School	
At Home	

Reward Stars

Lesson 16

Building Empathy, Continued

Empathy Icon

Students will continue to build empathy by considering how their interactions with others affect their emotions and through using of the metaphor of charging batteries with kindness. See lesson 15 for more background information on empathy.

Objectives

Students will be able to

- identify at least two ways they can "charge" their battery
- identify at least two ways they can "charge" others' batteries

Success Criteria

Students are able to

- define what the metaphor of "charging batteries" represents
- identify how they can charge their own battery
- understand the importance of charging not only their battery but others' batteries, too
- feel comfortable demonstrating empathy

Materials

- Preferred coloring utensils
- One copy per student of Charging Batteries worksheet
- One copy per student of My Kind Act worksheet
- One copy per student of My Kindness Plan worksheet

Things to Note

Avoid telling students their responses are incorrect. Instead, ask guiding questions or redirect them back to the task. Give them the option of asking a friend for help.

The first session in this lesson is split into two parts. If you are doing daily lessons, it is recommended that you conduct the first part in the morning and the second part later in the day. If you are teaching *Power Up* in one weekly lesson that covers all sessions, present Session 1, part 1 in the morning and Session 1, part 2 at Session 5 later in the day.

Session 16.1: How We Feel About Our Interactions

Check in with students on how they did with their commitment from last week. Ask, "Who would like to volunteer to share how they did proactively showing kindness?" Allow students a chance to share how they did on their commitments. If you find that the same students are sharing each week, encourage new students to share. If you have some students who never share, try to check in with them individually.

Improving Our Interactions as a Way to "Charge Our Batteries"

Part 1. In this lesson, the class will continue talking about empathy and consider how our social interactions affect our feelings and energy level. You will use the Charging Batteries worksheet and the image of the battery to reinforce the lesson.

Have students turn to the Charging Batteries worksheet in their workbooks. In this worksheet, there are pictures of pairs of batteries. You can tell students that at the top of the page, under the heading Start of Day, the first battery at top represents how good they feel about their interactions with others right now. The battery just below it represents how good they think others feel about interacting with them right now. Ask students to fill in their batteries according to how they feel about their interactions or how they others feel about interacting with them. You can tell them:

> On the top battery, I want you to color in how "charged" or "full" your battery is right now. In other words, how good do you feel about your interactions with others today? The more you fill in the battery, the better you feel about the social interactions you have had today. For example, I drew my battery mostly full, but not all the way full because I was running late this morning and didn't talk to one of the teachers as much as I like to in the morning. [Partially color in the battery to demonstrate.] *The second battery represents how charged you think others' batteries are after interacting with you today. If you have a positive interaction, their battery will become more charged. If you have a negative interaction, their battery will be less charged.*

Fill in Top Pair of Batteries in the Worksheet

Ask students to fill in the top battery in the worksheet to show how they feel about their interaction with others. Also have them color in the second battery below it on the worksheet to show how full they think the battery of other's is after interacting with them today.

Give students a couple of minutes to fill in their batteries. Walk around the room while students work and remind them that their batteries' charge can change, depending on their interactions with others.

At the end of the exercise, congratulate students on their work and let them know that the class is going to continue being kind to others. Have students put their worksheet away for now and let them know that at the end of the day or the next session, they will return to it and fill out the batteries located under the heading End of Day. You can tell them,

> *I want your goal to be filling up your battery and the battery of others. At the end of the day* [or the next lesson], *we are going to fill in the charges on the two batteries on the bottom of the worksheet. I want your batteries' to be full, so make sure you are being kind today!*

Return to the Charging Batteries Worksheet

Part 2: Have students get out their workbooks and turn to the Charging Batteries worksheet. Tell students,

> *You are going to fill in the pair of batteries on the bottom of the page. Just like the batteries you worked on earlier, the top battery represents how full your battery is, and the second battery below it represents how full others' batteries after interacting with you today* [this week]. *I want you to think about your interactions with others since we had our discussion this morning as you fill in the battery charges.*

Give students a couple of minutes to color in their worksheet batteries.

Students should understand that the goal is to pursue positive interactions and for everyone's "battery" to be as charged as possible. You can tell students that while our batteries' can get charged, they can also get drained. Our own batteries' can get drained when we are mean to others or do things that lead to us having negative interactions with others. We can also drain the battery of others by being mean to them. The less they enjoy their interactions with us, the more drained their battery is. The goal is for everyone's battery to be as charged as possible. If we charge someone else's battery, they are more likely to charge ours in return.

Have Students Review Their Work and Display the Skill Cutout

When students have finished, have them look at the Start of Day battery that represents their own charge. Ask them to compare it to the battery they just colored in. Which one is more charged? Allow students a chance to respond. Tell them, "Your battery is hopefully more charged because you were focused on having more positive interactions with others!"

Next have students look at the other person's battery in the Start of Day section of the worksheet and ask them to compare it to the other person's battery they just colored in. Which one is more charged? Allow students a chance to respond. Tell them, "The other person's battery is hopefully more charged because you were all working on spreading kindness, which helped others feel good."

Hang the charging batteries skill cutout on the board for students to see and refer to.

Session 16.2: Record Your Kind Acts

Have students use the My Kind Act worksheet to reflect on a kind act they have done. They can write about a recent kind act or something they did a long time ago. It should be something that they are proud to have done.

Students should answer each of the questions on the worksheet. They should be sure to include information about the kind act, about how they felt before and after they did the kind act, and about how they think the other person felt before and after.

Be sure that they also fill in the worksheet's batteries with their charges. Point out that the students' batteries appear on the left. They should color in the top left battery to show how fully charged their battery was before their kind act and color in the bottom left battery under it to show how charged it was after. Then, in the top battery on the right, they will fill out how fully charged the other person's battery was before they helped the person and in the bottom right picture, show how full the other person's battery was after you helped the person.

Walk around the room and ask students about their kind acts. Ask them questions that compare the batteries together (e.g., Which battery is more charged?). The batteries should get more charged for both the student and the person they helped.

Session 16.3: Make a Plan for Kindness

Have students use the My Kindness Plan worksheet to make a plan for how they are going to be kind this week. Ask students find the worksheet in their workbooks. Tell students that to make the plan to carry out a kind act they want to do, they will answer the questions on their My Kindness Plan worksheet. If they have time, they can draw a picture at the bottom of the page to go with their plan. Remind them of the purpose of the exercise before they begin: "Remember, the goal is to charge your battery and the battery of the person you are doing the kind act for."

As they work on their plans, walk around the room and ask what the student will do that will be kind. Give praise for their planned kind acts: "I saw a lot of great plans! I look forward to seeing and hearing about these kind acts."

Session 16.4: Remembering Acts of Kindness

For this session, have students share a time someone was kind to them and how it made them feel. While you may normally have students sit in a circle to make their commitments, it will be helpful to have students gather in a circle to discuss kindness.

Have students sit in a circle and take turns speaking, going around the room. Have students share what the individual did that was kind, how they felt before the kind act, and how they felt after the kind act. Encourage students by praising their work on the lesson: "I'm very proud of you and all of the kindness that you are spreading. Keep showing kindness!"

Session 16.5: The Commitment Circle

Have students gather into a circle to identify their commitments. To offer the prompt for the week, you can say,

> *Our prompt for our commitment circle this week is, What kind acts are you going to commit to? Remember, we want proactive commitments. For example, this week I am going to bring* [teacher's name] *coffee tomorrow morning.*

Go around the circle and have students make their commitments. Encourage them to make these commitments for both the home and school setting so they can see how these skills translate to the home setting. Remind them to make proactive commitments.

Reinforcing the Lesson

Throughout the day and week, ask students if their actions are charging others' batteries or draining them. If their answer is that they are draining the batteries, ask the students what they can do to charge their batteries and the batteries of other people.

Sample Letter to Parents and Guardians—Lesson 16

Dear Parent/Guardian,

This week, as part of our focus on social awareness skills in social and emotional learning, our class continued to learn about the importance of empathy and showing kindness to others. Students focused on identifying ways that they can improve how they feel about their interactions and how others feel about interacting with them. We called good interactions ways to charge our own batteries and the batteries of others. The kinder we are to others, the more fully charged both batteries become.

You can ask your child the following questions about the lesson:

- What does it mean to "charge batteries" in your classroom?
- How can you charge your battery?
- How can you charge the batteries of others?
- What are your plans to continue to charge your battery, and the battery of others?

Regards,

Charging Batteries

Start of Day:

End of Day:

My Kind Act

What was your kind act?

_____

_____

_____

How did you feel before your kind act?

_____

_____

_____

How did you feel after your kind act?

_____

_____

_____

How do you think the other person felt before your kind act?

_____

_____

_____

How do you think the person felt after your kind act?

_____

_____

_____

Your battery charge before your kind act: The other person's battery charge before:

Your battery charge after your kind act: The other person's battery charge after:

My Kindness Plan

How do you plan to show kindness?

_____

_____

_____

Who will receive this kind act?

_____

_____

_____

What materials will you need to complete this act?

_____

_____

_____

Where are you going to do this kind act?

_____

_____

_____

What are the steps you need to take to complete this act?

_____

_____

_____

Lesson 17

Working in a Group

Collaborative Group Member Icon

Students will learn the different roles people can play in a group, their specific role in a group, their strengths and their weaknesses when working in a group, and how to improve on a weakness to become a better group member.

Introduction

Students will be asked to take part in group work for the rest of their lives. Some students enjoy this work more than others, and some students are better at it than others. Working in groups gives students the chance to practice many of the skills they have learned and will learn in this curriculum. Students will have to communicate their needs, regulate themselves, be aware of what others are feeling, and effectively solve problems.

Being able to function in collaborative group work and in teams that can manage themselves has become a sought-after skill in the workforce. Employers want to see that group members can be innovative and meet the complex needs of project-based work (Magpili & Pazos, 2018). Teaching students to work in groups now will give them the foundation to successfully work in groups in the future.

Objectives

Students will be able to

- identify their role in a group
- identify four group roles and at least two strengths and two weaknesses of each group role
- create a plan to improve upon a weakness they have when working in a group

Success Criteria

Students are able to

- identify the four different types of roles group members can play
- understand what role they generally play in a group
- feel comfortable improving upon a weakness they have when working in a group

Materials

- One copy per student of the Group Roles worksheet
- One copy per student of the My Group Role Assessment worksheet
- One copy per student of the My Group Member Role Assessment worksheet
- One copy per student of the My Improvement Plan worksheet

Things to Note

It is important to remind students that no group role is wrong or inferior. Just like with anything, there are strengths and weaknesses with each group role. Students can work on enhancing their strengths while learning skills to improve upon their weaknesses.

Session 17.1: The Roles We Can Play in a Group

Check in on how students did on their commitments from last week. Ask them who would like to volunteer to share how they did completing their kind acts. Allow students a chance to share how they did on their commitments. If you find that the same students are participating each week, encourage new students to speak up. If you have some students who never share, try to check in with them individually.

Discuss Working in a Group

In this lesson, you will have students talk about working in groups and introduce the various roles that each group member plays. Begin by asking students to talk a little bit about their experiences in working in groups. The discussion should include the following questions, and you should allow time for students to respond to each:

> *Have you had good experiences when working in a group?*
> *Have you had bad experiences? Does everyone in a group*
> *always pull their weight? Does everyone always get along? Is*
> *there sometimes conflict? How is the conflict handled?*

Call on students to share their experiences about working in a group. They don't have to answer all of the above questions, but the point is to get them thinking and talking about their experiences working in groups.

After students have shared their experiences, recap what they shared and emphasize that working well with others in a group is a skill. You might say,

> *Some of you have had positive experiences working in a*
> *group, and some of you have had negative experiences. Your*
> *experience might have depended on the team members in*
> *your group, the assignment, or when the group took place.*

Working collaboratively with others is a skill that you will need for the rest of your life.

Ask students, "What do you think I mean when I say that being able to work in groups is a skill you will need?" Students should remember that they will need to work in groups in middle school, high school, and in most careers.

Conclude the discussion by reminding students that working in a group is an acquired skill. You don't expect them to be perfect at it right away. It takes time and practice. Now is the time to practice this skill instead of waiting until they have a job that depends, in part, on them being able to work constructively in a group with many different personalities.

At this point in this lesson, you will describe four different roles that a person can play in a group and have students discuss them. Let students know that each of these roles is named after a job position that demonstrates some of the role's traits. These four group roles are CEO (otherwise known as chief executive officer), lawyer, accountant, and entertainer.

Students should know that each group member role that the class discusses has its strengths and weaknesses. No role is wrong or bad. Let them know that it's important for us to recognize what role we have in a group and what role other group members have so that we can figure out how to work together in a constructive manner.

Review the Strengths and Weakness of the CEO Role

Ask, "What type of group role do you think the CEO would have?" After students respond, you should provide a definition of this role. You can say, "CEOs like to be in control. They are used to being in charge and getting to make decisions. They might tell others what to do, how to do it, and when to get it done."

Ask students to volunteer what they think the strengths of the CEO might be. Write student responses on the board. Extend the discussion by offering your explanation of the role. You can say, "The CEO's strengths include good leadership skills and being smart, big-picture focused, confident, and persistent."

Ask, "What might be some weaknesses?" Write student responses on the board. You can say, "A CEO's weaknesses might include rigidity, unwillingness to listen to new ideas, bossiness, and being off-putting to other group members who also want to contribute. "

Review the Strengths and Weaknesses of the Lawyer Role

Ask students what they think the lawyer's role might look like. After students respond, you can offer your definition. You can say, "Lawyers are determined to dissuade others from ideas and goals that do not align with their case. They have done the research and can back up their ideas."

Ask, "What do you think some strengths of the lawyer might be?" Write student responses on the board. When they have shared their thoughts, you can provide a definition: "Lawyers do a lot of research and back up their ideas. They are smart and able to see a situation from multiple perspectives in order to better argue a case."

Ask, "What do you think some weaknesses of the lawyer might be?" Write student responses on the board. When the students have shared their thoughts, you can offer the following: "Lawyers might not take other ideas into account. They might be judgmental and dismissive of ideas that don't align with their vision for the project."

Review the Strengths and Weakness of the Accountant Role

Ask students what kind of role they think the accountant might have in a group. After students respond, you can offer your explanation: "The accountant is very smart and works well with numbers. The accountant can get the job done without much input from others."

Ask, "What do you think the accountant's strengths are?" Write student responses on the board. When the students have shared their thoughts, you can say, "Accountants work really well by themselves. They don't need much help from others and are able to work through tough problems. The accountant enjoys a challenge and isn't afraid of hard work."

Ask, "What do you think the accountant's weaknesses might be?" Write student responses on the board. When the students have shared their thoughts, you can say, "Accountants can work so well by themselves that they might struggle to work well with others in a group. They might be quiet in the group and not want to contribute because they would rather just work on their own."

Review the Strengths and Weaknesses of the Entertainer Role

Ask students what they think the role of the entertainer is. After students have had a chance to respond, you can offer your explanation and say, "Entertainers are not afraid to have attention on them. They enjoy making others laugh and being around others. They might seek out social connection."

Ask students what they think the strengths of the entertainer are. Write student responses on the board. When the students have had a chance to share their thoughts, you can offer the following: "Entertainers are smart. They know that others need to laugh and have a good time in order to enjoy the social interaction of the group. They are able to make others laugh and enjoy themselves."

Ask students, "What do you think the entertainer's weaknesses are?" Write student responses on the board. After students have had a chance to share their thoughts, you can say the following: "Entertainers might be easily distracted and get off task. They might not contribute much to the group's project and might get others off track as well."

Consider What All the Roles Share

Conclude the discussion by having the students consider what all the roles have in common. After students have had a chance to respond, you should emphasize that all of these roles represent people who are smart. They all have goals and accomplish them in different ways. They all have strengths and weaknesses. Each takes a different role in the group, but each's strengths, when used correctly, can contribute to a well-run and productive group.

Add to the Group Roles Worksheet

Have students turn to the Group Roles worksheet in their workbooks. On the worksheet is a grid with descriptions of each of the group roles and each role's strengths and weaknesses. In the discussion, students will have come up with role characteristics that aren't listed in the worksheet. Have students add any strengths or weaknesses they identified to the descriptions in the worksheet.

Session 17.2: Practice Working in Group

In this session, students will practice working together as part of a group in a short activity. To form the groups, go around the room and have students count off from numbers 1 through 4. Students with the same numbers will group together. For example, all of the 1s will form a group, all of the 2s will form a group, etc. (If you have some groups of three, that is OK.) Assign each group a place in the room to work and present them with the group assignment: "In your groups, I want you to take a blank piece of paper and figure out as a group how to fold it into a bird."

Give students 3 minutes to complete the task and set a timer. As students work, walk around the room and observe. Don't resolve conflicts or arguments unless necessary.

Fill Out the My Group Role Assessment Worksheet

When time is up, have students stay in their groups and get out their workbooks. Ask them to complete the worksheet My Group Role Assessment to help them determine which group role they played in this activity.

After students answer the worksheet questions, they should tally their responses, following the directions at the bottom of the page. Once they have the total, ask them to identify which role they scored highest in and have them reread that role's strengths and weaknesses. Next, ask them to identify which role they scored the lowest in and to review that role's strengths and weaknesses. Some students might have a tie across roles, and that's OK. Some of the roles have similar qualities.

Allow students some time to work on the worksheet. When they are done, ask them to complete the My Group Member Role Assessment for the person in their group whose count-off number is one higher than theirs. For example, if their number was 1, they will do this assessment thinking about the student who was number 2 and that student's role in the group activity. The student with number 2 will complete the assessment for student number 3, and student number 3 will do the assessment for student number 4. Last, student number 4 will complete the assessment for student number 1.

Allow students some time to work on the role assessment worksheet. Once done, have students give the assessment to the student they assessed. After they have exchanged assessments, ask students to review the responses they received.

As students review their assessments, let them know that none of the responses are wrong or bad but they tell us how others might see us. To direct the discussion, you might say,

> *As you read your assessment, remember that none of the responses are wrong or bad. Compare their answers about you to the answers you wrote about yourself. Were they similar? Were you surprised by the responses?*

Have a discussion about the similarities and differences in answers. In concluding, let students know that sometimes we might think we are in one role but are perceived to be in another: "Our perception of ourselves might be totally different than how others perceive us. This isn't a bad thing, but it is something to be aware of, especially when working in groups."

Session 17.3: Becoming a More Productive Group Member

Now that students know what roles they tend to play in a group, they can begin to identify how they can become a more productive group member. In this session, students will identify their weaknesses as a group member and make a plan for improvement. Begin the session with a discussion on how we can be good group contributors, by asking the following prompt: "Remember, there is always room for improvement in every group role. What are some positive ways that people can contribute to a group?"

Write student responses on the board. Conclude by reading and summarizing some of the student's positive comments. You might say,

> *There are a lot of great ways that people can contribute to a group. They can listen to everyone's ideas, take notes, respectfully disagree, do their fair share of work, engage with group members, and be kind to others.*

Create an Improvement Plan

Have students return to their assessments in the My Group Role Assessment worksheet to begin to make an improvement plan. Ask them to look at the weaknesses listed for the role they had the highest number of points in at the bottom of the worksheet. In this exercise, students should identify which weakness they need to work on the most and what their plan for improving will be. Their plan should be as specific as possible so it's easy to measure and see if they have met their goals. To help them create measurable goals, you can offer some examples:

> *For example, if you like to keep to yourself, decide to make the conscious effort to say at least one thing for each topic discussed. If you like to entertain others, you can make the goal be to tell one joke after contributing two ideas or comments that aren't jokes.*

Have students write down their weakness, goal, and plan to improve on the My Improvement Plan worksheet. They should leave the Reflection section blank for now.

Practice in a Group Exercise

Now that students have their goals, let them know that they are going to practice putting their plan into action. Have students get into groups of four, dividing the class into groups in a way that works best for you, and then give the class the prompt for the activity:

> *"I want you to work with your group members to fold a piece of paper into a flower. Remember to put your improvement plan into practice."*

Walk around the room while students work and give them praise for their progress. After students have completed the activity, have them reflect on their experience by completing the Reflection section at the bottom of the My Improvement Plan worksheet. To get them started, you might ask, "How was the experience? Was it easy or hard to follow your plan? Did you have to constantly remind yourself of the plan? Did you meet your goal?"

Conclude the Exercise and Display the Skill Cutout

After students have finished writing their reflections, conclude the session by encouraging students to keep working on their plan. Let them know that being aware of our strengths and weaknesses helps us become more helpful group members. You might say,

> *Working in a group is hard. Improving upon our weaknesses can be hard too. The important thing to remember is that*

we keep practicing so we can get better. The more we practice the better we will do. No matter what role you have, no matter what role you are good at or what role you are bad at, you have a lot to contribute to any group. It's important that you are thoughtful in your interactions, and aware of your strengths and weaknesses. The goal is to become a collaborative group member. You want to listen to ideas nonjudgmentally, be open to ideas that are different than yours, and collaborate to accomplish the group's goal.

Add the working in a group skill cutout to the board or display area and let students know that when you see them being a productive group member, no matter the role they are playing, you will color in a bar for them.

Session 17.4: Play a Group Role

For this activity, students will play out a group role and have others in their group guess which role they had. You can have students stay in their same groups of three or four or split them up into new different groups. To begin, have each group write the four group roles (CEO, lawyer, accountant, entertainer) on separate pieces of paper. They, should fold the pieces of paper, mix up their order, and have each member choose a piece containing one of the four roles.

Tell the class that each member in their group should have a different role. Ask them not to tell the other group members what role they picked. Then offer them the prompt for the group activity:

In your groups, you are going to decide what shape, object, food, or animal you want to fold a blank piece of paper into. Once you have decided, you will create the object together as a group. The catch is you are going to have to play the role listed on your piece of paper during the group work.

Give them 5 minutes to complete the activity. Walk around the room while students work. Do not intervene unless necessary.

Have Students Guess the Roles Group Members Were Playing

Once done, come together as a whole group. Call on each group individually and have each of the group member try to guess what role that student was playing in their group and explain why they think so. After students have had a chance to guess their group members role, have a discussion about the exercise. Ask,

*Was it hard to play a different role than you normally would?
Were there parts you liked about that role? Were there parts
you disliked? How did other group members treat you?*

Session 17.5: The Commitment Circle

Have students gather into a circle. To present the prompt for this lesson's commitment circle, you can say,

> *Our prompt for our commitment circle this week is, How are
> you going to be a collaborative group member? For example,
> my group role is CEO. While I really enjoy being in charge of
> groups, I'm going to work on my improvement plan and be
> a collaborative group member by making sure that I listen to
> everyone else's ideas and really consider them rather than just
> deciding that my idea is best.*

Go around the circle and have students make their commitments.

Reinforcing the Lesson

As students work in groups throughout the lesson, remind them to work to their strengths and be aware of their weaknesses. Remind them that this is a great time to practice these skills, in the safety of their class.

Sample Letter to Parents and Guardians—Lesson 17

Dear Parent/Guardian,

This week, as part of our focus on social awareness skills in social and emotional learning, our class learned about working in a group and the different roles that each individual group member might play. Students focused on identifying their own role in the group and the strengths and weaknesses that come along with that role. It is important for students to understand the role they play in a group so they can ensure that they are being collaborative group members.

You can ask your child the following questions about the lesson:

- What role do you play in a group?
- What are the strengths of the role you play in a group?
- What are the weaknesses of the role you play in a group?

Regards,

Group Roles

The CEO (Chief Executive Officer)	The Lawyer
Strengths: good leadership skills, smart, able to see the big picture, confident, and doesn't give up.	**Strengths:** does a lot of research to back up ideas, smart and able to see a situation from multiple angles in order to argue a case.
Weaknesses: rigid, unwilling to listen to new ideas, bossy and off-putting to other group members who also want to contribute.	**Weaknesses:** even though able to take multiple perspectives on a situation, might not take other ideas into account. Might be judgmental and dismissive of ideas that don't align with a chosen vision for a project.
The Accountant	The Entertainer
Strengths: smart, works really well by themselves, doesn't need much help from others, and is able to work through tough problems. Enjoys challenges and is not afraid of hard work.	**Strengths:** smart, knows that others need to laugh and have a good time in order to enjoy the social interaction of the group. Able to make others laugh and enjoy themselves.
Weaknesses: might struggle to work well with others in a group. Might be quiet in a group and not want to contribute because of a preference to just work by themselves.	**Weaknesses:** might be easily distracted and go off task. Might not contribute much to the group's project and might get others off-track as well.

My Group Role Assessment

Circle the response that best represents your group role:

1. Do you like to be in charge?	Yes	No
2. Do you like to make others laugh?	Yes	No
3. Do you dread working in groups?	Yes	No
4. Do you enjoy social interactions more than getting the work done in groups?	Yes	No
5. Do you get frustrated with others who don't like your ideas?	Yes	No
6. Do you like to give group members tasks?	Yes	No
7. Are you often off task in the group?	Yes	No
8. Are you quiet in groups?	Yes	No
9. Are you vocal in groups?	Yes	No
10. Would you rather do the whole project yourself?	Yes	No
11. Can you see a situation from multiple perspectives?	Yes	No
12. Do you like to work with others?	Yes	No
13. Do you like to work alone?	Yes	No

How many "yes" answers did you give for questions 1, 5, 6, 9, 12? _____ (CEO)

How many "yes" answers did you give for questions 1, 5, 9, 11, 12? _____ (lawyer)

How many "yes" answers did you give for questions 3, 5, 8, 10, 13? _____ (accountant)

How many "yes" answers did you give for questions 2, 4, 7, 9, 12? _____ (entertainer)

My Group Member Role Assessment

Circle the response that best represents your group member:

1.	Do they like to be in charge?	Yes	No
2.	Do they like to make others laugh?	Yes	No
3.	Do they dread working in groups?	Yes	No
4.	Do they enjoy social interactions more than getting the work done in groups?	Yes	No
5.	Do they get frustrated with others who don't like their ideas?	Yes	No
6.	Do they like to give group members tasks?	Yes	No
7.	Are they often off task in the group?	Yes	No
8.	Are they quiet in groups?	Yes	No
9.	Are they vocal in groups?	Yes	No
10.	Would they rather do the whole project by themselves?	Yes	No
11.	Can they see a situation from multiple perspectives?	Yes	No
12.	Do they like to work with others?	Yes	No
13.	Do they like to work alone?	Yes	No

How many "yes" answers did you give for questions 1, 5, 6, 9, 12? _____ (CEO)

How many "yes" answers did you give for questions 1, 5, 9, 11, 12? _____ (lawyer)

How many "yes" answers did you give for questions 3, 5, 8, 10, 13? _____ (accountant)

How many "yes" answers did you give for questions 2, 4, 7, 9, 12? _____ (entertainer)

My Improvement Plan

My weakness:

_____

_____

_____

My goal:

_____

_____

_____

My plan:

_____

_____

_____

_____

_____

Reflection:

_____

_____

_____

_____

Respectfully Disagreeing

Respectfully Disagree Icon

In this lesson, students will learn how to respectfully disagree with others.

Introduction

Disagreeing with others is perfectly normal and should even be expected. While conflict is inevitable, there are benefits to conflict if it is handled correctly. Part of successful conflict resolution is the ability to disagree in a respectful manner. If both parties feel heard, understood, and validated, they are more likely to work together toward a common goal.

According to Awan et al. (2015) leadership skills that are sought-after include communication, team building, delegation, problem-solving, and decision-making. Being able to effectively disagree is crucial in order to effectively execute many of these skills. For example, effectively disagreeing with others demonstrates good communication, good coaching for others, helps resolve conflict through problem-solving and improves decision-making.

Objectives

Students will be able to

- respectfully disagree with at least one other person
- create a two-step formula they can use to disagree with others in a constructive manner

Success Criteria

Students are able to

- identify the formula their class created that will allow them to disagree respectfully with others
- understand the importance of knowing how to respectfully disagree with others
- feel comfortable practicing disagreeing with others

Materials

One copy of per student of the Respectfully Disagreeing Formula worksheet

Things to Note

This might be a difficult skill for students to master. Remind them that school is a safe place to practice respectfully disagreeing with others. When there is a disagreement in the classroom, direct students to utilize the formula they created. The more they practice respectfully disagreeing, the more comfortable they will become in using the skill.

Session 18.1: Learn About How to Disagree Respectfully

Begin the lesson by checking in on student commitments from the last lesson. Ask who would like to volunteer to share how they did in being a collaborative group member and allow students a chance to share how they did on their commitments. If you find that the same students speak up each week, encourage new students to participate. If you have some students who never share, try to check in with them individually.

Introduce the Concept of Respectfully Disagreeing

Begin the lesson activity with a discussion of what it means to disagree constructively while showing respect for the other person. Ask students to share their thoughts on what it means to respectfully disagree before offering your definitions. To begin the discussion, you can say, "In this lesson we are going to discuss respectfully disagreeing with others. What do you think it means to respectfully disagree with someone?"

After students respond, offer a definition or explanation. Use this definition to prompt a discussion about why the practice of respectfully disagreeing is important. Again, allow students to respond before you offer guidance or summarize with your own explanation of why it is important. You can say,

> *Respectfully disagreeing with others is when we take the time to listen to another person's point of view, without putting down that person's ideas. We listen and then present our own perspective. Why do you think it's important that we are able to respectfully disagree with others?*

Allow students to answer your question. After students respond, you should offer your explanation of why disagreeing respectfully is important. In summarizing, you could say,

> *It's important that we learn to respectfully disagree with others because it helps us be productive when solving a problem or resolving a debate. If we stop being respectful, then we have stopped trying to understand the other person's point of view. When we stop trying to understand the other person's point of view, we are cutting ourselves off from seeing a problem from multiple perspectives.*

While we might not change our minds after listening to the other person, it's good for us to be able to consider things we hadn't previously thought of. This can help us strengthen our ideas, and it can help us become open to other ways of thinking. We have a lot to learn from other people so it's important that we listen. In fact, it can sometimes be fun to get into a friendly debate with someone.

Practice Debating with a Partner

Have students divide up into pairs so that they can practice respectfully disagreeing. Pair the students up in a manner that works best for your class. Once students are in groups of two, let them know the assigned topic: What is the best dessert? You can also consider other topics, such as what is the best sport? What are the best toppings on a pizza? What is the best ice cream flavor? The topic should be one that is not controversial in nature.

Walk around the room while students practice debating. Don't intervene unless necessary.

Session 18.2: Create a Formula for How to Disagree

This lesson will ask students to recall their practice debate and the phrases and gestures that made them more willing to continue talking to their partner. Students will work from these collected phrases and gestures to make a formula for respectfully disagreeing. Begin the lesson by letting students know that now that they have practiced respectfully disagreeing with someone, you want them to think of phrases that they heard during the exercise that made them more open to listening to what the other person had to say.

Record Student Responses on a Whiteboard or Chalkboard

Let students share examples and write down the student responses on the board. To prompt the discussion, you can offer an example of a phrase that might be helpful in an argument. For example, you could share the following: "I heard you when you said _____, but _____. What phrases did you like?"

Collect Phrases to Use When Respectfully Disagreeing

Review the examples the students shared and work as a class with these phrases to assemble a formula for respectfully disagreeing. The formula should include phrases to use when reflecting the other person's statements and phrases for stating their own point of view. You can start the discussion by saying, "Based on your responses, let's create a formula we can use to disagree with others. What do you think it should start with?"

Guide students to start with words or phrases that validate what the other person said. An example could be, "What I heard you say was…"

After they have collected expressions that help with politely restating another's opinion, have students come up with a following phrase that allows them to state their point. For example, students might introduce their viewpoint by saying, "However…" or "Have you considered…" Let students have fun with this activity. The final formula can be as short or as long as needed. Write the formula somewhere that can be displayed in the room.

Complete the Respectfully Disagreeing Formula Worksheet

After collecting phrases and words for the respectfully disagreeing formula, let students know that you want them to write down the formula the class created in the worksheet Respectfully Disagreeing Formula that's in their workbooks so they can refer to it as needed.

At this point, hang the respectfully disagreeing skill cutout in the classroom for students to see and refer to.

Discuss Nonverbal Communication

Once students have recorded the phrases in their worksheets, begin a discussion of nonverbal behavior and its role in communication. Ask students to provide examples of how we might send messages without using words. You can say,

> Did you know that at least 55% of communication is nonverbal? Some argue that up to 93% of our communication is nonverbal. That means that the majority of the messages we give others aren't with our words. What are some ways that our body might send messages to others?

Have a discussion and write the responses on the board. Make sure to remind students that tone of voice; posture, such as leaning toward or away from a person; and eye contact or the absence of it, are all important parts of communicating. Students should be aware that not making eye contact or turning away from the person speaking can lead to communication breakdowns and misunderstandings. Nonverbal cues can also improve communication and the enjoyment derived from conversation.

To give students examples of nonverbal messages, you might say,

> If I make eye contact, nod, and lean in toward someone, they know that I am listening. If I look around the room, am on my phone, or lean away from the speaker, they might think that what they are saying isn't important to me. It's important that we focus on the speaker. By giving them our undivided attention, we send the message that what they are saying is important to us. We should be aware of what we are

*communicating to others nonverbally as we use our formula
for disagreeing.*

Session 18.3: Practice Debating as a Class

In this session, you will have students as a class practice using the formula they created to disagree respectfully. Select a fun topic for the class to practice using the formula. You can use the following example:

> *As a class, we are going to debate what the best type of music is. Raise your hand to respectfully disagree with what the person before you said. Use this time to practice using our formula for respectfully disagreeing. I will start. I think the best kind of music is* [insert your favorite type of music and exlpain why it is].

Have students practice respectfully disagreeing with each other when defending why their music is best. You can intervene and remind them to utilize the formula they developed. At the end of the debate, you can remind students that we all have different opinions about types of music. None of us are wrong in our opinions or thoughts, but it is important that we appropriately express them.

Session 18.4: Practice Debating with a Partner

Have students continue to practice respectfully disagreeing by using the formula the class developed. Let them know that it is important that we continue to practice this skill so that it comes easily. To begin the exercise, randomly pair each student with a partner and provide the prompt for their discussion: "You are going to discuss what you think the most important quality in a friend is. Don't forget to use the formula we created in order to make your point!"

Allow students a chance to practice respectfully disagreeing. Remind them to utilize the formula, intervening when you think it is needed for this activity and throughout the week.

Session 18.5: The Commitment Circle

Have students gather in a circle to name their commitments for the week. Offer your own commitment first to help students begin:

> *Our prompt for our commitment circle this week is, How many times are you going to use our formula to practice respectfully disagreeing this week? For example, I am going to use it at least three times at school and at least twice at home.*

Go around the circle and have students make their commitments. Encourage them to make these commitments for both the home and school settings so they can see how these skills translate to the home setting.

Reinforcing the Lesson

Throughout the week when students disagree, refer them to the formula you created to respectfully disagree. When they are calm, have them practice each using the formula to communicate to each other.

Sample Letter to Parents and Guardians—Lesson 18

Dear Parent/Guardian,

This week our class focused on learning how to respectfully disagree with others. This is a social awareness skill and part of social and emotional learning. In this lesson, we continued to learn about the importance of interacting with others in a positive manner. It is important for students to know how to respectfully disagree with others in order to prevent conflict from escalating and to allow everyone to feel heard.

You can ask your child the following questions about the lesson:

- How do you respectfully disagree with someone?
- What is the formula for respectfully disagreeing with someone?
- Can you describe a situation where being able to respectfully disagree might have changed the outcome of the argument?

Regards,

Respectfully Disagreeing Formula

Relationship Skills

Friendships

In this lesson, students will learn to identify qualities that are important to them in a friend as well as consider the qualities that they have to offer in a friendship.

Introduction

As students get older, they shift their focus from their families to their friends. Their friends' opinions and likes and dislikes start to matter more and more. As students meet new people and make new friends, they begin to determine what is important to them in a friendship and what isn't. Friends play a key role in many of the decisions we make and in helping us learn how to interact with others. They help us build necessary social skills in order to be successful in relating to others.

Stable friendships have been linked to improved academic, behavioral, and mental health outcomes (Ng-Knight et al., 2019). Cohen (2004) postulates that being socially connected is vital for well-being. Social support has also been linked to improved immune functioning and decreased risk of diabetes, cardiovascular disease, and mortality (Uchino, 2006). Teaching students how to make and maintain friendships will help improve their emotional and physical outcomes.

Objectives

Students will be able to

- identify the top three qualities that are important to them in a friend
- identify the top three qualities they have to offer in a friendship

Success Criteria

Students are able to

- identify what qualities they want in a friend
- understand what they have to offer in a friendship
- feel comfortable identifying peers that they think would make good friends

Materials

- One copy per student of the Qualities in a Friend worksheet
- Preferred writing/coloring utensils

Things to Note

Friendships can be a sensitive topic for students as they navigate through friendships and determine whether their current friendships are meeting their needs. Encourage students to consider what qualities they want in a friend. This does not mean they need to give up their current friends but instead that they could determine if all their needs are being met by their current friends. They might decide there is room for some new friends along the way.

Session 19.1: Identifying Qualities We Want in a Friend

Check in on how students did on their commitment from last week. Ask who would like to volunteer to share how they did at respectfully disagreeing. Allow students a chance to share how they did on their commitments. If you find that the same students participate each week, encourage new students to contribute. If you have some students who never share, try to check in with them individually.

Pick Your Top Four Qualities in a Friend

In this lesson, you will have students use the Qualities in a Friend worksheet to begin to talk about qualities they would like in a friend. Tell students to turn to the worksheet in their workbook. They will find various characteristics listed. Have students pick the top four qualities they would like in a friend and to list them in order of importance, with 1 being the most important.

Allow students time to work on this exercise. Walk around the room and offer encouragement and validation that it is a hard activity.

Session 19.2: Knowing the Qualities We Like to Have in a Friend

Remind students of the activity they completed in the first session when they worked hard to identify four qualities in a friend that were very important to them. In this session, have students return to the list in the Qualities in a Friend worksheet. Ask them to circle as many qualities in a friend as they want and that are important to them. If a quality isn't listed, students can write it on the worksheet.

Have students begin on the worksheet and circulate around the room while they work. Inquire about which qualities are important to them.

Discuss their Work on the Worksheet

When the students have finished, ask them why they think is important for us to know the qualities we want in a friend. After students have a chance to respond, you should extend the discussion by pointing out that it is important for us to be aware of the qualities we value most in a friend so that we can make good choices about making friends. You might say,

> *No person is bad, and no friend is bad. Everyone offers something different in a friendship. Sometimes a person's qualities go well with ours, and sometimes they don't. For example, honesty is very important to me. It would be difficult for me to be friends with someone who lied sometimes, even if just to spare my feelings. I would feel like I couldn't trust them and then we would most likely argue a lot. But someone else might value a friend who makes them feel good, even if it means there is a little bit of lying. Neither approach is inherently bad or wrong. It's just important for us to be aware of what we value in friendships.*

Session 19. 3: Understanding What We Offer a Friend

In this session, students will use the Qualities in a Friend worksheet to identify what qualities they can offer a friend. To begin, you can remind students that they have discussed what qualities they would like in a friend, but in this session, they will focus on what qualities they have to offer in a friendship. You might want to illustrate what people look for in friends. You could say, "For example, I'm a great listener. Many of my friends call me when they have a problem that they want to talk about because they know they will have my undivided attention."

Have students return to the Qualities in a Friend worksheet in their workbooks. Ask them to put a star next to the qualities that they have to offer in a friendship. When they are done, they should number the circled qualities, with number one identifying their strongest quality. Have them try to use a different color pen, marker, or crayon than they used to rank qualities in the previous activity.

Session 19.4: Share What You Identified in the Worksheet

For this exercise, you can have students gather in a circle and ask each of them to share what quality for them is the most important to have in a friend. Let them know you also want them to share what is the strongest quality they have to offer in a friendship. Ask students to listen when others speak to see if some list similar qualities or if others talk about different qualities that they value. They might be surprised by the responses that they hear!

Go around the circle and have students take turns sharing what quality they find most important in a friend and what their strongest quality is. Point out similarities in any responses. For example, you might say something like, "Johnny says he values honesty in a friend, and Jane says she is a very honest person."

At the end of the exercise, summarize what students reported. Note qualities students often named or ones that should be emphasized. For example, you could say,

> I heard a lot of our class mention that kindness is important to them. It seems that kindness is something everyone would benefit from. Let's make an effort for our class to focus on being more kind with each another.

Instead of kindness, you can mention another quality you heard students identify a lot.

Session 19.5: The Commitment Circle

Have students gather into a circle and provide the prompt for this week's commitment:

> Our prompt for our commitment circle this week is, How are you going to be a good friend? For example, I identified that I am a good listener to my friends. I am going to make sure I listen to at least two of my friends who need it.

Go around the circle and have students make their commitments. Encourage them to make these commitments for both the home and school setting so that they can see how these skills translate to the home setting.

Reinforcing the Lesson

Remind students throughout the week of the friendship qualities they identified as being most important to them. Encourage them to make some new connections in the class with students who have similar responses. Let them know that this does not mean they need to give up their current friends, but there is always room for new friends.

Sample Letter to Parents and Guardians—Lesson 19

Dear Parent/Guardian,

This week, as part of our focus on relationship skills in social and emotional learning, our class learned ways to make and maintain positive relationships with peers and adults. In this lesson, students focused on identifying qualities they would like in a friend as well as qualities they have to offer a friend. It is important that we are aware of what we want in a friend in order to build strong and lasting relationships.

You can ask your child the following questions about the lesson:

- What qualities do you want in a friend?
- What qualities do you have to offer a friend?
- Does this insight change how you think about any of your current friendships?
- Is there anyone in your class you were surprised to find had similar qualities that were important to you in a friend?

Regards,

Qualities in a Friend

Smart

Fun

Good Cook

Attractive

Good Listener

Gives you Gifts

Honesty

Accepting

Nonjudgmental

Respectful

Trustworthy

Generous

Encouraging

Shows Empathy

Loyal

Funny

Dependable

Supportive

Confident

Communicating Our Wants and Needs

"I" Statements Icon

In this lesson, students will learn how to effectively communicate their wants and needs through the use of "I" statements.

Introduction

Students often express themselves through their behaviors, and it can often be difficult to understand what the students' needs are or what the goal of their behaviors is. Nevertheless, behaviors are goal-oriented and can be understood to be in line with the goal the individual is attempting to achieve. Giving students an appropriate way to express their needs allows for all parties involved to address them.

"I" statements help students appropriately express themselves verbally so that they don't need to rely on communicating their wants and needs nonverbally. "I" statements present a formula for naming feelings and stating requests. They help individuals express what they are feeling, what made them feel that way, and what they need in order to feel better without putting the other person on the defensive (Nadig, n.d.). While they might not always get the resolution they wanted, they will get to voice their feelings, which as discussed earlier can lessen the intensity of the identified feeling.

Objective

Students will be able to utilize "I" statements at least two times a week to communicate their feelings, wants, and needs.

Success Criteria

Students are able to

- identify the format of an "I" statement
- understand when to utilize "I" statements
- feel comfortable using "I" statements

Materials

- One copy per student of the "I" Statements worksheet
- Cutout words from the Feelings worksheet
- Basket or container to hold feeling words

Things to Note

This is a difficult skill for students to master. Help them think through their "I" statements when they try to use them. Give a lot of praise for their progress and attempt at using the skill. Gently redirect them when they misidentify the formula or use it incorrectly. Be patient with them.

When using "I" statements, we should avoid not correctly identifying the feeling, placing blame on someone else, expressing only negative feelings, and displaying nonverbal behavior or body language that contradicts our words (e.g., smiling when stating that we are angry).

Session 20.1: Communicating What We Need and Want

Check in with students on their commitments from last week. Ask who would like to volunteer to share how they did at being a good friend. Allow students a chance to share how they did on their commitments. If you find that the same students are participating each week, encourage new students to participate. If you have some students who never share, try to check in with them individually.

Introduce "I" Statements

In this lesson, you will introduce the concept of "I" statements and have students practice by using the "I" statements worksheet. Begin by telling the class that using "I" statements is one way for students to be able to communicate what they are feeling and why: "We are going to talk about 'I' statements. What do you think an 'I' statement might be?"

Allow students a chance to respond. After this discussion, explain what "I" statements are and how they can help us communicate to others. You can say that "I" statements help us communicate our wants and needs to others. In an "I" statement, we state what we are feeling, what happened to make us feel this way, and what we need from the other person in order to feel better.

To let students know why using these statements can be helpful, you can say something like the following:

> *It's important that we are able to effectively communicate what is causing us to feel a certain way and what we need from another person in order to feel better. If we don't communicate what we need from others, we might*

*be disappointed when they do something different than we
expected. For example, this week I was upset when my mom
didn't call me on Sunday to check in like she usually does. I
was so upset that I ignored her messages on Monday morning. She kept asking me what was wrong, and when I finally
told her, she apologized and said she knew I was busy and
that she didn't want to bother me! If we had both communi-
cated a little better, she would have known that I wanted to
talk to her and I would have known that she was trying to
be respectful of my time!*

Practice "I" Statements Using the Worksheet

Have students practice creating "I" statements by using the formula in the "I"
Statements worksheet. Ask students to turn to the worksheet in their workbooks and draw their attention to the format for an "I" statement that appears
at the top of the page. In an "I" statement, we state what we are feeling, what
happened to make us feel this way, and what we need from the other person
in order to feel better. (These steps are represented in the "I feel," "when," and
"I need" parts of the statement that appears in the worksheet.)

For the exercise, have each student pick a person they want to communicate to. Tell them to not name this person out loud but to fill out the worksheet statement as if they were talking to this person. To demonstrate what
an "I" statement could look like, you could say, "For example, I would write
'I feel sad when my mom doesn't call me on Sunday like normal. I need to be
called every Sunday.'"

Another important component of "I" statements is that they don't include
the word *you* unless totally necessary. Let students know that when we say
"you," the other person might feel like we are accusing them of something and
they might become defensive. If this happens, the other person might become
upset or angry, and there might not be a positive resolution for everyone.

Assist Students and Display the Skill Cutout

Have students start on the worksheet and walk around the room and ask
them about what they are writing. Give gentle redirection if they are off
task. Encourage them to avoid using the word *you* as it can make others feel
defensive.

Hang the "I" statement skill cutout on the board for students to refer to
and see.

Session 20.2: Using "I" Statements to Communicate What We Feel

In this session, you will ask students to choose from slips of paper cut from
the Feelings worksheet. They will then create an "I" statement based on the

word they selected. As you are introducing the lesson, you can have a student cut out the worksheet words, fold the pieces of paper so that the word doesn't show, and put the paper in a basket or bucket.

When beginning the exercise, let students know that the class is going to continue practicing using "I" statements. Remind them that we use "I" statements to express how we feel, why we feel that way, and what we need from the other person. Just because we express what we need, doesn't always mean we will get it, but sometimes just letting someone else know how we feel is enough to make us feel better.

Pick a Word from the Feelings Worksheet and Create an "I" Statement

Tell students that you are going to walk around the room with a basket containing slips of paper. Each of the pieces of paper has a word for a feeling on it. The students are to grab one slip of paper and one feelings word out of the basket. This will be the feeling they are going to create an "I" statement for. You can offer them an example to illustrate how they can create the statement: "For example, if I grabbed the word *mad*, I would write, 'I feel mad when I'm pushed. I need my personal space to be respected.'"

Tell students that they can write their "I" statement on the "I" statements worksheet or on a blank piece of paper. Let them know that they will share this "I" statement with the class later, so they should make sure it is one they are comfortable sharing.

Walk round the room as students work and assist them with their statements. Praise well-worded statements and give encouragement when students work on perfecting their statements. ("Great job! I saw some great 'I' statements out there. 'I' statements don't always come easily so it's important to continue practicing using them!")

Session 20.3: Sharing Our "I" Statements

Have students gather into a circle and share the "I" statement they created using the word they chose. Remind students that these "I" statements are general examples. They are not and should not be directed to anyone in particular.

Have students read aloud from their worksheets the "I" statements they created. When the students have shared their work, conclude the session by encouraging them and reminding them that "I" statements may not get us what they want but they do help us reach a better understanding:

> *Great job class! I heard a lot of great "I" statements. Although using "I" statements doesn't mean that we will always get what we want in the end, they might help prevent an argument or help us compromise. We might then both get what we want!*

Session 20.4: Communicating What We Feel through an "I" Statement

Repeat Session 2's activity.

Session 20.5: The Commitment Circle

Have students gather in a circle and offer the prompt for the week's commitment:

> *Our prompt for our commitment circle this week is, When are you going to use "I" statements?' For example, this week I am going to use them at home when my family members don't want to do their chores.*

In the prompt, you can insert another example specific to you. Go around the circle and have students make their commitments. Encourage them to make these commitments for both the home and school setting so they can see how these skills translate to the home setting.

Reinforcing the Lesson

Continue to encourage students to use their "I" statements to communicate their wants and needs to adults and peers.

Sample Letter to Parents and Guardians—Lesson 20

Dear Parent/Guardian,

This week, as part of our focus on relationship skills and social and emotional learning, our class learned how to effectively communicate our wants and needs to peers and adults. Students practiced how to make an "I" statement. "I" statements are important because they help us better communicate to others our feelings and our wants and needs in a way that is constructive.

You can ask your child the following questions about the lesson:

- When can you use "I" statements?
- What is the format of an "I" statement?
- Why are "I" statements important?

Regards,

"I" Statements

I feel _____

when _____.

I need _____.

Feelings Bank	
mad	sad
angry	jealous
disgusted	happy
loved	enraged
bored	lonely
depressed	pleased
tired	suspicious
anxious	nervous
surprised	sick
stubborn	frustrated
amused	confident
excited	determined
indifferent	withdrawn

Feelings

mad	sad
angry	jealous
disgusted	happy
loved	enraged
bored	lonely
depressed	pleased
tired	suspicious
anxious	nervous
surprised	sick
stubborn	frustrated
amused	confident
excited	determined
indifferent	withdrawn

Building Social Skills Using the CREATE Acronym, Part I

Compliments Icon

Respecting Personal Space Icon

Eye Contact Icon

In this lesson, students will learn the first three components of the CREATE social skills acronym: compliments, respecting personal space, and eye contact.

Introduction

Social skills help students feel connected to others and the community around them. This can be through connections at home, at school, or in the wider community. Social skills help students relate to others and can even impact student academic achievement. In a study conducted by Davis et al. (2014), students with higher levels of social and emotional skills had higher grades than did their peers who reported lower levels of social skills.

Being able to read other's cues about personal space is important in having positive social interactions. Respecting personal space, understood as the distance that individuals work to keep between themselves and other people (Lough et al., 2015), is a trainable skill and an example of a social skill that students will learn in this lesson. When personal space is invaded, it can evoke feelings of discomfort and anxiety. An agreed-upon standard for personal space, however, can vary based on social and cultural dynamics and context. These nuances should be recognized in social skills training and can pose challenges for students.

Objective

Students will be able to identify at least three proactive social skills they can utilize when having a conversation with peers or adults.

Success Criteria

Students are able to

- identify the first three skills in CREATE
- understand the importance of using CREATE skills
- feel comfortable using CREATE skills

Materials

One copy per student of the Social Skills Assessment worksheet

Things to Note

When talking about social skills, be aware of any students with disabilities that you may have in the classroom. It can be difficult for many exceptional education students to engage in appropriate social skills. Really encourage these students to pick one skill they feel comfortable using and to practice it throughout the lesson period. Give extra praise when you see the skill being used. While students will learn eye contact as one of the lesson skills, it is important to note that in some cultures, it is rude to look people directly in the eyes.

Session 21.1: Learning about Social Skills

Check in with students on their commitments from last week. Ask, "Who would like to volunteer to share how they did using their 'I' statements?"

Allow students a chance to share how they did on their commitments. If you find that the same students contribute each week, encourage new students to participate. If you have some students who never share, try to check in with them individually.

Introduce the Concept of Social Skills

Begin with a discussion about social skills, asking students what social skills are and why they are important. For example, you might say, "In this lesson, we are going to talk about social skills. What do you think I mean by social skills? What are some social skills? Why do you think they are important?"

Allow students a chance to respond to each question before offering your thoughts. Conclude the discussion by defining social skills and how they are used. You can say,

> *Social skills are verbal and nonverbal techniques we use when interacting with others. I use social skills when I communicate with you, the principal, my family, and my friends. These skills help us build meaningful and lasting relationships.*

Introduce Three Social Skills Identified in the CREATE Acronym

Let students know that in the next few lessons they are going to learn six social skills. These skills are represented by the letters in the CREATE acronym. In this session, the class will focus on the skill represented by the letter C: compliments. You can begin by relating the skill to the acronym, defining it, and providing an example:

> *We are going to learn six social skills, represented by the word CREATE. We are going to start with the C. The C stands for compliments. We want to make sure we compliment people when they do something positive or that we like or think is good. If we don't tell them we like what they did, they won't know! For example, I might compliment my friend on listening to me by telling her she's a good listener. I might also compliment her clothes or something she is wearing. Compliments can make other people feel good about themselves, just like you feel good about yourself when you get a compliment.*

Have students practice giving compliments by asking them to pair up with a partner. (For this exercise, you can have the students partner with the person next to them or you can have them partner up in a different manner.) You can say, "I want you each to give the other person a compliment. Remember, a compliment is something that makes someone feel good about themselves."

Walk around the room while students practice complimenting each other and observe. Praise them for their work on compliments and help them if they get stuck.

Hang the compliment skill cutout on the board for students to see and refer to.

Session 21.2: Respecting Personal Space and Making Eye Contact

Remind students about the social skill they learned about in the previous session, giving compliments, and let them know that they are going to learn another skill that is named in the CREATE acronym. Rather than talk about the concept of personal space, for this lesson, you will try to illustrate what it is. Ask to get a volunteer for this skill.

Pick a volunteer that you know is good with personal space or make some time to discuss the activity with the student you will pick as a volunteer prior to the activity so they know what to expect and how to respond. Ask the volunteer a random question to begin a conversation. The question can be about the student's plans for the weekend or what the student's favorite book is. The topic doesn't matter. As the student volunteer answers, step closer. As you get into the student's personal space, the student should step back. Let the volunteer finish in responding to your question, thank this person, and then have the student return to her seat.

Discuss Respecting Personal Space

Ask students whether they noticed anything weird about the interaction you just had with the volunteer. After students respond, you can point out what happened when you crowded the volunteer (ex., "When I got too close to our volunteer, she stepped back away from me.")

Use the example to lead into the next social skill to cover, respecting personal space. Refer to the acronym when introducing it:

> *The R in CREATE stands for "respecting personal space." When we are talking with someone, we want to make sure we give that person enough space. We call this space around ourselves "personal space." If we get too close, the other person could feel uncomfortable or threatened. The person might show this by backing away or having a strong response to us. This could make us feel bad and confuse us as to why that person became upset. I like to pretend everyone has a small Hula-Hoop around them, and I give people that amount of space when talking to them. If you see someone backing up when you are talking to them, it's a good indication you have gotten into their personal space.*

Discuss Eye Contact

When you introduce eye contact, the last social skill students are going to discuss in the lesson, let them know that this skill is what the *E* in CREATE stands for. Begin by asking, "Why do you think eye contact is important?"

Allow students a chance to respond. After they respond, offer an explanation that mentions that making eye contact with people lets them know that they have our undivided attention and that we are interested in what they are saying. Be sure to provide some specific detail about how to practice eye contact and note that people in different countries and cultures may think that eye contact can be rude. You can say,

> *We don't have to stare people down, and we can occasionally look away and blink, but we want to make sure our eyes return to the speakers' faces so they know we are listening.*
>
> *You should know, too, that in some cultures it is rude to look someone in the eye when speaking. If you start talking to someone and this person doesn't look you in the eye, don't just assume that this person is being rude. It is also OK to let people know that you don't make eye contact in your culture. This helps them learn about you and your culture.*

Practice Eye Contact

In this exercise, students will conduct a conversation while not making eye contact and again while making eye contact. They can practice with the person next to them or with an assigned partner. Have students turn to their partners and talk about what their plans are for the weekend. Tell them,

"When you are talking to your partner, I want you to avoid eye contact. Make sure you don't look at each other."

Walk around the room while students complete this activity.

After the activity, have a discussion with students around the following questions. Allow time for responses after each question:

> *How did it feel when your partner didn't make eye contact with you? How did it feel not to make eye contact with your partner? Do you remember what your partner was talking about?*

After the discussion, have students get back with their partners, but this time, have them make eye contact during the conversation. Walk around the room and observe while students complete this activity.

After the activity, begin a discussion around the following questions, allowing time for responses after each:

> *How did it feel when your partner did make eye contact with you? How did it feel to make eye contact with your partner? Do you remember what your partner was talking about? What major differences did you notice between not making eye contact and making eye contact? Which do you prefer?*

Review the Lesson and Display the Skill Cutouts

Conclude the lesson by explaining the importance of these social skills. When we respect the personal space of others and make eye contact with them, we are telling them that they are important and what they are saying is important. Eye contact is a learned skill and, for some students, practicing it can feel uncomfortable at first. Encourage students and let them know the more we practice a social skill the better we will become at it.

Hang the respecting personal space and eye contact skill cutouts on the whiteboard or display area for students to refer to and see.

Session 21.3: Assess Your Use of the Social Skills

Let students know that they will evaluate how often they use the social skills that they have learned so far. Have them open their workbooks to the Social Skills Assessment worksheet. The worksheet lists the skills the class has talked about. At the top of the page in the first column on the left, ask the students to put the date. (They will complete this worksheet at a later date so ask them to keep the date section at the top of the second column blank for now.)

Ask students to go through the first three skills listed and circle the number in the left column that best describes how often they use those three skills. Tell them that the class will learn the other three skills in the next lesson so they should leave that area of the worksheet blank for now. The scale is as follows: 1= never, 2= not often, 3= half the time, 4= most of the time, 5=always. After students have assigned each skill a number that reflects how often they use the skill, they should circle one skill that they would most like to improve on this week.

Walk around the room while students work and ask questions about their worksheet and what they see as their strengths and weaknesses.

Session 21.4: Practice the Social Skills with a Partner

In this session, students will practice all the social skills they have learned while conducting a conversation with their partner. Students can team up with either the person sitting next to them or a person that you, the teacher, have assigned. If students have been working with the person next to them, try to pair them with someone new. You can introduce the activity as follows:

> *"We are going to practice using the skills we have talked about so far. I want you to turn to your partner and have a discussion about which superhero is your favorite. In the conversation, remember to use all of the skills we have talked about so far: giving compliments, respecting personal space, and making eye contact."*

Walk around the room while students work and remind them to utilize the learned skills.

Session 21.5: The Commitment Circle

Have students gather into a circle and offer the prompt for the week's commitment circle:

> *Our prompt for our commitment circle this week is, What skill are you going to work on first? Remember the skills we talked about are giving compliments, respecting personal space, and making eye contact. For example, this week I am going to work on making eye contact when I talk to people. I can easily become distracted and look away from them. I want them to know that what they are talking about is important to me.*

Go around the circle and have students make their commitments. Encourage them to make these commitments for both the home and school setting so they can see how these skills translate to the home setting.

Reinforcing the Lesson

Remind students throughout the day of the skills learned. Periodically quiz them on what the first three letters in CREATE stands for. Give praise when they remember even one of the skills.

Sample Letter to Parents and Guardians—Lesson 21

Dear Parent/Guardian,

This week, as part of our focus on relationship skills and social and emotional learning, our class learned three out of six of the social skills covered in the Power Up curriculum. Students can use the acronym CREATE to remember the social skills we covered this week and will cover next week. Students learned about the importance of offering compliments, respecting personal space, and making eye contact. These are represented by the C (compliments), the R (respecting personal space), and the first E (eye contact) in the CREATE acronym.

It is important that students have appropriate social skills to be able to start and hold a conversation with others.

You can ask your child the following questions about the lesson:

- What does the C stand for in CREATE?
- What does the R stand for in CREATE?
- What does the E stand for in CREATE?
- Which of these three skills is your strongest?
- Which of these three skills is your weakest?

Regards,

Social Skills Assessment

Complete the following assessment based on how often you use the skill.

1= never, 2= not often, 3= half the time, 4= most of the time, 5=always

	Date(s):					Date:				
Compliments	1	2	3	4	5	1	2	3	4	5
Respecting Personal Space	1	2	3	4	5	1	2	3	4	5
Eye Contact	1	2	3	4	5	1	2	3	4	5
Asking Questions	1	2	3	4	5	1	2	3	4	5
Taking Turns	1	2	3	4	5	1	2	3	4	5
Exhibiting Genuine Interest	1	2	3	4	5	1	2	3	4	5
Totals:										

Reflection

Consider the following questions: What was the difference in your totals? Did you improve on the skills that you circled? What did you do to ensure that you used the skill? Did your score go down in a specific area? If so, how can you improve in that area?

_____

_____

_____

_____

_____

_____

Building Social Skills Using the CREATE Acronym, Part 2

Asking Questions Icon

Taking Turns Icon

Exhibiting Genuine Interest Icon

Students will learn the last three components of the CREATE social skills acronym: asking questions, taking turns, and exhibiting genuine interest.

Introduction

A lack of conversational skills can negatively impact one's interpersonal relationships, employment, and overall wellness (Bambara et al., 2016). Students with social skills deficits often have difficulties in initiating or maintaining a conversation, talking about a new topic, asking follow-up questions, and taking turns. This lesson will focus on teaching students' social skills to close these gaps.

Taking turns is one of the important social skills addressed in this lesson, and it relates to the social skills of asking questions and exhibiting genuine interest. Being able to take turns will help students throughout their personal and professional lives. Practicing taking turns positively impacts students' play and increases positive interactions with peers (Stanton-Chapman & Snell, 2011). It leads students to be more absorbed in conversations, causing them to ask for clarification or elaboration when talking with others. Asking questions based on what the other person has said shows genuine interest. Together these skills demonstrate that the individual is invested in the discussion, which leads to more productive conversations and overall more positive social interactions.

Objective

Students will be able to identify at least three social skills they can utilize when having a conversation with peers or adults.

Success Criteria

Students are able to

- identify the last three steps in CREATE social skills acronym
- understand the importance of CREATE social skills

- feel comfortable using CREATE social skills

Materials

- One copy per student of the Questions worksheet
- One copy per student of the Social Skills Assessment worksheet (the worksheet started in Lesson 21)
- Two copies of the Matching Game (Session 4's optional activity)

Things to Note

Avoid telling students they are incorrect in lesson discussions and activities. Ask guiding questions to help them gain insight on what they could have done differently. Give students positive feedback for something they did correctly. When introducing social skills, be aware of the students with disabilities in the classroom. It can be difficult for many exceptional education students to engage in appropriate social skills. Encourage all students to pick one skill they feel comfortable using to practice throughout the week. Give extra praise when you see the skill being used.

Session 22.1: Asking Questions and Taking Turns

Check in on students' commitment from last week. Ask who would like to volunteer to share how they did practicing their social skill. Allow students a chance to share how they did on their commitments. If you find that the same students contribute each week, encourage new students to participate. If you have some students who never share, try to check in with them individually.

Review and Discuss the Skill Asking Questions

In this lesson, you will continue discussing social skills and begin by reviewing those covered in the last lesson. Remind students that in the last lesson they discussed the *C*, *R*, and *E* skills represented in the CREATE acronym. Do they remember what the letters stand for? After students respond, you can say, "The *C* stands for compliments, the *R* stands for respecting personal space, and the *E* stands for eye contact."

Tell students that in this lesson, they are going to learn about the *A*, *T*, and the *E* skills. Begin by defining the social skill of asking questions, the skill represented by the letter *A* in the acronym. To explain the skill, you can say,

> *The A stands for asking questions. When getting to know someone or talking to someone we already know very well, we want to show interest in them and their lives. Asking questions can help us get to know others better while building strong connections with them. When we first meet someone new, we can ask them about their interests. For example, we*

could ask about their favorite movies, songs, games, etc. If we have known someone for a while, we might want to ask about events happening in their life or about specific people in their life. For example, we could ask them about the birthday party they went to over the weekend or ask how their new dog is. Asking questions is a good way to start a conversation and to keep a conversation going.

Record Questions We Can Ask To Show Interest in Others

Ask the class to make a list of questions that they could ask someone in a conversation and write their questions on the class whiteboard. Tell them, "Let's make a list of questions we can ask when we first meet someone and a list of questions we can ask when we have known someone for a while."

Write the list of student questions on the board. Once done, have students write down the questions they might like to use in the Questions worksheet in their workbooks. Let them know that they can also add questions that didn't appear on the board. Allow students a chance to write down the questions in their workbook.

Discuss Taking Turns

Introduce the next skill, taking turns, by reminding students of the acronym and by asking them to share their thoughts:

> *The T in CREATE stands for taking turns. When we are talking with others, it is important that we take turns speaking. Why do you think this is important?*

After students respond you should provide an explanation, relating taking turns to showing interest and respect:

> *It's important that we all get a chance to be heard. If we want someone to listen to us when we are talking, we should show this person the same courtesy. By taking turns when talking, we show respect to others and let them know that what they are saying is important to us.*

Conclude the session by hanging the asking questions and taking turns skill cutouts on the bulletin board or display area for students to refer to and see.

Session 22.2: Expressing Genuine Interest

In this session, you will cover expressing genuine interest, the skill represented by the last letter in the CREATE acronym. Explain to students that when we are talking to someone, it is important that we exhibit genuine interest in what that person says. We can show interest by using some of the skills we have already discussed. We can also show interest in other people through our words and actions or behaviors.

Discuss Verbal and Nonverbal Gestures for Showing Interest

Ask the students, "What are some things we can say to exhibit genuine interest in other people?" Let students respond, and after the discussion, you can offer some examples: "We can repeat what they said, ask questions, and share our own related experiences."

Next, have the class consider nonverbal gestures to show interest. Ask, "What are some ways we can exhibit genuine interest without using words?"

After the discussion, you can say, "We can show genuine interest nonverbally by nodding our head, leaning toward the speaker, and making eye contact. These are all examples of active listening skills we can use."

Let students know that the more interest we show in what the speaker is saying, the more excited the other person will be to share. When it's our turn to talk, the speaker will likely return the favor and demonstrate genuine interest about what we have to say. You should stress that it is important not to try to fake genuine interest. We should instead work to be genuinely invested in what the other person is saying. It's easy to tell when someone isn't invested in a conversation and that can be frustrating for everyone and it can affect future interactions.

Practice Demonstrating Interest in Others

Have students get together with a partner to practice their social skills in a conversation. They can choose someone sitting close to them for their partner or the partner can be teacher assigned. You should just make sure that students work with new partners frequently so that they can practice these skills with different peers.

Ask students to take turns answering the question, "If you could visit anywhere in the world, where would it be and why?" As students answer the question and talk with their partners, they should practice the CREATE skills they learned about in the lesson.

Allow students a chance to talk. Walk around the room and observe while students discuss. Hang the exhibiting genuine interest skill cutout on the bulletin board or display area for students to see and refer to.

Session 22.3: Assess Your Use of the Social Skills

Have students use the Social Skills Assessment worksheet to assess how often they use the three social skills they learned in this lesson. Ask students to open their workbooks and to where the worksheet lists the skills they just covered. Have them go through each skill and circle the number in the left column that best describes how often they use this skill. They can add the date in the same area at the top of the worksheet where they wrote the date of their first skills assessment. Tell students to leave the second right-hand column blank for now. The scale is as follows: 1 = never, 2 = not often, 3 = half the time, 4 = most of the time, 5 = always.

Once students have completed their assessment, ask them to circle one to two skills that they would most like to improve upon this week. They should leave the Reflection section at the bottom of the Social Skills Assessment worksheet blank.

Walk around the room while students work on the assessment and ask them questions about what they see as their strengths and weaknesses.

Session 22.4: Matching Game

Note: Instead of making copies of the matching game worksheet for students to create game tiles from, you can project the worksheet on the wall or screen and have students draw the tile icons. This will make for a more time-consuming activity but will not require copies.

In order to let students practice the social skills and to have some fun, in this lesson, they will play a matching game where they will attempt to match icons as they turn game tiles face up. To begin, organize students into groups of three. Distribute copies of the Matching Game worksheet and ask the students to cut out the tiles for the matching game.

After they have cut tiles out, have students place the tiles face down on their table or desk. Tell them that in this game, they are each going to take turns flipping over two tiles at a time while the student flipping the tiles looks to find a match. The player turning tiles can only pick two to flip over on each turn. Students should watch and remember where tiles are so they can find a match when it is their turn. (If no match is found, the tiles should be returned to their face down position.) When students find a matching pair, they keep the set and get another turn.

Tells students that they will have a chance to practice taking turns, giving compliments, making eye contact, disagreeing respectfully if needed, and respecting personal space during this activity. The person with the most matches at the end wins!

Give students some time to play the game and practice the skills. Walk around the room while they work. Remind students of specific social skills they might benefit from using.

Session 22.5: The Commitment Circle

Have students gather into a circle and offer the prompt for this week's commitment circle:

> *Our prompt for our commitment circle this week is, What new skill are you going to commit to practicing first? The skills*

*we tried this week were asking questions, taking turns, and
exhibiting genuine interest. For example, this week I am going
to practice exhibiting genuine interest. I want people to know
I am invested in learning more about them.*

Go around the circle and have students make their commitments. Encourage
them to make these commitments for both the home and school setting so
they can see how these skills translate to the home setting.

Reinforcing the Lesson

Remind students to utilize the skills represented by the CREATE acronym.
Periodically quiz them on what CREATE stands for. At the end of the lesson
week, have students go back to their self-assessment and ask them to fill out
the last column to see how they have improved. You can say,

*We are going to revisit the self-assessment now that you have
had a chance to practice the skills. Write the date at the top
of the right hand column and circle the number in the right
column that best describes how often you use this skill. (The
scale is as follows: 1 = never, 2 = not often, 3 = half the time,
4 = most of the time, 5 = always.) When you are done circling
the numbers, add the total for each column and write a brief
summary about your progress on these skills.*

Reassure students on their progress: "It is important to remember that you
will not automatically get better at everything. If you show some improvement in one or two areas, that is great! Focus on one area at a time."

Sample Letter to Parents and Guardians—Lesson 22

Dear Parent/Guardian,

This week, as part of our continued focus on relationship skills and social and emotional learning, our class learned three social skills represented by the last three letters of our CREATE acronym. The skills are asking questions, taking turns, and exhibiting genuine interest. It is important that students have appropriate social skills to be able to start and maintain conversation with others.

You can ask your child the following questions about the lesson:

- What does the A stand for in CREATE?
- What does the T stand for in CREATE?
- What does the E stand for in CREATE?
- Which of these three skills is your strongest?
- Which of these three skills is your weakest?

Regards,

Social Skills Assessment

Complete the following assessment based on how often you use the skill.

1= never, 2= not often, 3= half the time, 4= most of the time, 5=always

	Date(s):					Date:				
Compliments	1	2	3	4	5	1	2	3	4	5
Respecting Personal Space	1	2	3	4	5	1	2	3	4	5
Eye Contact	1	2	3	4	5	1	2	3	4	5
Asking Questions	1	2	3	4	5	1	2	3	4	5
Taking Turns	1	2	3	4	5	1	2	3	4	5
Exhibiting Genuine Interest	1	2	3	4	5	1	2	3	4	5
Totals:										

Reflection

Consider the following questions:

What was the difference in your totals?

_____

_____

Did you improve on the skills that you circled?

_____

_____

What did you do to ensure that you used the skill?

_____

_____

Did your score go down in a specific area?

_____

_____

If so, how can you improve in that area?

_____

_____

Questions

The Matching Game

The Interview

Students will identify social skill strengths and weaknesses through observing a famous person and role model, and they will relate what they've observed to their own strengths and weaknesses.

Introduction

Role models, as Ahn et al. (2020) have defined them, are people who have had a strong and generally positive influence in someone's life. Role models are often used in education as a source of inspiration and even a way to help students identify possible career paths. Role modeling is so powerful that it was cited as a key theme in instilling clinical empathy in medical interns (Yazdi et al., 2019). It is important that we act in such a way that we can become positive role models for the students looking up to us for how to react and behave in certain situations. While we won't always be able to be a role model for all students, it is important to instill model positive behaviors and social and emotional skills.

Objectives

Students will be able to

- identify at least two social skill strengths in the identified role models interview
- identify at least one social skill weakness in the identified role models interview

Success Criteria

Students are able to

- identify social skill strengths and weaknesses in themselves and others
- understand the importance of social skills
- feel comfortable identifying what social skill they would like to work on

Materials

One copy per student of the Interview worksheet

Things to Note

Students often pick role models for this lesson's activity that they idolize. Be careful when critiquing the social skills displayed in the clips they choose. Make sure you speak about the social skill and not about the person, even if the person is someone you feel the student should not idolize. Do not make negative comments about the role model in the interview. For this exercise, you can have some students show their video clip to the group. If you do choose to have students share their clip, it is recommended you watch it first to ensure that it is appropriate.

This activity assumes that each student has access to a computer. If this is not the case, you should look up clips as a class and complete the activity together.

Session 23.1: Study an Interview of a Well-Known Person

Check in on students' commitment from last week. Ask who would like to volunteer to share how they did practicing their social skills. Allow students a chance to share how they did on their commitments. If you find that the same students contribute each week, encourage new students to participate. If you have some students who never share, try to check in with them individually.

Discuss Learning Social Skills from Observing Others

In this lesson, students will find a video clip of an interview with a person they look up to and discuss the social skills demonstrated in the interview. To begin, you can start with a discussion:

> Aristotle once said that "man is by nature a social animal whose inclination is to live in the company of others." Since we are social creatures who interact with many others, why do you think social skills are important? [Pause for discussion.]
>
> Aristotle meant that we enjoy social interactions. We like to be around other people and generally gravitate to them. Social skills are important because they help us connect to those around us and create meaningful experiences.

Find a Video Interview and Evaluate It Using the Interview Worksheet

To introduce the exercise, have students think about the social skills and relationship skills the class has talked about so far and tell them that for this lesson, you want them to think about a famous celebrity or role model that they look up to. This person could be a singer, actor, politician, author, or anyone they choose. The students should find one minute of an interview with this person and use the Interview worksheet in their workbooks to write down what social skills they notice the person using. (The video clip can be one minute from a longer interview. Students should just indicate the section they are studying for this activity by the time stamp.)

Remind students of the social skills the class has discussed: offering compliments, respecting personal space, making eye contact, asking questions, taking turns, and exhibiting genuine interest. Students can look for these skills and note them on the worksheet. They can also include other social skills that the class hasn't talked about.

Students should use the worksheet to rate how well the interview subject demonstrated each skill. In the blank areas below the listed social skills, students can add some other skills if they would like to. At the bottom of the worksheet, they will write down which skills the interviewed person demonstrated well and which skills they could improve on. Last, ask students to identify a skill that the interviewed person was good at and that they themselves will practice, using the interview subject as a model. Explain to students, "When we see others modeling a skill, it is easier to imitate."

Allow students a chance to search the internet for a video clip they would like to use. Remind students they are only looking to share one minute of the interview. Walk around the room while they work and provide assistance as needed. If each individual student does not have access to a computer, the teacher can put the students into groups (based on the number of computers available) to work on the activity together. If students do not have access to YouTube, have the entire class agree upon whom they would like to watch an interview of, and the teacher can play the video, allowing each student to independently complete the worksheet. The worksheet will be reviewed in the next sessions.

Note to teacher: You might want to consider having students send you the link they want to show the class, along with the specific one-minute time stamped section of video they want to show, so that you can preview the videos prior to the next session to ensure they are appropriate. You can instruct students to pause the video where they would like for the clip they want to show to start and hover over the progress bar across the bottom of the video, while it is paused. This should give them a time stamp for where the video is paused. They should then play the video and pause the video after one minute. Students can write down on their worksheet the time stamp that marks where they want the video to start.

Sessions 23.2–23.4

Have students share their findings with the class. Ask them to identify one minute of the video interview they picked and share it with the class. When sharing the video, students should tell the class how they scored the person on the Interview worksheet.

Have students present their video clips. Have them focus on describing the social skills demonstrated in the interview. They do not need to share what social skill they are going to work on based on the interview. This will be shared during the commitment circle in Session 5. If your students do not have 1-to-1 technology in the classroom, you can repeat Session 1's activity as a class, each day with a new clip.

Session 23.5: The Commitment Circle

Have students gather in a circle and offer the prompt for this week's commitment circle:

> *Our prompt for our commitment circle this week is, Based on the interview you found, what social skill are you going to work on? For example, I realized that I don't always ask my friends questions about things they are interested in. I'm going to do better about asking more questions.*

Go around the circle and have students make their commitments. Encourage them to make these commitments for both the home and school setting so they can see how these skills translate to the home setting.

Reinforcing the Lesson

Throughout the week, encourage students to observe social interactions on the school campus and identify the strengths and weaknesses of those interactions using the CREATE acronym. Encourage them to discuss their findings with you, if they feel comfortable and if time permits. You can also remind students that they should discuss their findings in private with you, rather than making their observations out loud where others can hear to ensure no feelings are hurt. Give students praise when you see them using social skills. Encourage students to also give each other praise when they see a social skill being used.

Sample Letter to Parents and Guardians—Lesson 23

Dear Parent/Guardian,

This week, as part of our focus on relationship skills and social and emotional learning, students looked up an interview of one of their role models. They watched the interview and made note of the specific social skills they saw their role model using. They then presented their findings to the class.

You can ask your child the following questions about the lesson:

- What person's video interview did you look up?
- What social skills did that person use well?
- What social skill could that person improve on?
- What skill did they use that you admired?

Regards,

The Interview

Interviewee's Name:

Time Stamp for 1-minute mark:

How often does your celebrity use the identified skill in their interview?

1 = Never, 2 = Sometimes, 3 = Half the time, 4 = Most of the time, 5= Almost always

Compliments	1	2	3	4	5
Respecting Personal Space	1	2	3	4	5
Eye Contact	1	2	3	4	5
Asking Questions	1	2	3	4	5
Taking Turns	1	2	3	4	5
Exhibiting Genuine Interest	1	2	3	4	5
	1	2	3	4	5
	1	2	3	4	5
	1	2	3	4	5

What skill(s) did they do well?

_____

_____

_____

What skills did they need to work on?

_____

_____

_____

Based on the interview, what skill would you like to improve on?

_____

_____

Responsible Decision-Making

Lesson 24

The Brain

Brain Icon

Students will learn the role the brain plays in critical thinking and problem-solving.

Introduction

While there are many parts of the brain that are integral to our survival, this lesson focuses specifically on the amygdala and the prefrontal cortex. These two areas of the brain have the ability to help us or hurt us when we are in the process of making responsible decisions.

The amygdala is part of our reptilian brain and is located within the temporal lobe. The amygdala is involved with associating experiences with emotions (Gupta et al., 2011). For example, if we walk by a house and a dog lunges at us, we will associate the experience of walking by that house with the fear of being bitten by a dog. The amygdala plays an important role in helping us identify and remember threats (Davidson, 2002).

The prefrontal cortex is not part of our reptilian brain. It wraps over our reptilian brain and is located behind our forehead. The prefrontal cortex has several functions that include controlling and organizing behavior, problem-solving, memory retrieval, and the reallocation of attention (Ramnani & Owen, 2004). Communication between our amygdala (which assesses threats) and our prefrontal cortex (which thinks through problems) is essential. If they are not communicating, then our emotions can take over and cause us to behave as if our survival were threatened.

Objectives

Students will be able to

- identify the role of the prefrontal cortex in decision-making
- identify the role of the amygdala in decision-making

Success Criteria

Students are able to

- identify the role of the prefrontal cortex and the amygdala in making decisions

- understand the importance of engaging the prefrontal cortex in decision-making
- feel comfortable utilizing self-management techniques to re-engage the prefrontal cortex

Materials

- One copy per student of the Brain worksheet
- Preferred coloring utensils

Things to Note

Avoid telling students they are incorrect in their answers in class. Instead, ask guiding questions or redirect them back to their task. Give them the option of asking a friend for help if they appear stuck.

Session 24.1: Understanding How Our Brain Functions

Check in on students' commitment from last week. Ask who would like to volunteer to share how they did practicing their social skill. Allow students a chance to share how they did on their commitments. If you find that the same students participate each week, encourage new students to contribute. If you have some students who never share, try to check in with them individually.

How Our Brain Processes Messages From the Body

In this lesson, you will help students understand how our brain takes in and processes messages from the body. You can use the following script:

> In this lesson, we are going to learn about our brain. We are going to learn how our brain receives and stores information. As we move through our day, our body takes in sensory data and sends messages to our brain. Sensory data is information that we get from our five senses. For example, when we touch sandpaper, our body experiences the sandpaper through our senses, and our brain stores information about that experience. We might determine that the sandpaper feels rough and appears to get lighter in color when it is used to sand something down. When we eat food, we take in information on whether the food is savory or sweet, if it is soft or chewy, if it is flavorful or bland, and we store information on whether we like that food or not.
>
> As our brain receives messages about our environment, neural pathways develop in our brain. Neural pathways look like

highways running all through our brain, and their function is to store information. When we don't have any information about an experience, our brains create new neural pathways to store that information. Our brain has what's called plasticity. This means that the brain re-wires itself and changes and isn't set in a certain way.

Study the Brain Worksheet

Have students retrieve the worksheet where they will find a drawing of the brain. Ask students to draw in some neural pathways, or highways. The picture of the brain already shows some lines but ask students to add in some more. They can use different colors to denote the different information that is held by each pathway.

Allow students a chance to work. Circulate while they work to comment on their pictures or to answer questions.

Session 24.2: The Prefrontal Cortex

Begin the class by asking if students have heard of the region of the brain called the prefrontal cortex: "Now that we have learned about how information is stored in our brain, we are going to learn about an area of the brain called the prefrontal cortex. Does anyone know what the prefrontal cortex does?" After students respond, you can explain its function by saying,

The prefrontal cortex is located in the front of our brain. [Point to your forehead.] Our prefrontal cortex evolved over time and grew over what was considered our "reptilian" brain. Our reptilian brain is located at the top of our spine. [Point to the back of your neck.] We will talk about this part of the brain in our next session.

The prefrontal cortex of our brain helps us with problem-solving. It analyzes our options in responding to the situations we might find ourselves in, and it allows us the chance to think through our actions. Not all species have the ability to utilize critical thinking and problem-solving skills like we do. The prefrontal cortex makes us different from other animals because we have the ability to think through our actions.

Color in the Prefrontal Cortex in the Worksheet

Ask students to turn to the Brain worksheet in their workbooks and have them color in the front part of the brain in the drawing, or the location of the prefrontal cortex. (You can demonstrate by coloring the region in your own worksheet.) Tell students, "You can use any color you want."

Session 24.3: The Amygdala

In the previous sessions, you will have talked about how our brain takes in sensory information and stores it, and the class will have learned about the prefrontal cortex, which enables higher-order thinking skills and allows us to think through situations. In this session, you will talk about the amygdala [uh-mig-duh-la]. You can use the following script to introduce the function of this part of the brain:

> *The part of the brain called the amygdala is located in an area known as the temporal lobe. The temporal lobe is located behind your ears [point to behind your ears]. The amygdala helps keep us safe. As we are going about our day, it is constantly checking for danger. If we come across something it perceives to be dangerous, our fear response takes over in order to propel us to take action to keep ourselves safe. These actions might include running away, fighting back, or standing still in order to avoid attention. As a result, the prefrontal cortex becomes less active, making it harder to use our critical thinking or problem-solving skills. This happens so that we can react quickly, because in a life-or-death situation, every second counts.*
>
> *For example, if you are walking on the sidewalk and you see something brown and long on the ground in front of you, your instinct would be to jump back in case it is a snake. Your amygdala helps you react quickly. Taking the time to think about the situation with your prefrontal cortex wouldn't help because in that time, if the object was a snake (and not a stick), it would bite you. Many times, the amygdala taking over can serve you well and keep you safe. But the amygdala doesn't always help us tell the difference between a life-and-death situation and a nonthreatening situation. Whether we are about to step on a snake or a stick our body has the same response.*
>
> *Our body is constantly taking in information. If it registers that we are angry or upset, it can cut off our connection to the prefrontal cortex and our ability to think through situations. This is why sometimes we feel like we have no control over our actions. Our amygdala takes over because it feels that we are in a life-and-death situation when we likely aren't.*

Discuss Self-Management Techniques

At this point, remind students about the self-management techniques they have learned. These can help return them to home mode. You can say,

It's important to be able to re-engage our prefrontal cortex before acting, especially when we find we are in fast-forward mode and that our amygdala might have taken over. This skill helps us make responsible decisions.

Think back to all the self-management techniques we learned. All of these are great ways to re-engage our prefrontal cortex and stop us from acting right away. By using a self-management skill, we give ourselves time to evaluate the situation, let our amygdala know we are safe, re-engage our prefrontal cortex, and determine the best course of action.

As I see you using your self-management strategies to help you manage your feelings and use your prefrontal cortex, I will give you a power bar.

Return to the Brain Worksheet and Display the Skill Cutout

Have students get out their workbooks and turn to the Brain worksheet. Ask them to color in part of the drawing where the amygdala would be. You can demonstrate where it is on your own worksheet. Let students use any color they want.

Hang the brain skill cutout on the board for students to refer to and see.

Session 24.4: How Our Brain Influences Our Actions

Have students partner up for an exercise that asks them to identify a time when they made a decision when their amygdala was in control. Remember to try to have all of the students work with different partners as frequently as possible. To begin the exercise, you can say,

I want you to tell your partner about a time when you used your amygdala to make a decision instead of your prefrontal cortex. What happened? How do you know that your prefrontal cortex wasn't in control? How did the situation turn out? How might the situation have turned out differently if you had used your prefrontal cortex to make a decision?

For example, I was stuck in traffic last week, and I started to get really angry. I know that I wasn't using my prefrontal cortex because I started honking my horn at other cars. Honking my horn didn't solve the problem since none of the cars had anywhere to go. We were all stuck in traffic. I ended up frustrated the whole time and angry that I was stuck in traffic. I'm sure I also frustrated other people. Had I taken some deep breaths, I wouldn't have honked my horn. I also would have been calmer and had a better start to my day without frustrating others.

Have students work with their partners on the exercise.

Session 24.5: The Commitment Circle

Have students gather in a circle and offer the prompt for this week's commitment circle:

> *Our prompt for our commitment circle this week is, How are you going to make sure you use your prefrontal cortex to make decisions? For example, I am going to do some deep breathing when I find myself in a situation that I know I need to think through.*

Go around the circle and have students make their commitments. Encourage them to make these commitments for both the home and school setting so they can see how these skills translate to the home setting.

Reinforcing the Lesson

Throughout the week, ask students if they were using their prefrontal cortex or their amygdala when they made a decision. If they say their amygdala, ask them how they could have re-engaged their prefrontal cortex. Also ask them if they had used their prefrontal cortex, how the situation might have turned out differently.

Sample Letter to Parents and Guardians—Lesson 24

Dear Parent/Guardian,

This week, as part of our class focus on responsible decision-making skills and social and emotional learning, we learned how two regions in the brain called the prefrontal cortex and the amygdala play a role in our decision-making. Students were able to identify how they can re-engage their prefrontal cortex when their amygdala is activated so that they can make responsible decisions.

You can ask your child the following questions about the lesson:

- What role does the prefrontal cortex play in making decisions?
- What role does the amygdala play in making decisions?
- How can you re-engage your prefrontal cortex when your amygdala is activated?

Regards,

The Brain

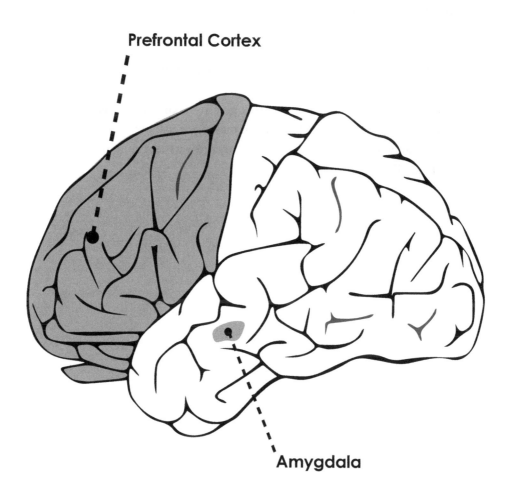

Prefrontal Cortex

Amygdala

MAGIC, Part 1

MAGIC Icon

Students will learn the first **two** steps in the responsible decision-making process known by the MAGIC acronym (*M*—manage emotions, *A*—assess the situation for possible solutions, *G*—gather pros and cons, *I*—identify bias, and *C*—choose the best decision). Students will learn to think through their options while considering their decisions impact not only themselves but on others as well.

Introduction

Responsible decision-making is a 21st century skill that is often valued in employees by hiring companies. In the Power Up curriculum, students have learned many skills that can be useful in making responsible decisions. They can use skills such as goal setting, time management, and communication to identify possible solutions and find the one that will be the most ethical for themselves and others. After a student is able to identify what they are feeling and manage that feeling, they can begin to think through making a responsible decision.

Objectives

Students will be able to

- identify at least two self-management strategies they can use to manage their emotions before making a decision
- identify at least two options available to them when making a decision

Success Criteria

Students are able to

- identify the first two steps in the MAGIC problem-solving process
- understand why it is important for them to think through their options
- feel comfortable coming up with multiple solutions to a problem

Materials

One copy per student of the MAGIC worksheet

Things to Note

In these exercises, encourage students to think through all of their options, even those that are unrealistic or that they know they wouldn't choose. This practice shows them that they always have a choice and a wide range of options available to them.

Session 25.1: Learning the Five Steps of Responsible Decision-Making

Check in on students' commitments from the previous lesson. Ask who would like to volunteer to share how they did calming themselves before making decisions. Allow students a chance to share how they did on their commitments. If you find that the same students contribute each week, encourage new students to participate. If you have some students who never share, try to check in with them individually.

Introduce the MAGIC Acronym

To begin the lesson on responsible decision-making, remind students about the last lesson about the brain and its role in critical thinking and problem-solving. We need to be able to use our critical thinking and problem-solving skills to make responsible decisions. Let students know that in this lesson, the class is going to learn five steps for making responsible decisions. Tell students that in order to get power bars colored in for this skill, they will need to demonstrate all five steps of the responsible decision-making process. Students will learn this process over the next two lessons, and at the end of the second lesson on the MAGIC process, they will be able to earn power bars. You can encourage them and let them know that this doesn't mean they can't start practicing what they learn in this lesson right away.

Discuss the First Step, Managing Emotions

Begin with a discussion of the first step in responsible decision-making, managing our emotions. You can say,

> *We are going to learn five steps that can help us make responsible decisions. The word magic can help us remember these five steps because each letter in the word represents a step in the process. The M stands for the first step: managing emotions. What do you think "managing emotions" means?*

Allow students a chance to respond. Praise answers that are appropriate and redirect students who share incorrect responses. Once students have shared their thoughts offer an explanation. You can say,

> *We talked a lot about managing our emotions in earlier lessons. Managing emotions is when we are able send messages*

*to our amygdala that everything is OK. The amygdala is the
part of our brain that helps us guard against danger. These
messages decrease the intensity of our feelings. They also allow
us to stay connected to our problem-solving prefrontal cortex
so that we can think through our problem with a clear head.*

Remind students that we can use any of the self-management techniques
the class practiced to help calm ourselves. Ask the class,

*What are some activities that have helped you manage your
emotions? Remember, the self-management skills we have
learned are pause, think, play; deep breathing; coloring mandalas; tracing finger mazes; progressive muscle relaxation;
reframing; placing worries into a worry box; wall push-ups
and stretching.*

Allow students a chance to share how they manage their emotions.

Session 25.2: the Assessing Options Step

This lesson focuses on the *A* in the MAGIC acronym, assessing the situation for
possible solutions. In introducing this step in responsible decision-making, let
students know that after we have managed our emotions, we are better able to
assess the options we have available to us. Some options are more realistic than
others, and some are more appealing. Stress that while we will ultimately pick
only one option, it is important to think through all options available. Knowing
our options can help us make the responsible and safe decision.

Discuss a Scenario and Practice Identifying Options

Have students discuss as a class a scenario in which they have to pick options
on how to respond. For example, you could say,

*Let's pretend that you came into the classroom and noticed
that your friends are all huddled together and whispering.
When they notice you, they quickly look away and keep whispering. You start to worry that they were talking about you.
What should you do? What are your options?*

Have students raise their hands and give options or describe what they might
do in response. Encourage them to list any option that comes to mind, even if
it isn't very realistic or feasible. Write their responses on the board.

Conclude the discussion by noting all the options the students identified
and encouraging them to be aware of their options before reacting:

*It's important to know that we have options when responding
to a situation. I want you to start thinking about all of the
options you have available to you when faced with conflict.*

Session 25.3: Listing Solutions to a Problem

In this session, students will use the MAGIC worksheet to create a list of possible solutions to a problem they have. Have students turn to the worksheet in their workbooks and ask them to think of a problem they are working through currently. Ask them to write a quick summary of the problem at the top of the worksheet. They should then list all possible solutions to the problem in the next section. Remind them to think of all of the solutions they can, even if they think they are silly and not realistic. The students should leave the rest of the worksheet blank for now.

Walk around the room and check in with students while they work. Suggest solutions they have not written down or might not have thought about.

After students are done with the worksheet sections, ask if any of them would like to share the problem they were brainstorming solutions for and the possible solutions they came up with. When students are sharing their work, don't indicate if you think a specific solution is appropriate or not. The idea is that they come up with solutions—whether they are good, bad, silly, right, or wrong. Thank students for their answers.

Session 25.4: Practicing Identifying Options

Work as a class to discuss another scenario. Ask for a volunteer to come up with a common problem that might be encountered at school that the class can discuss. Call on a student for a scenario. Be sure to call on a student you think might bring up a good topic with a lot of discussion points. Have students call out all possible solutions.

Session 25.5: The Commitment Circle

Have students gather in a circle and offer the prompt for this week's commitment circle:

> *Our prompt for our commitment circle this week is, How are you going to use the M in MAGIC to manage your emotions? For example, I'm going to take deep breaths when I encounter a problem so that I can use my prefrontal cortex to think through all of my possible options.*

Go around the circle and have students make their commitments. Encourage them to make these commitments for both the home and school setting so they can see how these skills translate to the home setting.

Reinforcing the Lesson

Remind students throughout the day of the options they have available to them. Encourage them to talk through these options and praise students when you see them make responsible decisions.

Sample Letter to Parents and Guardians—Lesson 25

Dear Parent/Guardian,

This week, as part of our focus on responsible decision-making and social and emotional learning, our class learned the first two steps in making responsible decisions. These steps are identified by the letters in the acronym MAGIC. The letter M stands for manage emotions, and the letter A stands for assess the situation for possible solutions. It is important for us to know our options so we can make the responsible decision. Next week we will learn the final three steps in the responsible decision-making process.

You can ask your child the following questions about the lesson:

- What does the M in MAGIC stand for?
- What does the A in MAGIC stand for?
- How will you manage your emotions when faced with conflict?

Regards,

MAGIC

Summary of the Problem:

_____

_____

_____

All Possible Solutions:

_____

_____

_____

Possible Solution #1	Possible Solution #2
Pros: Short-term: Long-term:	**Pros:** Short-term: Long-term:
Cons: Short-term: Long-term:	**Cons:** Short-term: Long-term:

Solution #1 Bias:

_____

_____

Solution #2 Bias:

_____

_____

Lesson 26

MAGIC, Part 2

MAGIC Icon

Students will learn the last three steps in the responsible decision-making process identified by the acronym MAGIC (*M*—manage emotions, *A*—assess the situation for possible solutions, *G*—gather pros and cons, *I*—identify bias, and *C*—choose the best decision). Students will weigh the pros and cons of their options, consider how their personal bias might affect their decision-making, and choose the best decision for themselves and others.

Objectives

Students will be able to

- identify at least two pros and two cons for each option available to them when making a decision
- identify previous experiences that might cause them to show bias in the decision-making process
- choose the decision that is best for them and for others

Success Criteria

Students are able to

- identify the last three steps in the MAGIC problem-solving process
- understand why it is important to weigh the pros and cons before making a decision
- feel comfortable using the MAGIC acronym to make responsible decisions

Materials

- Refer to the MAGIC worksheet from Lesson 24
- One copy per student of the Decision Impact worksheet

Things to Note

Encourage students to think through the pros and cons of each solution they are considering. This might be difficult for students. It's OK to point them in the right direction but try not to give them all of the answers. Instead, try to ask guiding questions.

Session 26.1: Gathering Pros and Cons

Check in on student commitments from last week. Ask who would like to volunteer to share how they did in managing their emotions, the M step in MAGIC. Allow students a chance to share how they did on their commitments. If you find that the same students are contributing each week, encourage new students to participate. If you have some students who never share, try to check in with them individually.

Introduce the Third Step in the Responsible Decision-Making Process

Begin the session by reviewing the last lesson and asking the class about the first two letters in the responsible decision-making acronym. Who remembers what they stand for? After the discussion, congratulate the students and reiterate that the *M* stands for managing emotions and the *A* stands for assessing for possible solutions.

Let students know that in this session, they are going to talk about the *G* in the acronym. Explain what the step is and ask to see if students understand what "pros" and "cons" might mean. You could lead the discussion as follows: "The *G* stands for gathering pros and cons. Who knows what pros and cons are?"

After students respond, you could explain that:

> *Cons are the drawbacks of a possible solution or decision. Drawbacks are things we don't like about what might happen if we made that choice. For example, if I want to watch TV instead of studying, a drawback would be that if I did that, I likely wouldn't get as good of a grade on the test. That is something that I wouldn't like. Pros are good aspects of the decision. For example, a pro of watching TV is that I will get some time to relax.*

List Pros and Cons in the MAGIC Worksheet

Have students turn to the MAGIC worksheet in their workbooks. In the last lesson, the students described a problem that they wanted to work through. They managed their emotions and came up with possible solutions. In this exercise, have the students circle their top two choices for solutions. After they have done that, they should write down their two possible solutions and create a pros and cons list for each possible solution in the columns at the bottom of the worksheet.

Students should consider both the short-term and long-term outcome of their solutions. To illustrate what you are asking for you could say,

> *For example, the disadvantages, or cons, of watching TV instead of studying would be I'd get a bad test grade. This would be a short-term impact. A long-term impact would be that I'd hurt my overall grade. Once I get a bad grade on a test, it's harder to boost my overall grade. The short-term advantage or pro of watching TV is that I would get to have some fun. The long-term pro of watching TV is that I might feel more relaxed.*

Give students time to complete the worksheet. Walk around the room while students work.

Session 26.2: Identifying Bias and Choosing the Best Decision

In this session, students are going to identify bias in their thinking and choose a decision option. Identifying our biases is the step after we have managed our emotions, assessed for solutions, and gathered the pros and cons of possible solutions. This step is represented by the *I* in MAGIC.

Have students return to the MAGIC worksheet in their workbooks. Ask them to write, under each pros and cons list, what bias they might have about possible actions or solutions to the problem. Take some time to define what bias means and make sure students understand this step. You can use the following language:

> *Bias means a judgment or feeling against something. It is a judgment that we make based on earlier experiences. For example, if your best friend and someone you didn't get along with entered into a costume contest and you were a judge, you might have a bias when voting because you want your friend to win.*

Allow students a chance to work on the worksheet and write down their biases.

Introduce the Fifth Step, Complete the Decision Impact Worksheet, and Display the Skill Icon

Choose is the last step in the responsible decision-making process and is represented by the *C* in MAGIC. Let students know that when we make a decision, we want to make sure that we are considering how it will impact everyone involved, not just ourselves.

Have students complete the Decision Impact worksheet. You can let students know that it serves as a guide to help them determine how their decisions will impact them and others. After the students have completed the worksheet, have them circle which possible solution would be the best for them and for everyone involved.

Walk around the room while students work and help them make their decisions. Hang the responsible decision-making skill cutout on the board for students to see and refer to.

Session 26.3: Using the Decision-Making Process

Now that students have had a chance to work through the steps of the MAGIC decision-making process in their worksheet scenario, in this session, you will have them discuss another scenario as a class. For this exercise, you can either give the class a scenario that frequently comes up in your class or you can ask students to come up with a scenario to discuss.

Ask Students to Identify Each Step in Responsible Decision-Making

After you identified the problem or challenge to discuss, ask students: "Now that we have our scenario, what is the first step?" Students should respond that the first step is to manage our emotions (the *M* in MAGIC). Follow up by asking,

> What are some ways we can manage our emotions in this scenario? Remember, the self-management skills we have learned are pause, think, play; deep breathing; coloring mandalas; tracing finger mazes; progressive muscle relaxation; reframing; placing worries into a worry box; wall push-ups and stretching.

After students respond, ask them what is the next step in our responsible decision-making process. Students should say that the next step is to assess the situation for possible solutions. Extend the discussion by asking, "What options do we have available to us in this situation?" Write all student responses on the board and encourage students to come up with as many options as possible. You might also suggest some options they might not have thought about.

After this discussion, ask the class, "What is the third step in the responsible decision-making process?" Students should respond that the next step is to gather the pros and cons. Once students have identified the step, encourage them to evaluate the options that the class has come up with. You can say, "Let's pick two of the possible options that are most probable. Which two do you think they are?"

Have students pick two options out of the scenarios listed and begin to identify the pros and cons of each option. Write their responses on the board after each of the questions about the first option. (What are the pros of our first option? What are the cons?) Ask them the same questions about the second option and write their responses on the board. (What are the pros of our second option? What are the cons?)

Once you have recorded their responses to the pros and cons of each option, ask students, "What is the fourth step in our responsible decision-making process?" Students should respond that the next step is identifying bias (the *I* in MAGIC). Ask students what bias they might have, based on previous experiences, about the first option? Write their responses on the board and ask them the same question about the second option. Again, record the students' responses on the board.

After recording students' thoughts about biases they might have, ask what the last step in the responsible decision-making process is. Students should respond that the last step in the MAGIC responsible decision-making process is to choose. At this point, return to the scenario and ask questions to help them choose a decision or course of action. You could ask, "How will each of these options impact us? How will each impact other people involved? Based on all of this information, what option should we choose? It is important that students remember to review what they learned through the previous steps and focus on considering the decision's impact on them and on others. The class might be divided on a response. If they are, it is OK. Ask them to justify their decision.

In concluding the discussion, congratulate students on their work and bring the focus to the benefits of a decision-making process: "Great job class! We really thought out our options so we could make a responsible decision. We might not always agree, and we might not always make the same decision and that's OK. The important thing is that the decision was well thought out and everyone was considered."

Session 26.4: Practicing with a Partner

Have students work through a scenario and practice decision-making with a partner. (You can assign partners in any manner that works best for your class). Let students make up a scenario or use one that one of the students is experiencing. In this exercise, ask the students to work through the five steps of the responsible decision-making process with their partners and discuss how the decision would impact those involved. Walk around the room while students work and assist as needed.

Session 26.5: The Commitment Circle

Have students gather into a circle and offer the prompt for this week's commitment circle:

> *Our prompt for our commitment circle this week is,*
> *When are you going to use the five steps of the responsible*

decision-making process? For example, this week I am going to use the five steps when trying to decide whether I should go grocery shopping or stay home and catch up on my shows.

Go around the circle and have students make their commitments. Encourage them to make these commitments for both the home and school setting so they can see how these skills translate to the home setting.

Reinforcing the Lesson

Remind students to utilize MAGIC when they need to make a responsible decision. If students experience conflict, have them walk through the steps in order to make a decision. If they have already made a poor decision, have them review the steps to determine what they could have done differently and what the possible outcome could have been instead. Remember to separate the students from their actions. They may have made an irresponsible decision but make sure they know that it does not reflect on who they are as a person or how you think about them.

Sample Letter to Parents and Guardians—Lesson 26

Dear Parent/Guardian,

This week, as part of our class focus on responsible decision-making and social and emotional learning, we continued to learn about the importance of thinking through our decisions in order to make the best decision possible. Students focused on learning the last three steps of the responsible decision-making process. These steps are represented by the last three letters in the acronym MAGIC, and they are gather pros and cons (G), identify bias (I), and choose an option (C).

You can ask your child the following questions about the lesson:

- What does the G in MAGIC stand for?
- What does the I in MAGIC stand for?
- What does the C in MAGIC stand for?
- Why is it important to use all of these steps to make responsible decisions?
- When are you going to use this acronym?

Regards,

MAGIC

Summary of the Problem:

_____

_____

_____

All Possible Solutions:

_____

_____

_____

Possible Solution #1	Possible Solution #2
Pros: Short-term: Long-term:	**Pros:** Short-term: Long-term:
Cons: Short-term: Long-term:	**Cons:** Short-term: Long-term:

Solution #1 Bias:

_____

_____

Solution #2 Bias:

_____

_____

Decision Impact

The Event: _____

Decision 1:

Decision 2:

How this impacts you:

How this impacts you:

How this impacts your family:

How this impacts your family:

How this impacts your teacher:

How this impacts your teacher:

How this impacts your school:

How this impacts your school:

How others are impacted:

How others are impacted:

Understanding Rules

Students will be able to identify the importance of rules and how following rules keeps everyone safe.

Introduction

School rules are necessary in order to create positive classroom environments and to establish fairness. When rules are established and made clear, then adults and students alike know what is expected of them and everyone else. Thornberg (2008) postulates that rules help give individuals a blueprint for their behaviors and the consequences of those behaviors. He identified four different types of rules: relational rules (rules for treating each other with kindness, ex., no bullying); structuring rules (rules to keep the classroom running efficiently, ex., raising one's hand to talk); protecting rules (rules to keep you safe, ex., no running in hallways); and etiquette rules (rules in regards to manners, ex., no chewing gum, no wearing hats). He found that students valued relational rules the most, and etiquette rules the least (Thornberg, 2008).

Objective

Students will be able to identify three rules and the purpose of those rules.

Success Criteria

Students are able to

- identify the importance of rules
- understand the consequences of not following rules
- feel comfortable discussing the importance of rules with their teacher and others

Materials

One copy per student of the My Country's Rules worksheet

Things to Note

During the activity, let students create whatever rules they want (as long as they aren't inappropriate). Remind students that they will need to justify their rule and explain its importance. Encourage students to utilize their training in respectfully disagreeing when debating rules.

Session 27.1: How Rules Keep Us Safe

Check in on student commitments from last week. Ask who would like to volunteer to share how they did using the five steps of MAGIC to make responsible decisions. Allow students a chance to share how they did on their commitments. If you find that the same students are contributing each week, encourage new students to participate. If you have some students who never share, try to check in with them individually.

Discuss How Rules Help Us Stay Safe

Introduce the topic of how rules keep us safe and ask students to share some examples. ("What are some rules that are in place to keep us safe?") Write down all student responses on the board so that you can have a deeper discussion about each rule when the students have finished listing examples. Have the class consider each rule listed on the board and offer some feedback. (You might say something like, "Great job class! Rules like keeping our hands, feet, and other objects to ourselves are in place to keep us physically safe.") Go through each and have students explain why they think the rule is in place and how it helps keep others safe.

Session 27.2: Create Rules for Your Own Country

Now that the students have talked about the importance of safety rules, in this exercise, you will ask them to work in groups of three to four to create rules for a small country. (You can assign students into groups in the manner that best suits your class.) Explain to students that this country will be run by each of them and their group members. Ask students to create rules that they think are fair and to explain why they think those rules are fair. Let them get creative! To get them thinking, you could offer an example: "Go deeper than the big and obvious rules countries have. Get creative! For example, a rule in my country might be that you can't work past 3 p.m."

Let students know that they will present these rules to the class in the next lesson so they should be sure they are confident in their rules. Students can use the My Country's Rules worksheet in their workbook to document their rules.

Walk around the room while students work. Do not give them input into their rules. Let them come up with the rules themselves. Remind students to use their CREATE social skills, the working in a group skills, and their responsible decision-making MAGIC skills.

Sessions 27.3 and 27.4: Continue the Project on Creating Rules

Allow students the chance to work in their groups on their country's rules.

Session 27.5: The Commitment Circle

Have students gather in a circle and offer the prompt for this week's commitment. You can say,

> *Our prompt for our commitment circle this week is, What classroom rule are you going to be better about following? For example, the classroom rule I'm going to be better about following is "being on time." Sometimes we are late when we go to lunch or other areas of the school. It's important that we are on time so we don't make other classes late. In order to do this, I'm going to have us start lining up a couple minutes earlier each time we need to leave the classroom.*

Go around the circle and have students make their commitments. Encourage them to make these commitments for both the home and school setting so they can see how these skills translate to the home setting. Make sure you follow through on the commitment you made.

Reinforcing the Lesson

Remind students throughout the day why rules are in place to keep us safe. Also remind them of the rules they created, especially if they are breaking a rule of their own making. If students are struggling with a rule, ask them why they think it is in place and what the consequences might be if they don't follow the rules.

Sample Letter to Parents and Guardians—Lesson 27

Dear Parent/Guardian,

This week, as part of our class focus on responsible decision-making and social and emotional learning, we learned why rules are in place and how they keep us safe. Students focused on identifying important classroom rules and creating rules for their own small country. It is important for us to all understand why rules are in place and how they often keep us safe so that we are more likely to follow them.

You can ask your child the following questions about the lesson:

- What rules do you think are most important for your classroom?
- What rules did your group come up with for your small country?
- Were there any rules that your group disagreed about?
- What were they?
- Were you for or against the rule?
- Why?

Regards,

My Country's Rules

Rules for My Small Country

In this lesson, students will listen to the rules each group created, provide feedback, and ask questions regarding the short- and long-term consequences of the rules.

Introduction

In this lesson, students will provide feedback to their peers on the rules they created for their small country. Hearing feedback will allow students to see their rules from a new perspective and will encourage them to think critically about the rules created by other groups. Nicol et al. (2013) found that when feedback is received from peers, it allows the individual to evaluate and reflect, increasing engagement in the feedback process. See the introduction in Lesson 27 for more information on the importance of rules.

Objective

Students will be able to identify at least one short-term and one long-term consequence of two of the rules they created for their country.

Success Criteria

Students are able to

- identify the importance of rules
- understand the short- and long-term consequences of rules
- feel comfortable discussing the importance of rules with their teacher and others

Materials

Completed copy of the My Country's Rules worksheet from Lesson 27

Things to Note

Encourage the class to utilize their skills of respectfully disagreeing, covered in a previous lesson, when they discuss the rules student groups have created.

Session 28.1: Present and Provide Feedback on the Created Rules

Check in on student commitments from last week. Ask who would like to volunteer to share how they did following the classroom rule they identified. Allow students a chance to share how they did on their commitments. If you find that the same students are contributing each week, encourage new students to participate. If you have some students who never share, try to check in with them individually.

Explain Students' Roles as Presenters and Class Participants

Now that students have created their small country's rules, in this session, they are going to present them to the class. Begin by reminding students of their work in the last lesson and let them know some guidelines for presenting the rules they created and for being a helpful listener. Tell the class that presenters will read each rule they created and explain their rationale for that rule. Once they are done, the rest of the class is going to ask questions about the rules the presenters created. The class is going to suggest rules they might want to consider or point out the short- and long-term consequences they might not have thought about.

You can show how the class can respond to presenters by offering example. You might say,

> For example, I shared earlier that a rule of mine would be that people couldn't work past 3 p.m. The consequences of that rule might be that I wouldn't be able to grocery shop when I get off work and I wouldn't be able to go out to eat dinner at a restaurant because no one would be working!

Have one group present the rules it created. If students in class don't point out consequences of the rules, you can challenge some of the rules. Model using the respectfully disagreeing formula the class created. Encourage students to have thorough discussions about each group's rules.

Sessions 28.2–28.4: Continue with the Presentations

Have the rest of the groups present the rules they created in the same fashion.

Session 28.5: The Commitment Circle

Have students gather in a circle and offer the prompt for this week's commitment circle:

Our prompt for our commitment circle this week is, What is a second classroom rule that you are going to be better about following? For example, last week I said I would work on being on time. This week I am going to work on my voice level. Sometimes I can be a little louder than the expected voice level in specific areas on campus.

Go around the circle and have students make their commitments. Encourage them to make these commitments for both the home and school setting so they can see how these skills translate to the home setting.

Reinforcing the Lesson

Remind students throughout the day why rules are in place and how they can keep us safe. Also remind them of the rules they created, especially if they are breaking a rule of their own making. If students struggle to follow a rule, ask them why they think it is in place and what the consequences might be if they didn't follow the rules.

Sample Letter to Parents and Guardians—Lesson 28

Dear Parent/Guardian,

This week, as part of our class focus on responsible decision-making and social and emotional learning, students presented to the class the rules they created for their small country. The class discussed the rules of each group and presented short- and long-term consequences of the rules that the presenters might not have considered. It's important for us to understand why rules might have been imposed so that we can better understand the purpose of the rules and be more likely to follow them.

You can ask your child the following questions about the lesson:

- What rules did other groups come up with that you agreed with?
- What rules did other groups come up with that you didn't agree with?
- Were you surprised by some of the short-term consequences of the rules your group came up with?
- Were you surprised by some of the long-term consequences of the rules your group came up with?

Regards,

Capstone Project

Becoming the Teacher

In this lesson, students will research a social and emotional learning skill that was not covered in this curriculum and teach it to the class. They will become experts in this skill and create a detailed plan to teach the class the identified skill.

Introduction

Having the student become the teacher allows the student to become an expert at what they are expected to teach. In this lesson, students will conduct their own research and put together a presentation. Through presenting the material, they will learn it in a more meaningful way and will become more confident in their ability to present the material. Lachner et al. (2018) found that when students gave an oral explanation of the material they learned, they tended to elaborate more than they would have if they had simply written down the explanation.

Objectives

Students will be able to

- identify one skill they will teach the class
- create one lesson plan with detailed information on how they will present the skill to the class both orally and visually

Success Criteria

Students are able to

- identify what skill they are going to teach the class
- understand the importance of this skill
- feel comfortable with the lesson plan they have created to teach this skill

Materials

- One copy per student of the My Skill Lesson Plan worksheet
- One copy per student of the Potential Skills to Teach worksheet
- Preferred coloring utensils

Things to Note

Encourage students to be as creative as possible in presenting the skill. Encourage them to find out as much as they can about the skill and encourage them to utilize different modes of presentation (e.g., video, visual, lecture etc.). This lesson does require students to prepare an oral presentation to the class in the next lesson. If you have students that are experiencing a lot of anxiety over presenting to the class, consider letting them film themselves teaching the skill and then playing the video for students to watch. You can also pair them with someone else or offer to help support them in teaching the skill. You can also work with them to reduce their anxiety so they are able to present to the class, if they would like.

Part of this lesson does ask students to do some research on their own. If students don't have their own devices to conduct research, you can have them work in groups, work together as a class to research each skill, or you can reserve a computer lab where 1:1 technology will be available.

Session 29.1: Choosing a Skill to Teach the Class

Check in with students on their commitments from last week. Ask who would like to volunteer to share how they did following their identified classroom rule. Allow students a chance to share how they did on their commitments. If you find that the same students are contributing each week, encourage new students to participate. If you have some students who never share, try to check in with them individually.

Identify a Skill to Teach

In this lesson, students will identify and research an SEL skill that hasn't been specifically taught in their class. They can pick their own skill or can identify one on the list provided at the end of this lesson. Students should present the skill verbally and use at least one visual in teaching it to the class. You can use the following script to present the exercise to the class:

> *In this lesson, we are going to focus on all of the social and emotional learning skills that we haven't covered. There are so many wonderful social and emotional skills to learn, but we only have so much time to cover them in our lessons. Because of this, you are each going to pick a social and emotional learning skill to teach the class. You are going to research this skill and then determine how you are going to teach this skill to the class. You can teach this skill however you think is best, but you will need to speak to the class and explain the skill and you will need to have at least one visual to go with your presentation. You can show videos, make posters, draw*

a picture, or use a PowerPoint presentation. Your goal is to make sure that your class learns the skill to the best of their ability.

Let students spend some time researching what skill they would like to teach to the class. Once students have identified a skill, write down which students are presenting which skill. You will want to try to ensure that each student has his or her own skill to present. Students can write down the skill they chose on the worksheet My Skill Lesson Plan.

Sessions 29.2–29.4: Creating a Lesson Plan

Once students have identified their skill, they will create a detailed lesson plan to teach this skill. The lesson plan should include the following elements: an explanation of the steps to complete the skill, a lesson objective, a detailed plan on how the student will teach the skill and what visuals they will use, and an icon representing the skill. After students present their skill, you can add their skill icon to the display with the other Power Up skill cutouts. To explain the lesson plan to students, you can use the following script:

In order to teach the skill, you will need to know the steps to complete the skill. For example, to practice deep breathing, you need to breathe in slowly through your nose, then hold your breath in your belly for a few seconds, and then breathe slowly out through your mouth. Those are the three steps.

In the lesson plan, you will also need to create an objective for your lesson. That means you will need to say what the class will be able to do after lesson. For example, students will be able to take a deep breath following the three-step process for deep breathing. You will also need to create a detailed plan for how you are going to teach the class this skill. Are you going to show an online video? Are you going to create a PowerPoint presentation? Are you going to create a poster? Your plan will need to include at least one visual. Be as detailed as possible. Last, you will need to make an icon to represent your skill.

You can create your plan and sketch your icon on the worksheet My Skills Lesson Plan. When you are done with your plan, you can draw a bigger version of your icon on a blank piece of paper. After you have taught your skill, I will add your icon to the display wall with the other skills.

For the remainder of the session, allow the students time to work on their projects. They will present these over the next couple of weeks.

Session 29.5: The Commitment Circle

If you would like to continue with the tradition of commitment circles, you can choose what you would like for your students to commit to that week. Think back on the previously learned skills and revisit ones that might need to be reinforced. You can also let students make their own commitments without a prompt. This will give you insight into what they feel they need to work on.

Reinforcing the Lesson

Encourage students to come back to their outlines and lesson plans throughout the week as they have new ideas.

Sample Letter to Parents and Guardians—Lesson 29

Dear Parent/Guardian,

This week our class focused on their capstone project. Students researched various social and emotional learning skills that haven't been taught yet and identified one they thought was important for their class to know. Students then identified steps or parts of the skill to learn in order to perform it, and they created a detailed lesson plan they will use to teach the class this skill. Next week, students will start presenting their skill to the class.

You can ask your child the following questions about the lesson:

- What skill did you choose?
- What are the steps to use this skill?
- How are you planning to teach this skill to your class?

Regards,

My Skill Lesson Plan

My skill is:

_____

_____

The steps for my skill are:

_____

_____

_____

_____

Lesson Plan

What is your objective?

_____

_____

How are you going to teach this skill?

_____

_____

_____

_____

_____

_____

Draft of your icon:

From *Power Up: Gamification Tools for Social and Emotional Learning,* © 2022 by J. Dombrowski.
Champaign, IL: Research Press (www.researchpress.com, 800-519-2707).

Potential Skills to Teach

How to say thank you	Reading body language
How to ask for help	How to be reliable
Digital citizenship	How to be trustworthy
How to forgive someone	Showing optimism
Perspective taking	Organizational skills
Being patient	Compassion
Giving praise	Understanding
Sharing	Integrity
Being a good sport when losing	Self-discipline
Giving criticism	Internal motivation
Accepting criticism	External motivation
Accepting no	Encouraging others
Good manners	Sharing ideas
Being flexible	Writing down ideas
Staying on task	Celebrating success
How to respond to peer pressure	Helping others
How to be a leader	Following directions

Lesson 30

Presenting My Skill

In this lesson, students will present the skill they have learned to the class and encourage the class to practice the skill. Having students teach the skills they have researched and learned gives them a sense of accomplishment and pride. See Lesson 29 for more background information.

Objective

Students will teach the class one skill they have researched and learned.

Success Criteria

Students are able to

- identify a skill they would like to teach the class

- understand the importance of the skill they are going to teach

- feel comfortable teaching their class this skill and providing a strategy to remember it

Materials

- One copy per student of the Skills Worth Knowing worksheet

- One blank piece of paper

Things to Note

Do not limit the students' creativity. Let them present their skills however they would like to -- providing the presentation is appropriate. Praise students for all the skills they taught. If time permits, review the lesson plan with each student a day or more before they present so they can feel confident in what they are presenting. You can take as many weeks as you would like for students to teach their peers these skills.

Sessions 30.1–30.5: Student Presentations

Before students begin their presentations, prepare the class to be good listeners. You can use the following script to introduce the activity:

This week we are going to learn social and emotional skills from our peers. When people are presenting, we want to make sure we give them our full attention. We should think of questions we can ask them about the skill, and we want to follow along with any activity they are asking us to participate in. Think about how you want your peers to treat you when you are presenting. That is how you should treat your peers.

Let students know that they can take notes on the skills they are learning on the Skills Worth Knowing worksheet in their workbooks. The presentations will take place over two or more weeks, so the class should really be able to practice learning the skills!

When students present their skills to the class, give lots of praise! It's hard to go in front of the class and present a skill. If prior to the presentation, a student expresses concern about the presentation or about being shy, encourage the student to create a video of them doing the skill so that the student doesn't have to speak directly to the class. You should also work with the students on ways they can decrease their anxiety and still present their skill. When students have made their presentations, hang their skill icons on the display wall for all students to refer to and see.

Reinforcing the Lesson

Remind students of all skills learned and encourage them to utilize them as needed. Once all students have presented their skills, you could choose to have a closing ceremony or party where the students celebrate their successes and share their favorite skills and when they have been helpful. Give students a lot of praise for all of their hard work!

Sample Letter to Parents and Guardians—Lesson 30

Note to teacher: The following letter to parents should be personalized. Look for suggested items to insert into the letter, but feel free to make any adjustments that you see fit! Remember, this is the conclusion to the skills that they have worked hard on for months, so the letter should convey pride in both the student and parent for the hard work they have put into the program and the progress they have made as a result of that work!

Dear Parent/Guardian,

We have concluded our *Power Up* social and emotional learning lessons for the year. It has been a pleasure working with your child. I am so proud of [student's name] progress and the hard work he/she/they put into these skills! [Student's name] worked exceptionally hard on mastering [insert skills].

You can ask your child the following questions about the lesson:

- What was your favorite skill you learned?
- What was your least favorite skill you learned?
- Has learning these skills been helpful?

Regards,

Skills Worth Knowing

Appendix A

Support Materials

Icon Cheat Sheet

*The Power Up Skill Cutouts for Display are available for download at **www.researchpress.com/downloads**. The icons, for reference, are showcased on the next two pages.*

Lesson 4	**Home**			
Lesson 5	**Rewind**			
Lesson 6	**Fast Forward**			
Lesson 7	**Triggers**			
Lesson 8	**Resiliency**			
Lesson 9	**Pause, Think, Play**			
Lesson 10	**Deep Breathing**	**Mandala**	**Finger Maze**	
Lesson 11	**Progressive Muscle Relaxation**	**Mindfulness**		
Lesson 12	**Reframing**	**Worry Box**	**Wall Push-Ups**	**Stretching**

Lesson 13	Goal Setting			
Lesson 15	Kindness			
Lesson 16	Empathy			
Lesson 17	Collaborative Group Member			
Lesson 18	Respectfully Disagree			
Lesson 20	"I" Statements			
Lesson 21	Compliments	Respecting Personal Space	Eye Contact	
Lesson 22	Asking Questions	Taking Turns	Exhibiting Geniune Interest	
Lesson 24	Brain			
Lessons 25 and 26	MAGIC			

Sample Tallying Sheet

Skill	Student Initials														
Home Mode															
Rewind Mode															
Fast-Forward Mode															
Triggers															
Resiliency															
Pause, Think, Play															
Deep Breathing															
Mandala															
Finger Maze															
Mindfulness															
Progressive Muscle Relaxation															
Worry Box															
Wall Push Ups															
Stretching															
Reframing															
Goal Setting															
Kindness															
Charging Batteries															
Groupwork															
Respectfully Disagreeing															
"I" Statements															
Compliments															
Personal Space															
Eye Contact															
Asking Questions															
Taking Turns															
Genuine Curiosity															
Prefrontal Cortex															
MAGIC															

Power Up Board

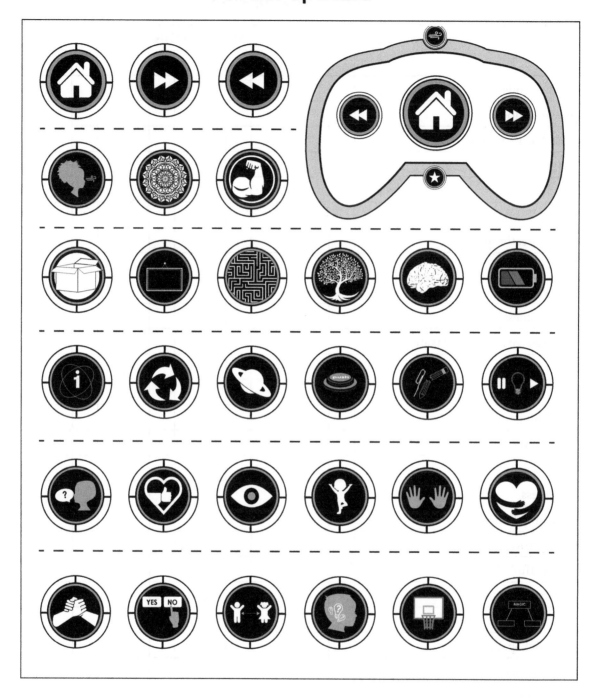

From *Power Up: Gamification Tools for Social and Emotional Learning,* © 2022 by J. Dombrowski. Champaign, IL: Research Press (www.researchpress.com, 800-519-2707).

Power Up for Small Groups

Small group interventions on social and emotional learning (SEL) can provide a range of personal and academic benefits for children. When students are not making gains through the use of school-wide, universal interventions, small group interventions should be considered. Green et al. (2019) found that when students are exposed to SEL in the small group setting, teachers see a decrease in behavioral issues and an increase in students' ability to self-regulate and to develop more-positive relationships with peers.

The *Power Up* curriculum in small group format offers a fun, game-based approach to teaching core SEL skills. Students learn the skills while earning icons and advancing across the Power Up board. In the small group format, the group focuses on one of the five domains of SEL: self-awareness, self-management, social awareness, relationship skills, or responsible decision-making. Designed to be facilitated in once-a-week sessions held outside the classroom, the Small Group program can run from 6-8 weeks, depending on the group's needs. In this section of the curriculum, you will find guidance on implementing the program in the small group format, the Power Up board for each SEL domain, Lesson 1, and support materials for communicating with teachers and parents and guardians.

Implementing the Small Group Format

In order for small groups to be as successful as possible, facilitators should consider their own experience and skill set in implementing the curriculum. Successful SEL small group programs feature appropriate and attainable student goals, positive reinforcement, experienced facilitators, and space reserved for the sessions (Humphrey et al., 2009). Before starting your small group sessions, you should answer the following questions: When are you going to run your group? How often are you going to meet? Where are you going to meet? Do you need to reserve this space? Prior to implementing the group, do you need any training on how to address sensitive topics or mental health concerns? How can you receive this training? How are you going to ensure that you are consistent in implementing the interventions? How are you going to communicate to the teacher the skills the students learned? How are you going to support teachers so that they can be consistent in reinforcing the skills? How are you going to communicate with parents? How are you going to empower students? After you have established the foundation for your group, you will be able to start the Power Up lessons for small groups.

Power Up lessons help students build skills in each of the five domains of SEL. Lessons 4-8 in the main curriculum focus on self-awareness, Lessons 9-13 are on self-management, Lessons 14-18 address social awareness, Lessons 19-23 cover relationship skills, and Lessons 24-28 focus on decision-making. Final lessons in the full curriculum cover comprehensive skill practice. The Small Group curriculum format allows students to concentrate on the skills in one SEL domain, while attending once-a-week sessions.

In order to run the small group, facilitators will start with Small Group Lesson 1 found in the section Power Up for Small Groups and then proceed to the five lessons identified for the domain the group is focusing on. For example, if the group is learning self-awareness, facilitators will begin with Small Group Lesson 1 and then proceed to Lessons 4 through 8, the five lessons covering self-awareness skills.

Each domain has five lessons, and with Small Group Lesson 1 included, the group will run for six weeks, covering six lessons. Facilitators can also extend the small group sessions by including the capstone project from Lessons 29-30. They can also use the optional Session 4 scripts to extend some lessons into more than one week.

While lessons in the full program are divided into five sessions with the last two sessions being devoted to practice and commitment circles, lessons in the Small Group format include sessions 1–3 and 5. Each Small Group lesson is meant to be completed in 30-45 minutes. Facilitators will follow the directions and scripts for each lesson and complete sessions 1–3 and 5 in each weekly group. Session 4 script is optional. Facilitators might need to make some minimal rewording of some lessons, since they won't be covering the whole curriculum. They should also read through Small Group Lesson 1 prior to the start of the group, as some logistical issues might need to be considered.

Using the Power Up Game Board and Icons

In the Small Group program, each SEL domain has its own Power Up board. The board's icons represent the skills to be learned in that domain and covered in the group. Students will each have their own Power Up board, and the students' goal is to earn all four bars for each icon on the Power Up board. (The Small Group Power Up boards can be found Power Up for Small Groups Support Materials.)

Each icon is enclosed within a circle that is divided into four segments, or power bars. When a student is observed using the SEL skill, the student receives a bar, and the segment is colored in. When all four bars have been colored in, the student has earned the icon and "powered up." The student gets to color in the icon.

To fill in the power bars, facilitators can either ask the student's teachers to report how often the student used the learned skills throughout the week, or they can ask the student to tell about times they used the skill. If facilitators think the student is making up stories about when they used the skill, that is OK. Facilitators should still give them credit as the student is still identifying times they could have used or can use the skill.

When the student "powers up" on a skill, there should be a reward available. These do not have to be monetary in value. Rewards can be given out during free time at the end of the group meeting, or if the school has a positive behavior support plan, facilitators can use that for rewards as well. For example, some schools have a form of "school bucks" that can be turned in for prizes. The school bucks might serve as rewards for the Power Up students. Rewards can also be worked out with the students' teachers. Some teachers might be willing to give the student a homework pass or extra recess time.

The Power Up board also features a controller with a home, fast-forward, and rewind buttons. The controller is used as a tool to describe different states of feeling that students might experience. The home mode represents our resting state. In the home mode, the individual is at peace and, as a result, is productive. In the home mode, heart rate and breathing is normal, and the individual is alert and able to concentrate. This mode represents feelings, such as happiness, love, and contentment. In a gaming context, home mode is where players start the game. Energy levels are normal, health levels are high, and players are able to complete their missions.

In the rewind mode, we have low levels of energy (as if we were moving in reverse), which results in poor concentration and low productivity. In the rewind mode, individuals might feel weighed down, tired, and unmotivated. As a result, they are not very productive. In a gaming context, rewind mode is when the character has low energy levels and struggles to complete or even start missions. Rewind mode includes feelings like boredom, loneliness, and fatigue.

The fast-forward mode is characterized by high levels of energy (as if we were moving in fast-forward motion). The increased energy makes it hard to be productive because it interferes with concentration. In the fast-forward mode, individuals might experience an increased heart rate or heavy breathing, or they might fidget. In the gaming context, fast-forward mode is when a game character might use a booster (or special ability) to complete a task. This extra boost, however, makes it harder to control the character, resulting in a failed mission. This mode includes emotions like frustration, anger and feeling or acting silly.

Facilitators can read more about these modes in Lessons 4-8 in the self-awareness domain. If facilitators are not covering the self-awareness domain, they will need to review with students the three different modes their feelings can fall into as these modes and the controller on the Power Up board will be referenced throughout the curriculum.

Support Materials

You will need to regularly communicate with the teachers, administrators, and support staff who work with the student about the skills the group is working on. Keeping them informed will help them track students' use of the skills and help you recognize and award students. The Small Group Lessons Summary in the curriculum gives an overview of the activities and skills practiced in the group intervention. Power Up facilitators should distribute it to teachers and staff or use it as a resource in describing program lessons. You can find the Small Group Lesson Summary in the section Power Up for Small Groups Support Materials.

Each week the students will learn an SEL skill, which should be reinforced by the student's teacher. In order to support the teachers, facilitators can email them a brief summary of the skill learned. In drafting the email, Small Group facilitators can draw on the brief descriptions in the Lessons Summary included in the Small Group curriculum. These descriptions can be edited or modified. The emails should be brief so as not to overwhelm the teacher and should just include the meat-and-potatoes basics of what the teacher should know to help increase follow-through.

The sample Parent Permission Slip can be used as a guide for creating an introduction to the program. Facilitators can copy and use and edit it as needed. The school name and the group's focus and meeting time will need to be inserted in the form's blanks. A sample weekly report letter to parents and guardians is included at the end of each lesson. Every parent letter is also available in an adaptable Microsoft Word document as part of the download identified on the copyright page. Further tips on implementing *Power Up* appear in the curriculum introduction and overview chapters.

Small Group Lesson 1: Introduction

In this lesson, students will get to know other group members and the purpose of the group.

Introduction

The first lesson in your small group begins with an icebreaker. Icebreakers are a popular way to build a sense of community and are used in many settings. Miller et al. (2017) found that students who participated a relationship-building program had more positive relationships with their peers, enjoyed school more, had fewer behavioral issues, and achieved a better academic performance. Starting the group off with an icebreaker activity will allow students to get to know one another, and it will increase feelings of connectedness and set a positive tone for the group. This activity will also give them the opportunity to get to know you better and will start the process of building trust and rapport that you will be working on throughout the year.

Objectives

Student will be able to

- learn at least three things they have in common with at least two group members
- identify the purpose of the group

Success Criteria

Participants can

- identify at least three things they have in common with at least two group members
- understand the purpose of the group
- feel comfortable learning skills and strategies with group members

Materials

- Paper and pencil
- A copy of the Power Up board for small groups
- The Things We Have in Common worksheet
- A Power Up icon for display
- Workbook folder or binder, one per student

Things to Note

The following lesson is meant to be completed in one 30-45 minute session. All Small Group programs will complete this Lesson 1 and then proceed to the five lessons in the domain, following a once-a-week session format. If as group facilitator, you want your group sessions to run longer to give your participants more practice, you can conclude sessions with lessons 29-30. As another option, a session 4 activity can also be included. Groups will use the Power Up board specific to the domain they are focusing on. (The Power Up boards for use in Small Group session can be found in the Power Up for Small Groups Support Materials section.)

Lesson 1: Icebreaker Activities and Introduction to *Power Up*

Introduce the Program and SEL Skills

Facilitators should introduce themselves, welcome participants, and explain the lesson timeline. As facilitator, you could say the following:

> *Welcome to our group. My name is (your name and background here). Your teachers have told me so much about you and I am happy to meet you. We are all going to work together to learn some new skills. It is important that you learn these skills so you can be leaders on the campus for other students who might need to learn these skills as well. Our group is going to go for six (or insert another amount) weeks. We will meet on (date and time). In our group, we are going to learn about (domain name, ex. self-awareness, self-management, social awareness, responsible decision-making, or relationship skills. Use the appropriate description below to explain the domain that the group will focus on.)*

- **Self-Awareness.** Self-awareness is when we are able to tell what we are feeling. We also have insight into who we are. For example, I know my strengths and weaknesses, my morals and my values. In this group, we are going to gain insight into ourselves and our feelings.

- **Self-Management.** Self-management is when we are able to manage our big emotions. We are able to demonstrate impulse control and utilize skills to keep ourselves calm so we are able to make good decisions. We are also able to set and manage goals that are important to us and manage our time effectively. In this group, we are going to learn how we can control our emotions when they feel out of control and learn how to set and achieve goals.

- **Social Awareness.** Social awareness is when we are able to think about others' thoughts and feelings. We might be able to see a problem from their point of view, or we might demonstrate empathy. In this group, we are going to learn how we can demonstrate empathy and kindness to others.

- **Relationship Skills.** We use relationship skills to not only make new friends but also to maintain friends that we already have. Relationship skills also help us start and maintain conversations and work well in a group. In this group, we are going to learn relationship skills so that we can put ourselves in a good position to have positive interactions with others.

- **Responsible Decision-Making.** Responsible decision-making skills help us make decisions that are best for ourselves and others. In this group, we will learn how we can think through our options, weigh the pros and cons of possible outcomes, and make the best decision for ourselves while also considering others.

Introduce Power Up Board and Icons

Once students know the focus of the group, you can introduce the Power Up board and what the icons represent and how to earn them. In describing the board, make sure to explain that the board shows that participants are using the skills they are learning. You could say,

> *Throughout our group, we will learn new skills. As we learn these new skills, you will be asked to practice them. I have already talked to your teacher, and (s)he is going to help track you using your skills.*
>
> *Each skill is represented by an icon. (Facilitators should distribute the Power Up boards so students can see the icons.). Each icon is inside a circle. The circle is made up of four segments. These are the power bars. To earn a power bar, you must practice using the skill on your own outside of our group. Each time you are seen using a skill, you will get a bar filled in. When you have earned four bars, you will have "powered up" and earned the icon. When you "power up" you will be able to color in the icon.*

If you want to give rewards for powering up, you can name the reward at this point. Rewards can be something like a pencil or a couple minutes of free time that you give the group, or you can work out a reward with the teachers.

If you are focusing your small group on the self-management, social awareness, relationship skills or responsible decision-making domain, you will need to review information about the three modes on their controller: home, fast-forward, and rewind modes. You will also need to review what feelings would be included in each mode. You can say,

> *If you look at the controller on your Power Up board, you will notice that it has three different modes. The first mode, the home mode, is found in the center of your controller. The home mode is when you feel relaxed and at ease. You are able to complete tasks and are productive. Your heart rate and breathing are normal, and your muscles feel relaxed. This mode represents feelings such as happiness, contentedness, and love. In a game, this would be when your character is just*

starting out and they have normal energy and health levels. As a result, they are able to complete their tasks and missions.

On the left side of the controller, you will see the rewind mode. The rewind mode is when you have low energy levels and you feel as if you are moving in reverse. As a result, you are not productive and struggle to finish or even start tasks. Your body might feel heavy and you might be tired. In a game, this would be when your character is running low on energy and as a result, is unable to start or finish missions. This mode houses feelings such as sadness, boredom, and loneliness.

The last mode is the fast-forward mode. This mode is found on the right side of your controller. The fast-forward mode is when you have high energy levels and feel as if you are moving quickly, or in fast-forward. Due to the high energy levels, you might struggle to concentrate and/or finish the task you started. You might fidget because of your extra energy, and your heart rate and breathing might be fast. In a game, this is when your character might use a booster to boost their skills, and as a result, they are harder to control. Your character might not finish the mission or might fail the mission. This mode houses feelings such as frustration, anger, and excitement. It is important to know these modes because we will be referring to them throughout our group.

Introduce the Icebreaker Activity

Let students know that they are going to do an icebreaker activity in which they will get to know the members in their group. You could introduce the activity by saying, "While we will focus on these skills and modes in the coming weeks, today we are going to take the time to get to know each other, since we will be spending a lot of time together!"

Pair the students up and give them a blank piece of paper and a pencil or pen. If you have an odd number of students, pair someone with you. It's good for students to see that they have things in common with adults too.

Have students write down everything they can find that they have in common with their partner. Explain that they have five minutes for the activity, and set a timer for five minutes. To explain the activity, you could say,

I want you to work with your partner and write down everything that you can find you have in common. You can use The Things We Have in Common worksheet as a guide. You will have five minutes.

When they are done, have students tally up the number of things they found in common with the other person and see which pair has the most in common.

Have the partners share with the group their top three favorite things they have in common. Pair the students up with a new partner and have them repeat the exercise.

Review the Activity

Answer student questions. It is important that students feel comfortable in the group and feel as if it will be a positive experience versus a punishment. If you have some time left over, challenge the whole group to find things they all have in common:

> *Even if you weren't paired with every student, we got a lot of good information about everyone! We will certainly be getting to know each other better over the coming weeks. Does anyone have any questions about our group?*

Introduce the Commitment Circle

At the end of each lesson, the group will form a commitment circle. In the circle, participants should establish how they will practice the skill they learned through the following week. This is their commitment. Facilitators will provide a prompt based on the lesson. The prompt is in the form of a question that the participants should answer. Commitments should be an action the participant can realistically complete in a defined period of time, whether that is over a week or the length of the program. It should be specific and should usually include how many times the participant will take the action or practice the skill.

Have students stand together and form a circle at the end of the lesson. Introduce the concept of commitment and a commitment circle. Explain that commitments made in the commitment circle will outline how they will try to practice their new skill. Ask students to make and describe their commitment for the week. You could say,

> *At the end of each group, we are going to make a commitment circle. In our commitment circles, we will answer a question based on our lesson. You will make a commitment to practice what we learned in our lesson over the coming weeks. A commitment is an obligation or promise to do what we say we are going to do. When you make a commitment, make sure that your commitment is something you can carry out. You don't want to make commitments you know you can't keep.*
>
> *Our prompt for our commitment circle this week is, How are you going to get to know more about the group members over the next six weeks? For example, you could say, "I am going to*

sit by someone new each week so I can get to know everyone better."

Go around the circle and have students make their commitments.

Small Group Power Up Game Boards

Self Awareness

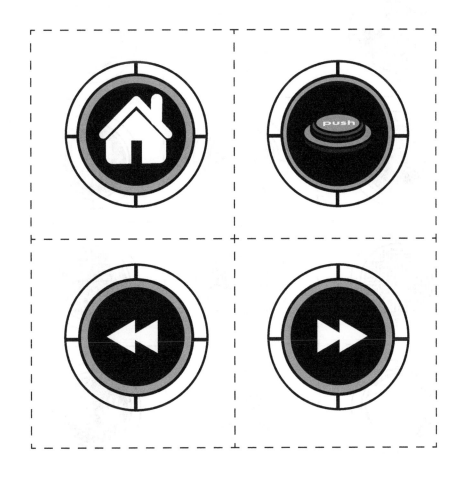

Self Management

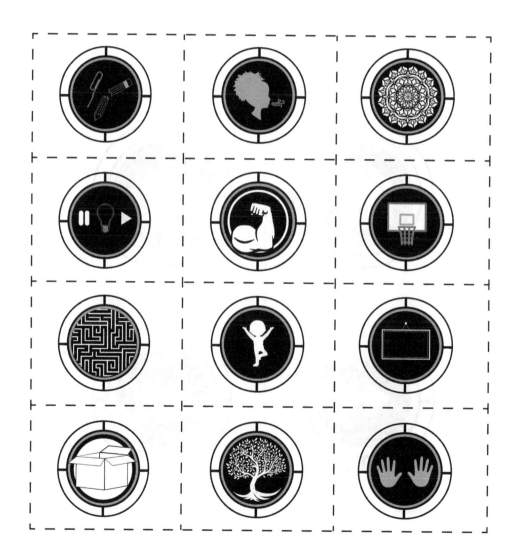

Social Awareness

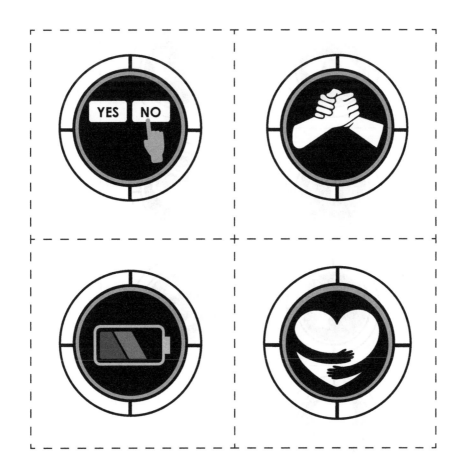

Relationship Skills

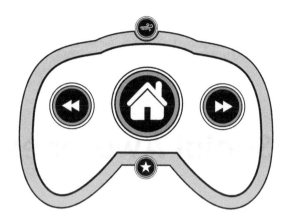

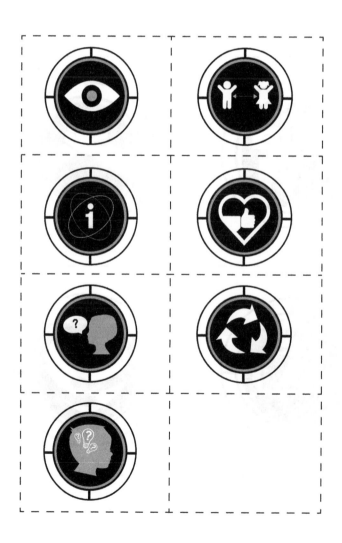

Responsible Decision Making

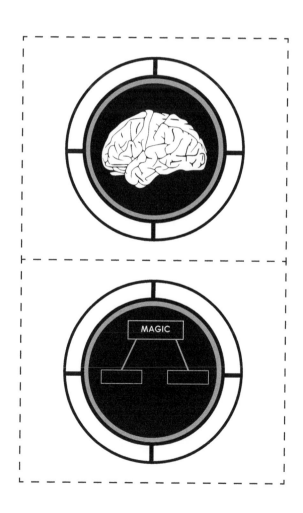

Power Up Support Materials for Small Groups

Small Group Lessons Summary

(Numbering refers to lessons in full curriculum)

Lesson 1 for All Groups. Lesson 1 focuses on establishing the group's purpose and an icebreaker activity. Identifying commonalities with their peers is encouraged.

Groups on Self-Awareness

Lesson 4. Lesson 4 focuses on the home mode on the Power Up controller and the feelings the home mode houses. In the home mode, students are relaxed and productive. They are able to accomplish their daily tasks. Home mode emotions include feeling happy, content, relaxed, and loved. Identification of home mode feelings is encouraged.

Lesson 5. Lesson 5 focuses on the rewind mode on the Power Up controller and the feelings it represents. In the rewind mode, students have low energy levels that result in low productivity. They struggle to complete or even start daily tasks. They experience feelings such as tiredness, boredom, and sadness. Identification of rewind mode feelings is encouraged.

Lesson 6. Lesson 6 focuses on the fast-forward mode on the Power Up controller and the feelings it covers. In the fast-forward mode, students have high energy levels with low levels of productivity. The extra energy they experience makes it difficult for them to successfully complete a task. They might experience feelings such as anger, frustration, and excitement in the fast-forward mode. Identification of fast-forward mode feelings is encouraged.

Lesson 7. Lesson 7 focuses on triggers for various feelings and experiences. Situations, people, places, things, or objects that might cause students to experience certain feelings are identified. Students identifying triggers for various modes is encouraged.

Lesson 8. Lesson 8 focuses on resiliency. An unwound paperclip that bends when an object (or obstacle) pushes against it, instead of breaking the way a wooden pencil would, is presented as an example of resiliency. Students will be encouraged to identify opportunities to be adaptable like the paperclip and overcome challenges.

Groups on Self-Management

Lesson 9. Lesson 9 focuses on the self-management strategy of pause, think, play. With this strategy, students are encouraged to pause (or stop), think about their options, and then play, or move forward with the best option for themselves and others. Students are encouraged to use the pause, think, play strategy.

Lesson 10. Lesson 10 focuses on the self-management strategies of deep breathing, finger mazes, and coloring mandalas. The use of deep breathing, finger mazes, and coloring mandalas is encouraged. If mandalas are not available, students are encouraged to draw their own.

Lesson 11. Lesson 11 focuses on the self-management strategies of progressive muscle relaxation (PMR) and mindfulness. With PMR, each muscle group is relaxed one at a time. With mindfulness, there is a focus on the present and the here and now. The focus is not on things that happened in the past or things that will happen in the future. The use of progressive muscle relaxation and mindfulness is encouraged.

Lesson 12. Lesson 12 focuses on the self-management strategies of placing worries in a worry box, reframing, doing wall push-ups, and stretching. Worries can be placed in a worry box to temporarily get them out of students' heads so they can focus. Negative thoughts will be reframed into positive ones. Lastly, movement can be used to self-regulate. This can be done through stretching or wall push-ups. The use of the worry box, reframing, wall push-ups and stretching is encouraged.

Lesson 13. Lesson 13 focuses on setting smaller goals in order to reach a "big" goal. Time management skills will also be reviewed. The use of goal setting and time management skills is encouraged.

Groups on Social Awareness

Lesson 14. Lesson 14 focuses on identification of the individuals in the student's social support systems. These individuals help support the student when they are feeling overwhelmed or in need. These social supports can include family, friends, teachers, and community members. The use of social support systems is encouraged.

Lesson 15. Lesson 15 focuses on acts of kindness and the definition of empathy. Empathy is understanding and caring about what others are feeling. Demonstrating random acts of kindness is encouraged.

Lesson 16. Lesson 16 continues to focus on empathy. Engaging in acts of kindness can "charge" batteries (or make one feel good) while charging the batteries of others (making others feel good). Demonstrating random acts of kindness to charge their batteries and the batteries of others is encouraged.

Lesson 17. Lesson 17 focuses on group roles. Group roles include the CEO, lawyer, accountant, or entertainer. Each group role has its strengths and weaknesses: the CEO has good leadership skills but struggles to listen to other points of view, the lawyer is a good researcher but is judgmental, the accountant can work through tough problems but struggles to work in a group, and the entertainer brings enjoyment to the group but struggles to stay on task. Insight into their group role's strengths and weaknesses is encouraged.

Lesson 18. Lesson 18 focuses on skills for respectfully disagreeing with others. A formula for respectfully disagreeing will be agreed upon by the group. The formula is [insert your group created formula]. The use of the formula for respectfully disagreeing is encouraged.

Groups on Relationship Skills

Lesson 19. Lesson 19 focuses on desired qualities in a friendship (both in a friend and in the student). Continued identification of desired qualities in a friend is encouraged, as well as demonstrating desired qualities.

Lesson 20. Lesson 20 focuses on communication of wants and needs through "I statements." The format of an "I statement" is as follows: "I feel _____ when _____. I need _____." The use of "I statements" to communicate wants and needs is encouraged.

Lesson 21. Lesson 21 focuses on the first three social skills represented in the acronym CREATE. The acronym can help students remember learned social skills. The C stands for compliments, the R stands for respecting personal space, and the E stands for eye contact. The use of giving compliments, respecting personal space, and making eye contact is encouraged.

Lesson 22. Lesson 22 focuses on the social skills represented in last three letters of the CREATE acronym. The A stands for asking questions, the T stands for taking turns, and the E stands for exhibiting genuine curiosity. The use of asking questions, taking turns, and exhibiting genuine curiosity is encouraged.

Lesson 23. Lesson 23 focuses on reviewing recorded interviews of role models. Strengths and weaknesses of the interviewees are identified. The use of a social skill that needs strengthened by each student is encouraged.

Groups on Responsible Decision-Making

Lesson 24. Lesson 24 focuses on two regions in the brain: the prefrontal cortex and the amygdala. The prefrontal cortex is where problem-solving and critical thinking occur. The amygdala, by contrast, is constantly looking for threats and can shut off our connection to the prefrontal cortex when overwhelmed. The use of self-management strategies to reconnect the prefrontal cortex and the amygdala in order to solve problems is encouraged.

Lesson 25. Lesson 25 focuses on the first two steps in the MAGIC decision-making process. The *M* stands for managing emotions. The *A* stands for assessing for possible solutions. The use of a self-management strategy to remain calm and think through possible solutions is encouraged.

Lesson 26. Lesson 26 focuses on the last three steps of the MAGIC decision-making process. The *G* stands for gathering the pros and cons of each possible outcome, the *I* stands for identifying biases (how previous experiences impact decisions made now), and the *C* stands for choosing the best option for all. The use of weighing the pros and cons to decide the best outcome for everyone is encouraged.

Lesson 27. Lesson 27 focuses on the importance of rules. Students will be asked to establish rules for a small nation. Following rules to keep everyone safe is encouraged.

Lesson 28. Lesson 28 focuses on the presentation of the rules students created for their small nations in the previous lesson. Short- and long-term consequences of the rules will be discussed. Continued reflection on the short- and long-term consequences of rules is encouraged.

Supplementary Capstone SEL Lessons for All Groups

Final Two Lessons (Lesson 29-30 full curriculum). Each group participant completes a capstone project in which he or she identifies an SEL skill not yet taught. Group members research and teach the skill to group members. Practice in using each skill is encouraged.

Parent Permission Slip

Dear Parent(s) or Guardian(s),

   This letter is to inform you that your student has been selected to participate in a small group for social and emotional learning at _____ Elementary. The group will focus on the _____ domain of social and emotional learning. In this domain, students will learn about _____.

   These groups will take place on _____ at _____ a.m./p.m. during _____. Please elect your decision below and return this form to your child's teacher by _____. I look forward to working with your child!

   If you have any questions, feel free to contact me:

Name: _____

Email: _____

Phone: _____

Please check one of the following statements and sign and date the bottom of the consent form.

☐ Yes, I give consent for my child to participate in the social and emotional learning group.

☐ No, I would not like my child to participate in the social and emotional learning group at this time.

Student Name: _____

Teacher Name: _____

Parent Name: _____

Parent Signature: _____

Date: _____

Power Up Lessons for the Virtual Classroom

Virtual Lesson 1: Digital Citizenship

Note to the teacher: In this lesson, students will research what digital citizenship is and how to show digital citizenship in the virtual classroom. The purpose of this lesson is to set the stage for positive interactions in a virtual format. Having students take charge of their digital learning community and setting expectations for themselves and their peers will help create a positive classroom community in which ideas can be shared and discussed respectfully.

Instructions to the Student

Research what digital citizenship is and pick one way to demonstrate digital citizenship. Your post should be two paragraphs. The first paragraph should explain in detail what digital citizenship is, and the second paragraph should describe a way to demonstrate digital citizenship.

After you have posted your response, read posts from at least **three** other classmates and comment on how their definitions of how to show digital citizenship will help make the virtual classroom an engaging and safe place to be.

Instructor Follow-Up

After students have all made their posts, teachers should compile their posts into a master list of digital citizenship attributes. As the instructor, you can review and vet the list and add any attributes you would like to the master list. Post this master list and have students comment, agreeing to demonstrate these attributes to the best of their abilities.

Two attributes that are strongly recommended for inclusion are confidentiality and engaging responses. It is important to remind students that they need to be comfortable with the whole class knowing the information they are sharing. Students should think out their responses to others and make them engaging. They should also make sure that all posts are getting responses and have comments. Students should not respond only to the same people. They should also keep other students' responses confidential so everyone feels comfortable sharing.

Other attributes you might want to consider including are using appropriate language, writing in full sentences, posting responses that do not contain profanity or inappropriate material, being respectful of all students, responding equally to all students' posts rather than just the same students' posts, managing time appropriately, creating a safe space for all, using technology to solve problems, and posting accurate data.

There will be times when a student might share inappropriate information. Quietly take down the post and follow your school procedures in approaching the student and making a referral to the school counselor. Students should keep all information shared by peers confidential.

Virtual Lesson 2: Getting to Know Me

Note to the teacher: In this lesson, students will reflect on what makes them them. They will identify their likes, dislikes, strengths, and weaknesses. Students will share their responses with the class in order to allow them to begin the process of getting to know one another. Instructors can use the following paragraphs for the student assignment.

Share a Post about Yourself

Think about what makes you *you*. What are some of your hobbies? What is your favorite food? Where is your favorite place to visit? Do you have siblings? Who do you live with? Do you have pets?

Create a discussion post in which you write all about you. Try to include at least **10** facts about yourself. Try to make these interesting and fun. Make sure that whatever you share, you are OK with your entire class and teacher knowing.

Respond to Five Other Posts

While other students are busy reading about you, you will be busy reading about them. Pick at least **five** posts from other students and read them thoroughly. After you have read through each post, think about what you would like to know about that person. Ask that student your question. For each of the **five** posts, ask at least **one** question. Don't forget to check back on your original post to answer questions that your peers have asked you!

Virtual Lesson 3: Getting to Know You

Note to the teacher: In this lesson, students will reflect on what stereotyping and discrimination is and their personal experiences with stereotyping and discrimination. Students will work to identify ways that they can demonstrate inclusivity and equality in various settings. You can use the following language and prompts for the student assignment.

Reflection on Stereotyping and Discrimination

This lesson asks you to reflect on several questions leading up to your discussion post. You can silently answer these in your head, write your responses down on a piece of paper, or discuss with an adult in the home.

Look up the definition of stereotyping. Reflect on the following questions in your head or write your answers down on a blank piece of paper. What is stereotyping? What are some common stereotypes you have heard? Are stereotypes always accurate?

Categorizing people is a dangerous practice because it doesn't allow us to get to know the person we are making assumptions about. You are missing out on getting to know someone who may or may not fall into the category you have tried to place them in. Has anyone ever made a stereotype about you? How did it feel?

Look up the definition of discrimination. Reflect on the following questions in your head or write your answers down on a blank piece of paper. What is discrimination? What are some ways people can be discriminated against? What is the negative impact of discrimination?

Inclusion and equality are two ways that we can combat stereotyping and discrimination. Inclusion is when we make sure that everyone is included no matter their gender, skin color, ethnicity, or culture. Equality is when everyone is treated equally.

Create a Post about Inclusion

Write a post in which you answer the following questions:

- How can you practice inclusion and equality in your home and community?

- What pledge would you like to make to your classmates? For example, *I pledge to treat everyone with kindness.*

Respond to **two** peers posts. Comment on their plans for inclusion and equality. Would their plan make you feel included? Would their plan make you feel like their equal?

Virtual Lesson 4: The Home Mode

Note to the teacher: In this lesson, students will learn about the first mode on their game controller: the home mode. They will learn what feelings are in the home mode, and will be able to identify what the home mode looks, feels, and sounds like for them. You can use the following language and prompts for the student assignment. Don't forget to include the Power Up *controller visual with the following instructions to students!*

Introduction to the Controller

Review the Power Up controller included with the lesson materials. This controller features three modes: the home mode, fast-forward mode, and rewind mode. In the home mode, we are relaxed and at rest (as a game character might feel as they start their missions.) As a result, we are productive. (Game characters are able to complete their missions.) In the rewind mode, we have lower energy levels and feel as if we are moving in reverse. In this mode, we are less motivated and less productive. (A game character might be unable to complete missions due to low energy levels.) In the fast-forward mode, we have increased energy levels that make it hard to concentrate. Due to the extra energy, we might also struggle to be productive (as a game character might feel when their energy boosts get in the way of them completing their missions.)

Introduction to the Home Mode

We are going to talk about the home mode on our controller first. The home mode is located in the center of our controller. Our home mode houses feelings that make us feel at rest and relaxed. We are able to regulate ourselves and use our critical thinking skills. As a result, we can concentrate and are more productive. In the home mode, our heart rate and breathing are normal, and our muscles are relaxed. Emotions in home mode might include happy, relaxed, calm, loved, and content. For example, when we start playing a game, our character usually has full health and normal energy levels. They are in good shape to begin their mission.

Explore Home Mode Feelings

Use the internet or an online dictionary to search for a list of words for feelings. After you have a list, go through it to identify feelings that you experience in the home mode. For example, happy, relaxed etc. What feelings did you find that would represent being in the home mode? In the first part of your discussion post, write down your list of **five** feeling words that you identified as home-mode feelings.

After you have listed your **five** feelings, pick one of the home mode feelings that you relate to the most. In the second part of your post, write about how you feel when you experience this emotion.

Answer the following questions in your discussion post:

- What does your face look like when you experience this feeling?

- How does your body move when you experience this feeling?

- What sounds might you make when you are experiencing this feeling?

- Do you enjoy the experience of this feeling?

After you are done, read at least **two** other discussion posts and comment on how they experience the feeling they selected. Do you experience it in the same way or differently?

Virtual Lesson 5: The Rewind Mode

Note to the teacher: In this lesson, students will learn about the second mode on their game controller: the rewind mode. They will learn what feelings are in the rewind mode and will be able to identify what the rewind mode looks, feels, and sounds like for them. Instructors can use the following language and prompts for the student assignment. Don't forget to include a copy of the Power Up controller!

Introduction to the Rewind Mode

In our last lesson, we learned about the home mode and found the icon for it on our Power Up board controllers. In this lesson, we are going to talk about the rewind mode. In the rewind mode you feel as if you have low energy levels and poor concentration that contribute to poor productivity. Your body might feel heavy and you might feel exhausted all the time. For example, imagine you are a game character with low energy levels. These low energy levels will cause the character to take longer to complete missions or cause them to not be able to complete the mission at all. Feelings in this mode might include being sad, disappointed, bored, tired, or worried. On your controller, the rewind mode is on the left-hand side, next to the home mode.

Explore Rewind Feelings

Use the internet or an online dictionary to search for feelings words. After you have made a list, go through it to identify feelings that you would experience in the rewind mode. For example, you might have the words *sad, lonely, disappointed*. What feelings did you find that would represent the rewind mode? In the first part of your post, write your list of **five** feeling words you identified as rewind mode feelings.

After you have listed these **five** rewind mode feelings, pick one of the rewind mode feelings that you relate to the most. In the second part of your post, write about how you feel when you experience this emotion.

Answer the following questions in your discussion post:

- What does your face look like when you experience this feeling?

- How does your body move when you experience this feeling?

- What sounds might you make when you are experiencing this feeling?

- Do you enjoy the experience of this feeling?

After you are done, read at least **two** other discussion posts and comment on how they experience the feeling they selected. Do you experience it in the same way or differently?

Virtual Lesson 6: The Fast-forward Mode

Note to the teacher: In this lesson, students will learn about the last mode of their game controller: the fast-forward mode. They will learn what feelings are in the fast-forward mode and will be able to identify what the fast-forward mode looks, feels, and sounds like for them. Instructors can use the following language and prompts for the student assignment. Don't forget to include a copy of the Power Up controller!

Introduction to the Fast-forward Mode

We have discussed the home mode and the rewind forward mode and found the icons for them on our Power Up controllers. The last mode we will talk about is the fast-forward mode. In the fast-forward mode, you feel high levels of energy and as a result, struggle to be productive. Your heart might race, your palms might sweat, and you might fidget. Think of a game character who is using their special abilities, or boosters, but struggles to control them. The high energy levels results in them making mistakes and being unable to complete their mission. Feelings that might fall into this category include being frustrated, angry, excited. The fast-forward mode is found on the far right side of your controller.

Explore Rewind Mode Feelings

Use the internet or an online dictionary to search for feelings words. After you have made a list, go through it to identify feelings that you would experience in the fast-forward mode. For example, you might have words like *frustrated*, *angry*, etc. What feelings did you find that would represent being in the fast-forward mode? In the first part of your discussion post, write down your list of **five** feeling words that you identified as home mode feelings.

After you have listed these **five** feelings, pick one of the fast-forward mode feelings that you relate to the most. In the second part of your post, write about how you feel when you experience this emotion.

Answer the following questions in your discussion post:

- What does your face look like when you experience this feeling?

- How does your body move when you experience this feeling?

- What sounds might you make when you are experiencing this feeling?

- Do you enjoy the experience of this feeling?

After you are done, read at least **two** other discussion posts and comment on how they experience the feeling they selected. Do you experience it in the same way or differently?

Virtual Lesson 7: Triggers

Note to the teacher: In this lesson, students will focus on identifying their triggers for each of the three modes. Triggers can be people, places, situations, things, colors, or sensations that cause students to feel a specific emotion. Students will learn that one thing can trigger different people into different modes. Students will also learn the connection between feelings, thoughts, and behaviors.

If students share something concerning, you should check in with that particular student. If you feel uncomfortable, consult with a school counselor or an administrator on how to proceed. Use your judgment to determine if you should delete the post.

Instructors can use the following language and prompts for the student assignment.

Defining Triggers

Triggers are events, people, places, situations, or things that cause us to feel a specific way. Triggers can be both pleasant and unpleasant. Events, people, places, situations, or things can cause us to be triggered into any of the three modes we have discussed. For example, seeing my friends might trigger me into the home mode (feeling happiness and content). Not seeing my friends might trigger me into the rewind mode (experiencing sadness).

Everyone is different, and everyone has different triggers for each mode. For example, homework might trigger one person into rewind mode because with it, they experience boredom. It might trigger another person into fast-forward mode because they experience frustration when faced with homework.

All of our feelings, thoughts, and behaviors are connected. For example, if you do poorly on a math test, you might feel sad. Feeling sad might result in thoughts like, "I can't do this," "I'll never get a good math grade again," or "I wasted my time studying." Having these thoughts might cause you to decide not to study for your future tests. Feelings, thoughts, and behaviors are all connected.

Discover Your Triggers

Create a list of events, people, places, situations, or things that might trigger you into each mode. You do not need to explain why each thing triggers you into a specific mode. Present only the information that you are comfortable sharing with the entire class. You can make your own personal list at home of triggers that you don't feel comfortable sharing with everyone.

Pick **one** trigger off of your list to think about further. What feeling would you experience as a result of that trigger? What thoughts would come up? What behaviors might occur? Do this for each of the modes (home, fast-forward, rewind).

Create a Post

Post a list of at least **three** triggers for each mode and expand on **one** trigger for each mode, explaining why that specific thing causes you to experience that mode. Once you have uploaded your post, comment on **three** other posts. In your responses, you can **agree** that what your classmate discussed in detail also triggers you into that mode, or you can **disagree** and identify what mode it would have triggered you into and why. Remember, no reactions or triggers are wrong. They are unique to each person. Sometimes you will be triggered to have the same reaction as someone else, and sometimes you won't.

Virtual Lesson 8: Resilience

Note to the teacher: In this lesson, students will learn about resilience and about bouncing back from and overcoming challenges. Students will be given the metaphor of bending like an unwound paper clip or snapping like a wooden pencil as an image of how people can respond when presented with obstacles. Instructors can use the following language and prompts for the student assignment.

Defining Resilience

For this week's post, you will research and formulate your own definition of resilience. What is resilience? What does it look like?

Imagine you have a paper clip that you have unwound so that it is long and straight. If you held the paper clip on each end and, without letting go, forcefully pressed it against the edge of a countertop, what would happen to the paper clip? (It will likely bend.)

Now, imagine taking your pencil and doing the same thing. What would happen to the pencil? (It will likely break.)

When you encounter tough situations, would you rather be like the paper clip that bends and adapts or like the pencil that breaks and snaps when met with adversity?

Write a Story of Resilience

Research the background of a famous person that you look up to. Write a discussion post about a time when this person demonstrated resilience. What obstacle did they meet in life? How did they overcome that obstacle? What would have happened if they hadn't demonstrated resilience? What might their circumstances look like now?

After you have posted your discussion, respond to **one** other post. Before replying, read the post thoroughly and then research the famous person that the post refers to. Find another example of when this famous person demonstrated resilience. Describe this example in your response to your peers' post.

Think about how you are going to respond when you are met with difficult situations. Are you going to bend like the paper clip or snap like the pencil?

Virtual Lesson 9: Pause, Think, Play

Note to the teacher: In this lesson, students will learn their first self-management strategy of pause, think, play. With this strategy, students are taught to pause when they encounter a difficult situation, manage their emotions, think about their options, and then choose (or play) the option that is best for themselves and others.

Introduction to Self-Management Strategies

Self-management strategies help us to calm down our bodies and minds when we are experiencing difficult feelings. We are most likely to use our self-management strategies when we are in the rewind or fast-forward mode. We might be angry, frustrated, sad, jealous, excited, or experiencing some other difficult feeling. Self-management strategies help us move back to home mode so we are able to think through our actions.

The first self-management strategy we are going to learn is pause, think, play. The three steps to pause, think, play are as follows:

- **Pause:** Stop what you are doing.
- **Think:** Identify the options you have available to you.
- **Play:** Go with the best option for you and others.

Practice these steps this week when you experience a difficult feeling or situation.

Post about Using the Pause, Think, Play Strategy

After you have practiced this skill, answer the following questions in a discussion post:

- What happened that triggered you to use the pause, think, play skill?
- Was it easy to use?
- Were you able to follow the steps?
- Did you make a better decision because you used this skill?
- How did the situation turn out?
- How could the situation have turned out differently if you hadn't used this skill?

Respond to **two** peers' posts about their experience using the strategy. Congratulate them on using the skill successfully or encourage them to keep trying the skill.

Virtual Lesson 10: Deep Breathing, Mandalas, and Finger Mazes

Note to the teacher: Don't forget to attach the Power Up controller, Mandalas, and Finger Mazes worksheets for students to refer to. In this lesson students will learn three new self-management skills that they can use to reduce their energy levels. These skills will be most helpful when students find themselves in the fast-forward mode and need to return to the home mode.

Introduction to Deep Breathing, Mandalas, and Finger Mazes

In this lesson, we will practice three different strategies to reduce our energy levels: deep breathing, coloring mandalas, and tracing finger mazes. Deep breathing is a self-management strategy that helps us relax our bodies. For example, it can slow a racing heart, relax tense muscles, and help clear our heads. To learn the skill, we will practice using the controller on our Power Up board. On the bottom of the Power Up controller, there is a star. On the top, there is an image of a puff of breath. We will time our breaths in and breaths out by slowly tracing our finger around the edge of the controller. To begin, place your finger on the star at the bottom of the controller. As you trace the outline of the controller, moving up and to the left, you will breathe in slowly. The idea is to slow your breathing, so it is important not to trace the controller too quickly. When you reach the breath symbol at the top of the controller, slowly breathe out while you finish tracing the controller, moving down and to the right and back to the star. Repeat this pattern another two to four times or until you feel calmer and more relaxed.

The second calming strategy we will practice is coloring mandalas. Coloring mandalas is a good way to decrease anxiety and serves as a good distraction. Mandalas are generally in the shape of a circle and have symmetrical patterns within them. You can color the mandala however you would like, as there is no set formula. The idea is for you to focus on coloring the mandala in a manner that is relaxing to you. You can use a pre-drawn mandala, or you can create your own mandala to color. The attached Mandala worksheet can serve as a guide for you as you create your own mandala to color.

Finger mazes are another great way to shift our focus. Some finger mazes have dead ends and wrong turns while others only have one way to the center. Using finger mazes helps us shift our focus from a stressful situation to something that is nonthreatening and unrelated to the stressful situation. Use the attached Finger Mazes worksheet to practice following a finger maze. Take your finger, place it at the beginning pathway and trace the maze from start to finish.

Practice deep breathing, finger mazes, and coloring mandala strategies this week when you experience a difficult feeling or situation.

Discussion Posts

After you have practiced these skills, answer the following questions in a discussion post:

- Which skill was your favorite?

- What happened that triggered you to use this skill?

- Was it easy to use?

- Were you able to follow the steps?

- If you used the skill because you faced a difficult situation, were you able to make a better decision about how to respond to it because you used this skill?

- How did the situation turn out?

- How would the situation have turned out differently if you hadn't used this skill?

Respond to **two** peers' posts about their experience using a strategy. Congratulate them on using the skill successfully or encourage them to keep trying the skill.

Virtual Lesson 11: Progressive Muscle Relaxation and Mindfulness

Note to the teacher: In this lesson, students will learn two new self-management strategies they can use to reduce their energy levels. Don't forget to distribute the Progressive Muscle Relaxation worksheet before this lesson! You will also need a short video that walks students through how to practice mindfulness. It is recommended that you film yourself practicing this skill. Filming a video of you using mindfulness is preferable as it models to the student that adults they know use this skill. You can use the instructions in the face-to-face lessons to film the video. As an alternative, you can identify one or two short videos on YouTube for students to watch. Be sure to post the video(s) so students can see them.

Introduction to Progressive Muscle Relaxation

Progressive muscle relaxation is a self-management strategy in which we alternate between tensing and relaxing muscle groups in our bodies while breathing in and out. As we breathe in, we focus on the tension and stress in a particular muscle group while physically tensing those muscles. When we breathe out, we relax those muscles and imagine that the tension and stress in that muscle group is moved out of us with our breath. We continue until that group of muscles is relaxed and then move to the next muscles groups. We focus on each muscle group from our feet up to our head until all are relaxed.

Introduction to Mindfulness

Mindfulness is the practice of focusing on the present. When people are being mindful, they use their five senses to focus on the world around them. They don't worry about something that happened in the past or try to plan for the future. They practice being in the present moment and focusing on what is happening around them at that time. Practicing mindfulness helps improve our ability to manage stress and decreases symptoms of anxiety and depression.

Practice the Skills

Progressive muscle relaxation. Practice using progressive muscle relaxation using the attached visual of the different muscle groups as an aid. You will start with the muscles in your feet. As you breathe in, physically tense the muscles in your feet by scrunching them up and focus on any stress or tension they hold. As you breathe out, relax your feet and imagine any of the tension and stress you feel leaving your feet with your breath out. Repeat with several breaths until your feet are relaxed, then move to the next muscle group on your Progressive Muscle Relaxation worksheet. Repeat the process, moving from your feet to your head.

Mindfulness. After you have practiced progressive muscle relaxation, watch the guided mindfulness video your teacher posted. Listen to the prompting on the video and practice being mindful.

Practice these strategies this week when you experience a difficult feeling or situation.

Discussion Post about Using the Skills

After you have practiced these skills, answer the following questions in a discussion post:

- Which skill was your favorite?
- What happened that triggered you to use this skill?
- Was it easy to use?
- Were you able to follow the steps?
- Did you make a better decision because you used this skill?
- How did the situation turn out?
- How would the situation have turned out differently if you hadn't used this skill?

Respond to **two** peers' posts about their experience using a strategy. Congratulate them on using the skill successfully or encourage them to keep trying the skill.

Virtual Lesson 12: Worry Box, Reframing, Wall Push-ups, and Stretching

Note to the teacher: In this lesson, students will learn four new self-management strategies they can use to improve their mood and increase their energy levels. These strategies are creating a worry box (where they can leave their worries), using movement (wall push-ups and stretching), and reframing (taking a negative thought and seeing it in a positive manner).

Don't forget to attach the Stretching worksheet.

Introduction to Worry Boxes, Reframing, and Movement

In this lesson, we will learn four new self-management strategies. You will create a worry box to hold your worries, learn how to reframe negative thoughts and situations, and practice movement and exercise through wall push-ups and stretching. These self-management techniques can help reduce anxiety and depression and improve overall mood.

Create a Worry Box

For our first activity, we are going to create a worry box. To start, write down on a piece of paper the things that are worrying you. Leave enough space between each worry so that you can cut them out and separate them.

After you have written down each worry, cut or rip the paper so that each one is on its own piece of paper. After you have done this, find a small box, hat, or other container that you can use to keep the slips of paper with your worries. If you are able, decorate the box or container. Put the slips of paper in your container, and when you do so, imagine that you are letting that container temporarily hold your worries for you. While the worry box won't get rid of your worries, it can hold them while you focus on what you need to get done at the moment, giving you a break from carrying those worries, and as a result increases your energy levels.

Reframe a Thought

Get out a piece of paper and write down a negative thought you are currently having. After you have written it down, crumple up the paper into a small ball. After you have done that, uncrumple the ball of paper and smooth it out. (It is OK if the paper rips.) Put this paper to the side. Get out a fresh piece of paper. Write down the same thought, but change it so that it is now positive. For example, instead of thinking "I *have* to read for thirty minutes today" think "I *get* to read about how to make delicious cookies today."

Set this piece of paper next to the crumpled up paper. Which one looks better? Which one sounds better? When you have negative thoughts, does it make you feel like a crumpled and ripped piece of paper or a fresh and crisp piece of paper? When you have positive thoughts, does it make you feel like a crumpled and ripped piece of paper or a fresh and crisp piece of paper?

Changing thoughts on an event or experience from negative to positive ones is called "reframing." You are taking a negative thought about an experience and viewing that experience again in a positive manner, as if you were putting a nice new frame on it.

Reframing is a skill that takes a lot of practice. To try the skill, you can reframe the following thoughts:

- No one likes me.

- I'm not good at anything.

- I'm not popular.

- Write your own example to reframe.

Save your answers and include them in your discussion post for the lesson.

Try Wall Push-ups and Stretching

For our last two strategies, let's get moving! Exercise can help lift our mood and give us energy. One exercise we can try is stretching. Stretching is a great way to relax your muscles and help you shift your focus from negative or worrisome thoughts. Use the Power Up stretching worksheet to identify a stretch you would like to try. Do not do any stretches you aren't sure how to do properly. If the stretch hurts, **stop**. Stretching shouldn't hurt.

The second way to incorporate movement is to do wall push-ups. To practice, find a sturdy wall and place your palms flat against the surface with your arms extended out straight in front of you. Lean in toward the wall, bending your elbows, as if you were doing a push-up. Try to do as many wall push-ups as you can. Remember, the exercise shouldn't hurt. If it does, **stop**.

Practice these strategies this week when you experience a difficult feeling or situation.

Post about the Skills You Have Practiced

In the first part of your post, list your positive reframings of the negative thoughts listed above.

After you have had a chance to practice the skills, answer the following questions in a discussion post:

- Which skill was your favorite?

- Was it easy to use?

- Were you able to follow the steps?

- What happened that triggered you to use this skill?

- Did you make a better decision because you used this skill?

- How did the situation turn out?

- How would the situation have turned out differently if you hadn't used this skill?

Respond to **two** peers' posts about their experience using a strategy. Congratulate them on using the skill successfully or encourage them to keep trying the skill. Read their reframed thoughts. Give them at least one other way they can reframe their own thought.

Virtual Lesson 13: Goal Setting and Time Management

Note to the teacher: In this lesson, students will learn about goal setting and time management. Students will identify a goal they would like to work on, break it down into smaller steps they can take to achieve their goal, set deadlines, and identify times they are going to take to work towards their goal. Don't forget to attach the Goal Setting worksheet!

Introduction to Goal Setting and Time Management

In this lesson, we will practice how to set goals for ourselves. To begin, write down one short-term goal you would like to accomplish. You can either print the attached Goal Setting worksheet, or you can copy down the worksheet prompts onto a blank piece of paper. A short-term goal is a goal that you would like to achieve in the near future. Getting a good grade on a test next week or reaching the next level in a game you are playing by tonight is an example of short-term goals. Next, write down one of your long-term goals. A long-term goal is a goal that you would like to accomplish in the next several months or years. For example, graduating from elementary school, joining a sports team in middle school, or going to college are long-term goals.

Create a Plan to Reach a Goal

Once you have identified these two goals, pick one goal that you would like to focus on. This will be referred to as your "big" goal. Consider your "big" goal. What are three smaller goals you can break this goal into and that would help you reach your big goal? When should you achieve each of these small goals? What is your deadline for each? Deadlines refer to when you would like to have the goal accomplished. Write your responses on the Goal Setting worksheet.

    See an example of goal setting below.

Long-term goal: Learn how to draw.

    Smaller goals:

1. Research a drawing book that will help me learn to draw. Deadline: one week from now.

2. Order the book I have chosen and study it. Deadline: two weeks from now.

3. Start practicing drawing for 30 minutes each day. Deadline: three weeks from now.

Set Time Aside to Achieve Your Goal

After you have broken up your big goal into smaller goals and set deadlines for the smaller goals, consider your day. When are you going to work on these smaller goals? On the back of your Goal Setting worksheet, write down each hour of the day, and next to each hour, write down what you typically do during that time. For example, at 6:00 p.m. I make and eat dinner. At 7:00 p.m., I watch TV.

Now that you have written down how you spend your time each day, consider when you will work on your goals. This might require you to decrease your time doing something else. Once you have decided when you are going to work toward your goal, cross out the other activity and add working on your goal to your calendar.

Start putting your plan into practice.

Create a Discussion Post

After you have practiced the goal setting skill, answer the following questions in a discussion post:

- What goal are you working toward right now? This goal can be different than the one you worked on in this lesson's activity. Make sure you are comfortable with the entire class reading your responses.

- What are some smaller goals you can break your "big" goal into?

- How do you plan to manage your time in order to achieve your goals?

- What are you going to add to your schedule?

- What are you going to remove from (or decrease time spent on) your schedule?

- How do you feel about making these adjustments to your schedule?

Respond to **two** peers' posts. Give each peer **one** suggestion on another small goal they could work on that would be helpful for them in reaching their big goal. Give them encouragement on their way to meeting their goals!

Virtual Lesson 14: Social Supports

Note to the teacher: In this lesson, students will work to identify those individuals in their support systems. These individuals might include family and friends, school supports, or community supports. Students will also explore how those individuals support them, and how they can support then in return.

Introduction to Social Support Systems

Social support systems are made up of those individuals in our lives who help us when things are tough. Social support systems can include family and friends, people at school, and people in the community. Friends and family members that are in your support system can include people in your immediate or extended family. They also include your close friends. These are people who are there for you and people you can trust.

School members that are in your support system might include your teacher, counselor, administrators, or another trustworthy adult at the school. These are people you can talk to and ask for help. Community members in your support system are people in the community that can help you. These might include people from your after school program, a coach, your neighbors, or church members. These are people you know are invested in your well-being.

Discussion

Answer the following questions in a discussion post:

- What family members are in your social support system?
- What school members are in your social support system?
- What community members are in your social support system?

Respond to at least **two** peers' posts about their support systems. Look for people that other students listed in their support system that you hadn't considered. Could these kinds of people be supports for you as well?

Virtual Lesson 15: Empathy and Acts of Kindness

Note to the teacher: In this lesson, students are going to learn about empathy and its importance. They will also identify ways they can show empathy and kindness.

Introduction to Empathy

This week, you are going to learn about empathy and engage in acts of kindness. Empathy is understanding and caring about what others are feeling. Empathy is important because it helps us see others' perspectives and builds social connections and support. It is important to show others that we care about them, and we will hopefully get the same kindness in return.

Acts of kindness can include things like doing your chores without being asked, walking the neighbor's dog when asked, helping carry in the groceries, letting your sibling play with your toys, or making your friend some cookies.

For this lesson activity, you will do one act of kindness for three different people.

After completing your kind acts, answer the following questions in a discussion post:

- Why is empathy important?
- What would the world look like if we didn't have empathy?
- What was one of your kind acts?
- How did you feel before you engaged in your act of kindness? How did you feel after your kind act?
- How do you think the other person felt before your act of kindness? How do you think they felt after?
- Why do you think it is important to show others kindness?

Respond to at least **two** peers' posts. Praise them for their kind act and then comment on their responses.

Virtual Lesson 16: Charging Batteries

Note to the teacher: In this lesson, students will be introduced to the metaphor of a recharging battery to show the impact kindness can have on ourselves and others. As we have positive interactions with others, our batteries get fully charged. As we have negative interactions with others, our batteries can become drained.

Introduction to Charging Batteries

Imagine that people had a battery that represented how they were feeling at that moment. If their battery was full, they had energy, were happy, and felt satisfied overall. If their battery was empty, they had very little energy, felt down, and didn't feel good about themselves.

Now imagine that we could charge these batteries by being kind to people and that we could charge other people's batteries by being kind to them. The kinder we were the more everyone benefited.

Activity

For this exercise, you will do one act of kindness for three different people this week and then create a post about what you did.

Answer the following questions in your discussion post:

- What was one of your kind acts?

- How did you feel before your kind act?

- How did you feel after your kind act?

- Do you feel like your battery became even a little bit more charged after your kind act?

- How do you think the other person felt before your kind act?

- How do you think the other person felt after your kind act?

- Do you think the person's battery became even a little bit more charged because of your kind act?

Respond to at least **two** peers' posts. Give them praise for their kind act and then comment on their responses.

Virtual Lesson 17: Working in a Group

Note to the teacher: In this lesson, students will learn about the different roles that an individual can play in a group: CEO, lawyer, accountant, and entertainer. They will learn the strengths and weaknesses of each role and determine which role they play in a group. Students will identify areas of improvement.

Please distribute the Group Roles Assessment worksheet and the Group Roles worksheet in advance of this lesson.

Introduction to Working in Groups

There will be many times throughout your life when you will need to work in a group. You might need to work in groups virtually or in middle school, high school, or in your workplace. Working in groups can be challenging. Some people enjoy it while others don't.

In this lesson, you will complete the Group Roles Assessment worksheet to determine which group role you are most like. After you have taken the assessment, read the role descriptions in the Group Roles worksheet.

Discussion Post

Focus on the role that you score the highest in and answer the following questions in a discussion post:

- What group role did you score highest on in the assessment?
- Do you agree with the role you got?
- What are your strengths when working in a group?
- What are your weaknesses when working in a group?
- How can you improve upon one of your weaknesses when working in a group?

Respond to at least **two** peers' posts. Read their comments how they are going to improve upon their weakness and give them some additional ideas.

Virtual Lesson 18: Respectfully Disagreeing

Note to the teacher: In this lesson, students will learn about the importance of respectfully disagreeing with others. They will also create a formula that they can use to respectfully disagree.

Respectfully Disagreeing

Learning to respectfully disagree with others is an important skill. Being able to express your own opinions, thoughts, and ideas without intentionally hurting anyone's feelings is vital to having productive conversations.

In this exercise, brainstorm or look up several different ways in which people can respectfully disagree with others. Create a formula you can refer to when respectfully disagreeing with someone. Your formula should include specific phrases that you can say and any postures, gestures, or facial expressions that can be used with the phrase you created.

Answer the following questions in a discussion post:

- What is your formula for respectfully disagreeing with someone?

- Why do you think this is an important skill to have?

- What nonverbal cues can you use to respectfully disagree with someone?

Respond to at least **two** peers' posts. Comment on their formula for how they would respectfully disagree with others.

Virtual Lesson 19: Qualities in a Friend

Note to the teacher: In this lesson students will work to identify what qualities are important to them in a friend, and what qualities they have to offer in a friendship. Don't forget to attach the Qualities in a Friend worksheet!

Introduction to Qualities in a Friend

Everyone has ideas on what a quality friend is. Sometimes people value honesty over all else, and sometimes people value loyalty over all else. There are many different qualities we might value.

Assignment

For lesson, review the list on the Qualities in a Friend worksheet. Pick the four most important qualities you would like in a friend. Label them in order of importance, with 1 being the most important one.

Answer the following questions in a discussion post:

- What quality was the most important to you? Why?

- What other qualities did you choose? Why?

- What other qualities would you add to your list? Why?

Respond to at least **three** peers' posts. Comment on the qualities they chose and why you might agree or disagree that those are important qualities. If you are disagreeing remember to respectfully disagree!

Virtual Lesson 20: "I" Statements

Note to the teacher: In this lesson students will learn how to communicate their wants and needs by using "I" statements. Students will practice using "I" statements.

Introduction to "I" Statements

When communicating with others, it is important that we effectively communicate how we are feeling and what we need from the other person to resolve issues. If we aren't clear about exactly what upset us and exactly what we need from the other person, the other person might not know how to respond to us. Not communicating how we are feeling can lead to hurt feelings and to people lashing out or withdrawing.

To practice effectively communicating your feelings, you can use the formula below, which is also referred to as an "I" statement.

I feel _____

when _____.

I need _____.

In the first blank after "I feel," you name what you are feeling. (To help with this, you can think back to the feelings vocabulary words from the self-awareness lessons.) The more specific you are the better.

In the second blank after "when," you state what made you feel that way. Again, you should be specific. If the other person is unclear on what upset you, they might unintentionally upset you by doing it again.

In the last blank after "I need," you say what you need to feel better or resolve the issue. While you might not always get the resolution you want, expressing your needs gives you voice.

When using "I" statements, it is also important that we don't accuse or blame the other person. In order to avoid this, we should keep from using the word *you*. We can use "I" statements not only to express anger or frustration but also to thank someone and take the time to appreciate them when they do something we like or that we think is positive. It's important that we express when we like what someone did so they know to do it again.

The following are examples of "I" statements:

- I feel angry when I'm called names. I need people to use kind words.

- I feel frustrated when I'm doing math homework. I need assistance with completing it.

- I feel happy when dinner is made for me. I need help in getting dinner!

Assignment

Use "I" statements three times this week and answer the following questions in a discussion post:

- Who did you use the "I" statement with?
- What did you say?
- How did you feel before you used the statement?
- How did you feel after you used the statement?
- How do you think the situation would have turned out differently if you didn't use "I" statements?

Virtual Lesson 21: Social Skills Part 1

Note to the teacher: In this lesson, students will learn the first three social skills represented by the acronym CREATE. These are compliments (C), respecting personal space (R) and eye contact (E). Students will be encouraged to practice these skills.

Introduction to CREATE

Whether we are meeting someone new or talking to an old friend, it is important that we have a toolbox of social skills we can use. Social skills help us to build connections with others, make new friends, maintain current friendships, and help us actively engage in conversations. When we are invested in what we are saying and what the other person is saying, we are more likely to build stronger connections with others.

In the Power Up program, we are going to learn six social skills. The word *CREATE* is an easy way to remember them because each letter represents one of the skills. The first three social skills we will cover are compliments (C), respecting personal space (R), and eye contact (E):

Compliments. When you are interacting with others, you should say nice things to them. You can tell them you like something about their appearance or you can compliment something they did. Compliments make other people feel good, which also make us feel good.

Respecting personal space. When you are talking to or interacting with others, you should make sure that you aren't too close to them. If you invade their personal space, they could feel uncomfortable, angry, or scared. To help gauge how much personal space someone needs, you can pretend that everyone has a Hula-Hoop around them. The Hula-Hoop acts as a barrier, and you shouldn't enter the space in someone else's Hula-Hoop unless you are given permission.

Eye contact. When you are talking with someone, you should look that person in the eyes. This lets the speaker know that you are listening to what is being said. This also keeps you involved in the conversation. If you aren't looking at the speaker, it's easier to become distracted.

Making eye contact can be awkward and uncomfortable at first. The more you practice, the better you will get at it. You should know, too, that in some cultures, it is rude to look others in the eye. If you find that someone doesn't look you in the eye, don't assume that this person is not listening. It is also OK to tell others that in your culture you don't look people in the eye when speaking.

Assignment

Practice the skills of giving compliments, respecting personal space, and making eye contact this week.

Answer the following questions in a discussion post:

- Which skill was the easiest to use?

- Which skill was the hardest to use?

- Did you notice a difference in your conversations when you used these skills?

- Did you notice a difference in your relationships with your family and friends when you used these skills?

Respond to at least **two** peers' posts. Encourage them to continue to use skills they felt were hard and praise them for skills they found easy to use. You can always ask for tricks or tips on skills that you found hard to do as well.

Virtual Lesson 22: Social Skills Part 2

Note to the teacher: In this lesson, students will learn the last three social skills represented by the CREATE acronym. These are asking questions (A), taking turns (T), and exhibiting genuine interest (E).

Social Skills Part 2

In this lesson, we are going to learn about three social skills that are represented by the last three letters in the acronym CREATE. Remember, *C* stands for compliments, *R* is respecting personal space, and *E* is eye contact. The social skills we'll cover for this lesson are asking questions (the *A*), taking turns (the *T*), and exhibiting genuine interest (the last *E*).

Asking questions. When you talk with others, it is important to ask questions. You can ask questions about them or ask about the topic being discussed. You shouldn't change the topic of the conversation, but enhance it instead. Showing interest allows other people to share more about what interests them and increases the chances that they will ask you about topics that interest you.

Taking turns. When talking with others, you should each get your fair share of talking time. If you give others in the conversation time to share their thoughts and opinions, they will likely show you the same respect by asking you to share your thoughts.

Exhibiting genuine interest. When you exhibit genuine interest in other people while they are talking, you are allowing them to talk about something that is important to them. This allows you to build a stronger connection with them, and gives you the opportunity to learn something new.

Assignment

Practice the social skills of asking questions, taking turns, and exhibiting genuine interest this week.

Answer the following questions in a discussion post:
- Which skill was the easiest to use?
- Which skill was the hardest to use?
- Did you notice a difference in your conversations when you used these skills?
- Did you notice a difference in your relationships with your family and friends when you used these skills?

Respond to at least **two** peers' posts. Encourage their progress in using the skills they felt were hard. Praise them for their work on skills they found easy to use. You can always ask for tricks or tips on using skills that you found hard as well.

Virtual Lesson 23: Role Models

Note to the teacher: Instead of having students put the link to the interview in their discussion post right away, you can ask them to email it to you to review for appropriateness. After you approve the video, they can make their discussion post with the video and answers to the questions.

In this lesson, students will watch an interview with a famous person that they look up to. As they are watching the interview, they will be on the lookout to determine which social skills the famous person was good at and which social skills they could improve on.

Introduction to Role Models

Find a short video clip of a celebrity or famous person that you look up to. Watch the clip and look for when the person uses CREATE social skills (giving **c**ompliments, **r**especting personal space, making **e**ye contact, **a**sking questions, **t**aking turns, and **e**xhibiting genuine interest). Remember, this video clip should be appropriate for school and appropriate for the entire class to watch.

Activity

In your discussion post, include the video clip and answer the following questions:

- Did the celebrity give compliments?
- Did the celebrity respect personal space?
- Did the celebrity make eye contact?
- Did the celebrity ask questions?
- Did the celebrity take turns speaking?
- Did the celebrity exhibit genuine interest?
- Which skill was their strongest?
- Which skill was their weakest?

Respond to at least **two** peers' posts. Watch the videos they selected and share your thoughts on which of the person's social skills were the strongest and which skills were the weakest in the interview.

Virtual Lesson 24: The Brain

Note to the teacher: In this lesson, students will learn about two different parts of their brain: the prefrontal cortex (responsible for problem-solving and critical thinking) and the amygdala (the threat-detection center). They will learn how these two parts of the brain are connected.

Introduction to the Brain

Using our problem-solving and critical thinking skills is important to making responsible decisions. The part of the brain called the prefrontal cortex is responsible for our higher-order thinking. We use this part of the brain to solve problems and think through situations logically.

Our amygdala is the threat-sensing area of our brains. Our amygdala is constantly searching for threats in order to keep us safe. When we feel threatened, our amygdala overrides our prefrontal cortex and releases adrenaline, which prepares us to fight or run in order to survive.

Our brain doesn't always know the difference between a life-threatening situation and one that only seems threatening. It doesn't always know the difference between our response to what's dangerous or our response when we are frustrated about something like being stuck in traffic. Our amygdala has the same reaction. This can be a problem because we don't always have access to the problem-solving part of our brain when we might be in challenging situations.

When we are presented with a situation in which we might become frustrated, angry, or experience any other unpleasant feeling, it is important to remember to use a self-management strategy such as mindfulness, deep breathing, or movement. This tells the amygdala that we are not in danger, and it allows us access to our prefrontal cortex so we can think through our decisions.

Activity

Read through the following questions in which you consider the differences between using your amygdala to solve problems and using your prefrontal cortex to solve problems.

Answer the following questions in a discussion post:

- Write about a time that you used your amygdala to make a decision rather than your prefrontal cortex. Remember to share only things you are comfortable with all of your peers' knowing. How did this situation turn out?

- If you had used a self-management strategy in this situation, how might the situation have turned out differently?

- Write about a time that you used your prefrontal cortex to make a decision rather than your amygdala. Remember to share only things you are comfortable with all of your peers' knowing. How did this situation turn out?

- If you had used your amygdala to solve the problem instead, how might the situation have turned out differently?
- Did the situation in which you used your amygdala or the prefrontal cortex to solve the problem turn out better?

Respond to **two** peers' posts. Name **one** benefit to using their prefrontal cortex in the situation they wrote about.

Virtual Lesson 25: MAGIC

Note to the teacher: In this lesson, students will learn the first two steps of the decision-making process. There are five steps in total, and they are represented by the acronym MAGIC. Students will learn that the M stands for managing emotions and the A stands for assessing the situation for possible solutions.

Introduction to MAGIC

When making decisions, you can use the acronym MAGIC to guide you. It spells out the steps in responsible decision-making. The *M* in MAGIC stands for managing emotions. When you encounter a problem that you need to solve, you should manage your emotions first. Everyone does this differently. You should use the self-management technique that works best for you. Remember, the self-management skills we have learned are pause, think, play; deep breathing; coloring mandalas; tracing finger mazes; progressive muscle relaxation; reframing; placing worries into a worry box; wall push-ups; and stretching.

The second step in the MAGIC decision-making process is *A* or assessing the situation for possible solutions. Before we make a decision we should consider all of the solutions we have available to us. Every problem has many solutions, and we should make a list of all of the possible solutions before deciding what we want to do.

Activity

Answer the following questions in a discussion post:
- What is a problem that you or someone you know is faced with right now? (Remember, only share information you are comfortable with everyone knowing.)

- How are you going to manage your emotions when thinking about and responding to this problem?

- What are all of the possible solutions to the problem?

Respond to **three** peers' posts. Give them ideas for other possible solutions they haven't considered.

Virtual Lesson 26: MAGIC Part 2

Note to the teacher: In this lesson, students will learn the last three steps in the MAGIC decision-making process. These steps are gathering the pros and cons (G), identifying bias (I), and choosing the best decision for yourself and others (C).

MAGIC Part 2

In this lesson, we will learn the steps in the responsible decision-making process known as MAGIC. Remember, the *M* in MAGIC stands for managing emotions. The *A* stands for assessing the situation for possible solutions. We are going to learn about the *G*, *I*, and *C* now.

The *G* stands for gathering the pros and cons of your top two to three possible options. Pros are likely positive outcomes of choosing a particular option or solution. (They are things or events you would like to have happen.) The cons are the likely negative outcomes of choosing a particular option or solution. (They are things or events you would not like to have happen.) There are pros and cons to all possible solutions, so it's important to consider all of them when making a decision.

The *I* in MAGIC stands for identify your bias. When you identify your bias, you consider how your previous experiences may influence your judgments in the decision-making process. For example, if you like to listen to country music and you were asked to pick the music for a school dance, you would be biased about the type of music you'd want to choose. Look at your top couple of solutions. What previous experiences have you had that might create a bias in your decision-making?

Lastly, the final step *C* stands for choose. After you have all of the information, you can choose which solution would be best for you and all others involved.

Activity

Answer the following questions in a discussion post:
- Think about the problem you discussed in your last post. Pick your top two or three solutions. What are the pros of each solution? What are the cons of each solution?
- What pre-existing bias do you have?
- What is the best solution for you?
- What is the best solution for others involved?

Respond to **three** peers' posts. Suggest pros and cons that they might not have considered. Name at least **one** pro for the solution they ultimately chose.

Virtual Lesson 27: Responsible Decision-Making: Understanding Rules

Note to the teacher: In this lesson, students will learn the importance of rules. Students will identify rules they do and don't agree with and offer an explanation as to why they do or don't agree with those rules.

Introduction to the Purpose of Rules

Many rules are in place to keep us safe. While we might not agree with all rules, there is a reason they were put in place in the first place.

Activity

Answer the following questions in a discussion post:

- Name two rules you agree with and why you think they are important. These can be rules at home, at school, or in the community. For example, one rule people might think is important is to keep our hands, feet, and all other objects to ourselves and away from others because this keeps people physically safe.

- Name two rules you don't agree with and explain why you don't agree with them and why you think they were put into place.

Respond to at least **two** peers' posts. In your response, give additional reasons why the rules your peers don't agree with were put into place.

Virtual Lesson 28: Rules for My Small Country

Note to the teacher: In this lesson, students will work to create rules for a small country. They will be asked to justify their rules and consider the short-term and long-term consequences of those rules.

Discussion Post

Answer the following questions in a discussion post:

- If you were running a small nation, what would your top 10 rules be?

- Why did you choose these rules?

- What are the short-term and long-term consequences of these rules?

Try to be creative in making your rules! For example, one rule might be, "No one can work after 3 P.M."

Respond to at least **three** peers' posts. Review the rules they created for their small country. Do you agree with these rules? Why or why not? What might some unintended consequences be of these rules? For instance, in our example rule, if no one worked past 3 p.m. then people wouldn't be able to go to restaurants to eat dinner or get medical care later in the day.

Virtual Lesson 29: Researching

Note to the teacher: In this lesson, students will research a social and emotional learning skill that hasn't been taught yet and create a plan to teach this skill to the class.

Introduction to Researching SEL Skills

Note to the teacher: Make sure each student identifies a different skill to teach. If students appear stuck, you can give the bulleted suggestions below:

There are so many valuable social and emotional learning skills. We have learned many of them, but there are still a lot more to learn! In this lesson, you will research a social and emotional learning skill that you think is valuable to know. You can pick a skill you want to teach or ask the teacher for ideas. Be sure to email your teacher for approval to take on the skill you want.

You will be responsible for teaching the class this skill next week. Once you have received approval to teach the skill you picked, spend time creating a presentation to teach others how to perform the skill. For your presentation, you can create a video, PowerPoint presentation, or flyer with step-by-step instructions on how to master the skill. Get creative!

- Apologizing
- Asking for help
- Showing forgiveness
- Perspective taking
- Having patience
- Giving praise
- Sharing
- Showing sportsmanship
- Accepting "no"
- Giving constructive criticism
- Receiving constructive criticism
- Being flexible
- Staying on task
- Not giving into peer pressure
- Demonstrating the importance of body language
- Being reliable
- Being trustworthy
- Demonstrating optimism
- Demonstrating organizational skills
- Being compassionate

- Being understanding
- Showing integrity
- Demonstrating self-discipline
- Showing time management skills
- Encouraging others
- Sharing ideas
- Celebrating success
- Following directions
- Helping others

Virtual Lesson 30: Presenting the Skill

Note to the teacher: In this lesson, students will present the skill they researched. Students will also learn new skills from their peers. After all students have presented, thank them for their participation in this program and praise them for all the progress they have made!

Presenting Your Skill

In this lesson, you will present your skill to the class in a post. Make sure you include a couple steps to follow in performing the skill in order to fully master it. To teach the skill, you can create a video, PowerPoint presentation, or poster to present your skill.

Respond to at least **five** peers' posts. Thank them for presenting the skill and give them an example of a time that you will try this skill.

References

Adeyemo, D. A. (2007). Moderating influence of emotional intelligence on the link between academic self-efficacy and achievement of university students. *Psychology Developing Societies, 19*, 199–211.

Ahn, J. N., Hu, D., & Vega, M. (2020). "Do as I do, not as I say": Using social learning theory to unpack the impact of role models on students' outcomes in education. *Social and Personality Psychology Compass.* https://doi.org/10.1111/spc3.12517

Aldwin, C. (2007). *Stress, coping, and development: An integrative perspective* (2nd ed.). Guilford Press.

Alego, J. (2001). The labyrinth: A brief Introduction to its history, meaning and use. *Quest, 89*(1), 24–25.

Alvarez, T., Bunei, M., Arst, A., Cormack, K., Allen, A., & Noah, E. (2018). *How anger affects the brain and body* [Infographic]. Better Health Channel. https://www.nicabm.com/how-anger-affects-the-brain-and-body-infographic/

American Psychiatric Association. (2017). Diagnostic and statistical manual of mental disorders: DSM-5. Arlington, VA.

Apostol S., Zaharescu L., Alexe I. (2013). Gamification of learning and educational games. *International Scientific Conference eLearning and software for Education, 2*(67).

Arguedas, M., Daradoumis, T., & Xhafa, F. (2016). Analyzing how emotion awareness influences students' motivation, engagement, self-regulation, and learning outcome. *Journal of Educational Technology & Society, 19*(2), 87–103.

Aspinwall, L. (2011). Future-oriented thinking, proactive coping, and the management of potential threats to health and well-being. *The Oxford hand-book of stress, health, and coping,* 1–35. https://doi.org/10.1093/oxfordhb/9780195375343.013.0017

Awan, H., Ahmed, K., & Zulqarnain, W. (2015). Impact of project manager's soft leadership skills on project success. *Journal of Poverty, Investment and Development, 8*(2), 37–89.

Bandura, A. (1977). *Social Learning Theory.* Prentice-Hall.

Bandura, A. (1989). Human agency in social cognitive theory. *American Psychologist, 44*(9), 1175–1184. https://doi.org/10.1037/0003-066X.44.9.1175

Bandura, A., & Wood, R. (1989). Effect of perceived controllability and performance standards on self-regulation of complex decision-making. *Journal of Personality and Social Psychology, 56,* 805–814.

Bambara, L. M., Cole, C. L., Kunsch, C., Tsai, S., & Ayad, E. (2016). A peer-mediated intervention to improve the conversational skills of high school students with Autism Spectrum Disorder. *Research In Autism Spectrum Disorders, 27,* 29–43. https://doi.org/10.1016/j.rasd.2016.03.003

Barchard, K. (2013). Does emotional intelligence assist in the prediction of academic success? *Educational and Psychological Measurement,* 840–858.

Belfield, C., Bowden, B., Klapp, A., Levin, H., Shand, R., & Zander, S. (2015). The economic value of social and emotional learning. Retrieved from https://www.cfchildren.org/wp-content/uploads/research/sel-columbia-univ-benefit-cost-report-2015.pdf

Bi, Y., & Liu, Y. (2019). Creating mandalas reduces social anxiety in college students. *Social Behavior and Personality: An International journal, 47*(10), 1–10. https://doi.org/10.2224/sbp.8410

Blair, C., & Diamond, A. (2008). Biological processes in prevention and intervention: The promotion of self-regulation as a means of preventing school failure. *Development and Psychopathology, 20*(3), 899–911. https://doi.org/ 10.1017/s0954579408000436

Boulton, M. J., Don, J., & Boulton, L. (2011). Predicting children's liking of school from their peer relationships. *Social Psychology of Education, 14,* 489–501.

Boylan, F., Barblett, L., & Knaus, M. (2018). Early childhood teachers' perspectives of growth mindset : Developing agency in children. *Australasian Journal of Early Childhood, 43*(3), 16–24. https://doi.org/10.23965/AJEC.43.3.02

Brugniaux, J. V., Marley, C. J., Hodson, D. A., New, K. J., & Bailey, D. M. (2014). Acute exercise stress reveals cerebrovascular benefits associated with moderate gains in cardiorespiratory fitness. *Journal of*

Cerebral Blood Flow and Metabolism, 34(12), 1873–6. https://doi.org/10.1038/jcbfm.2014.142

Cammorta, J., & Romero, A. (2006). A critically compassionate intellectualism for Lantino/a students. *Multicultural Education,* 16–23.

Cardaciotto, L., Herbert, J., Forman, E., Moitra, E., & Farrow, V. (n.d). The assessment of present-moment awareness and acceptance: The Philadelphia Mindfulness Scale. *Assessment, 15*(2), 204–223. https://doi.org/10.1177/1073191107311467

CASEL. (2018). *Core SEL Competencies.* CASEL. Retrieved from https://casel.org/core-competencies/

Casey, B. J., Giedd, J. N., Thomas, K. M. (2000). Decision-making and problem-solving in adolescents who deliberately self-harm. *Biological Psychology 54,* 241–257.

Claessens, B. C., Van Eerde, W., Rutte, C. G., & Roe, R. A. (2007). A review of the time management literature. *Personnel Review, 36,* 255–276.

Cohen, S. (2004). Social relationships and health. *The American Psychologist, 59,* 676–684. https://doi.org/10.1037/0003-066X.59.8.676

Collie, R. J., Shapka, J. D., & Perry, N. E. (2011). Predicting teacher commitment: The impact of school climate and social-emotional learning. *Psychology in the Schools, 48*(10), 1034–1048. https://doi.org/10.1002/pits.20611

Damon, W., Lerner, R. M., & Eisenberg, N. (2006). *Handbook of child psychology: Social, emotional, and personality development* (6th ed.). New York: Wiley.

Davidson, R. J. (2002). Anxiety and affective style: role of prefrontal cortex and amygdala. *Biological Psychiatry, 51*(1), 68–80. https://doi.org/10.1016/s0006-3223(01)01328-2

Davis, A., Solberg, V. S., de Baca, C., & Gore, T. H. (2014). Use of social emotional learning skills to predict future academic success and progress toward graduation. *Journal of Education for Students Placed at Risk, 19*(3–4), 169–182. https://doi.org/10.1080/10824669.2014.972506

Denham, S. A. (2006). Social-emotional competence as support for school readiness: What is it and how do we asses it? *Early Education and Development, 17,* 57–89.

DeRosier, M. E., & Lloyd, S. W. (2011). The impact of children's social adjustment on academic outcomes. *Reading & Writing Quarterly: Overcoming Learning Difficulties, 27,* 25–47.

Dicheva, D., Dichev, C., Agre, G., & Angelova, G. (2015). Gamification in education: A systematic mapping study. *Educational Technology & Society, 18*(3), 75–88.

Dierdorff, E., Fisher, D., & Rubin, R. (2019). The power of percipience: Consequences of self-awareness in teams on team-level functioning and performance. *Journal of Management, 45*(7), 2891–2919. https://doi.org/10.1177/0149206318774622

Dishion, T., & Tipsord, J. (2011). Peer contagion in child and adolescent social and emotional development. *Annual Review of Psychology, 62*(1), 189–214. https://doi.org/10.1146/annurev.psych.093008.100412

Durlak, J. A., Domitrovich, C. E., Weissberg, R. P., & Gullotta, T. P. (2015). *Handbook of social and emotional learning: research and practice.* Guilford Press.

Durlak, J. A., Weissberg, R. P., Dymnicki, A. B., Taylor, R. D., & Schellinger, K. B. (2011). The impact of enhancing students' social and emotional learning: A meta-analysis of school-based universal interventions. *Child Development, 82*(1), 405–432. https://doi.org/10.1111/j.1467-8624.2010.01564.x

Dweck, C. S. (2016). Mindset: The new psychology of success (Updated edition). Penguin Random House.

Dweck, C. S. (1999). Self-theories: Their role in motivation, personality, and development. Psychology Press.

Eisenburg, N. (2000). Emotion, regulation, and moral development. *Annual Review of Psychology, 51*(1), 665–697.

Elliot-Johns, S. E., Booth, D., Rowsell, J., Puig, E., & Paterson, J. (2012). Using student voices to guide instruction. *Voices from the Middle, 19*(3), 25–31.

Epstein, F. (2006). Relationship between low cholesterol and disease. *Annals of the New York Academy of Science, 748*(1), 482–490.

Erdley, C., & Nangle, D. (2001). Children's friendship experiences and psychological adjustment: Theory and research. *New Directions for Child and Adolescent Development, 91*, 5–24.

Ernst, M., Pine, D. S., Hardin, M. (2006). Decision-making and problem-solving in adolescents who deliberately self-harm. *Psychological Medicine 36*, 299–312.

Evans, G. W., & Rosenbaum, J. (2008). Self-regulation and the income-achievement gap. *Early Childhood Research Quarterly, 23*, 504–514.

Fabelo, T., Thompson, M. D., Plotkin, M., Carmichael, D., Marchbanks, M. P., & Booth, E. A. (2011). Breaking schools' rules: A statewide study of how school discipline relates to students' success and juvenile justice involvement. *New York: Council of State Governments Justice Center.*

Faiella, F., & Ricciardi, M. (2015). Gamification and learning: a review of issues and research. *Je-LKS : Journal of e-Learning and Knowledge Society, 11*(3). https://doi.org/10.20368/1971-8829/1072

Fan, R., Varamesh, A., Varol, O., Barron, A., Van De Leemput, I., Scheffer, M., & Bollen, J. (2018). *Does putting your emotions into words make you feel better? Measuring the minute-scale dynamics of emotions from online data.* ArXiv. https://doi.org/10.48550/arXiv.1807.09725

Fried, R., Karmali, S., Irwin, D., Gable, F., & Salmoni, A. (2018). Making the grade: mentors' perspectives of a course-based, smart, healthy campus pilot project for building mental health resiliency through mentorship and physical activity. *International Journal of Evidence Based Coaching and Mentoring, 16*(2), 84–98. https://doi.org/10.24384/000566

Galinsky, A. D., Maddux, W. W., Gilin, D., & White, J. B. (2008). Why it pays to get inside the head of your opponent: The differential effects of perspective-taking and empathy in strategic interactions. *Psychological Science, 19*, 378–384. https://doi.org/10.1111/j.1467-9280.2008.02096.x

Galinsky, A. D., & Moskowitz, G. B. (2000). Perspective-taking: Decreasing stereotype expression, stereotype accessibility, and ingroup favoritism. *Journal of Personality and Social Psychology, 78*, 708–724. https://doi.org/10.1037/0022-3514.78.4.708

Gallant, S. N. (2016). Review article: Mindfulness meditation practice and executive functioning: Breaking down the benefit. *Consciousness And Cognition, 40*, 116–130. https://doi.org/10.1016/j.concog.2016.01.005

Gallardo, L., Barrasa, A., & Guevara-Viejo, F. (2016). Positive peer relationships and academic achievement across early and midadolescence. *Social Behavior and Personality: An International Journal, 44*(10), 1637–1648. https://doi.org/10.2224/sbp.2016.44.10.1637

Gendron, B. P., Williams, K. R., & Guerra, N. G. (2011). An analysis of bullying among students within schools: Estimating the effects of individual normative beliefs, self-esteem and school climate. *Journal of School Violence, 10*(2), 150–164. https://doi.org/10.1080/15388220.2010.539166

Gifford-Smith, M. E., & Brownell, C. A. (2003). Childhood peer relationships: Social acceptance, friendships, and peer networks. *Journal of School Psychology, 41*, 235–284.

Goleman, D. (1995). *Emotional Intelligence.* Bantam Books.

Goubert, L., & Trompetter, H. (2017). Towards a science and practice of resilience in the face of pain. *European Journal of Pain, 21*, 1301–1315. https://doi.org/10.1002/ejp.1062

Green, J. H., Passarelli, R. E., Smith, M. K., Wagers, K., Kalomiris, A. E., & Scott, M. N. (2019). A study of an adapted social–emotional learning: Small group curriculum in a school setting. *Psychology in the Schools, 56*(1), 109–125. https://doi.org/10.1002/pits.22180

Gullo, G., Capatosto, K., & Staats, C. (2019). *Implicit bias in schools: a practitioner's guide*. Routledge.

Gupta, R., Koscik, T. R., Bechara, A., & Tranel, D. (2011). The amygdala and decision-making. *Neuropsychologia, 49*(4), 760–766. https://doi.org/10.1016/j.neuropsychologia.2010.09.029

Hagger, M., Hardcastle, S., Chater, A., Mallett, C., Pal, S., & Chatzisarantis, N. (2014). Autonomous and controlled motivational regulations for multiple health-related behaviors: between- and within-participants analyses. *Health Psychology and Behavioral Medicine: An Open Access Journal, 2*(1), 565–601. https://doi.org/10.1080/21642850.2014.912945

Han, H., & Johnson, S. D. (2012). Relationship between students' emotional intelligence, social bond, and interactions in online learning. *Educational Technology & Society, 15*(1), 78–89.

Hardy, S., Dollahite, D., Johnson, N., & Christensen, J. (2015). Adolescent motivations to engage in pro-social behaviors and abstain from health-risk behaviors: A self-determination theory approach. *Journal of Personality, 83*(5), 479–490. https://doi.org/10.1111/jopy.12123

Harvard Health Publishing. (2006). *Anger: Heartbreaking at any age*. Harvard Health Publishing. Retrieved from https://www.health.harvard.edu/heart-health/anger-heartbreaking-at-any-age

Harvard Health Publishing. (2017). *How depression affects your thinking skills*. Harvard Health Publishing. Retrieved from https://www.health.harvard.edu/depression/how-depression-affects-your-thinking-skills

Hawker, D., & Boulton, M. (2000). Twenty years' research on peer victimization and psychosocial maladjustment: A meta-analytic review of cross-sectional studies. *The Journal of Child Psychology and Psychiatry and Allied Disciplines, 41*(4), 441–455.

Hawley, P., Little, T., & Card, N. (2007). The allure of a mean friend: Relationship quality and processes of aggressive adolescents with pro-social skills. *International Journal of Behavioral Development, 31*(2), 170–180. https://doi.org/10.1177/0165025407074630

Hefner, J., & Eisenberg, D. (2009). Social support and mental health among college students. *American Journal of Orthopsychiatry, 79*, 491–499. https://doi.org/10.1037/a0016918

Himmelstein, K. W., Bruckner, H. (2011). Criminal-justice and school sanctions against non-heterosexual youth: A national longitudinal study. *Pediatrics, 127*, 49–57.

Humphrey, N., Lendrum, A., Wigelsworth, M., & Kalambouka, A. (2009). Implementation of primary social and emotional aspects of learning small group work: A qualitative study. *Pastoral Care in Education, 27*(3), 219–239.

Hunter, M. (2011). Perpetual self conflict: self awareness as a key to our ethical drive, personal mastery, and perception of entrepreneurial opportunities. *Contemporary Readings in Law and Social Justice, 3*(2), 96.

Iannucci, B. (2013). Emotional Intelligence: A Quantitative Study of the Relationship Among Academic Success Factors and Emotional Intelligence. ProQuest Dissertations Publishing. Retrieved from https://search.proquest.com/docview/1448579431

Jolliffe, D., & Farrington, D. (2006). Examining the relationship between low empathy and bullying. *Aggressive Behavior, 32*(6), 540–550. https://doi.org/10.1002/ab.20154

Jones, D. E., Greenberg, M., & Crowley, M. (2015). Early social-emotional functioning and public health: The relationship between kindergarten social competence and future wellness. *American Journal of Public Health, 105*(11), 2283–2290. https://doi.org/10.2105/ajph.2015.302630

Kapp, K. M. (2007). Tools and techniques for transferring know-how from boomers to gamers. *Global Business and Organizational Excellence, 26*(5), 22–37.

Kim, J., & Cicchetti, D. (2010). Longitudinal pathways linking child maltreatment, emotion regulation, peer relations, and psychopathology. *Journal of Child Psychology and Psychiatry, 51*(6), 706–716. https://doi.org/10.1111/j.1469-7610.2009.02202.x

King, K., Lengua, L., & Monahan, K. (2013). Individual differences in the development of self-regulation during pre-adolescence: Connections to context and adjustment. *Journal of Abnormal Child Psychology, 41*(1), 57–69. https://doi.org/10.1007/s10802-012-9665-0

Kiss, M., Kotsis, A., & Kun, A. I. (2014). The relationship between intelligence, emotional intelligence, personality styles and academic success. *Business Education & Accreditation, 6*(2), 23–34.

Koegel, L. l., Navab, A., Ashbaugh, K., & Koegel, R. L. (2016). Using reframing to reduce negative statements in social conversation for adults with Autism Spectrum Disorder. *Journal Of Positive Behavior Interventions, 18*(3), 133–144.

Kurdi, V., Archambault, I., Briere, F., & Turgeon, L. (2017). Need-supportive teaching practices and student-perceived need fulfillment in low socioeconomic status elementary schools: The moderating effect of anxiety and academic achievement. *Learning and Individual Differences, 65*, 218–229.

Lachner, A., Ly, K.-T., & Nuckles, M. (2018). Providing written or oral explanations? Different effects of the modality of explaining on students' conceptual learning and transfer. *Journal of Experimental Education, 86*, 344–361. https://doi.org/10.1080/00220973.2017.1363691

Lambert, N. M., Fincham, F. D., & Stillman, T. F. (2012). Gratitude and depressive symptoms: The role of positive reframing and positive emotion. *Cognition & Emotion, 26*, 615–633. https://doi.org/10.1080/02699931.2011.595393

Landers, R. N. (2014). Developing a theory of gamified learning: Linking serious games and gamification of learning. *Simulation & Gaming, 45*(6), 752–768. https://doi.org/10.1177/1046878114563660

Laursen, E., Moore, L., Yazdgerdi, S., & Milberger, K. (2013). Building empathy and social mastery in students with autism. *Reclaiming Children and Youth, 22*(3), 19–22.

Libbrecht, N., Lievens, F., Carette, B., & Cote, S. (2014). Emotional intelligence predicts success in medical school. *Emotion, 14*(1), 64–73.

Lieberman, M. D., Inagaki, T. K., Tabibnia, G., and Crockett, M. J. (2011). Subjective responses to emotional stimuli during labeling, reappraisal, and distraction. *Emotion 11*, 468–480. https://doi.org/10.1037/a0023503

Liem, G. D., & Martin, A. J. (2011). Peer relationships and adolescents' academic and non-academic outcomes: Same-sex and opposite-sex peer effects and the mediating role of school engagement. *British Journal of Educational Psychology, 81*(2), 183–206. https://doi.org/10.1111/j.2044-8279.2010.02013.x

Losen, D., & Gillespie, J. (2012). *Opportunities Suspended: The Disparate Impact of Disciplinary Exclusion from School.* The Civil Rights Project. https://files.eric.ed.gov/fulltext/ED534178.pdf

Lough, E., Hanley, M., Rodgers, J., South, M., Kirk, H., Kennedy, D., & Riby, D. D. (2015). Violations of personal space in young people with Autism Spectrum Disorders and Williams Syndrome: Insights from the social responsiveness scale. *Journal Of Autism & Developmental Disorders, 45*(12), 4101–4108.

Lucian, M. (2017). The effects of teacher-student relationships on academic achievement-a college survey. *Annals of Philosophy, Social and Human Disciplines, 1*, 39–51.

Luciana, M. (2013). Adolescent brain development in normality and psychopathology. *Development and Psychopathology, 25*, 1325–1345. https://doi.org/10.1017/S0954579413000643

MacLeod, S., Musich, S., Hawkins, K., Alsgaard, K., & Wicker, E. (2016). The impact of resilience among older adults. *Geriatric Nursing, 37*(4), 266–272. https://doi.org/10.1016/j.gerinurse.2016.02.014

Magpili, N. C., & Pazos, P. (2018). Self-managing team performance: A systematic review of multilevel input factors. *Small Group Research, 49*(1), 3–33. https://doi.org/10.1177/1046496417710500

Mantzios, M., & Giannou, K. (2018). When did coloring books become mindful? Exploring the effectiveness of a novel method of mindfulness-guided instructions for coloring books to increase mindfulness and decrease anxiety. *Front. Psychol, 9*, 56. https://doi.org/10.3389/fpsyg.2018.00056

Marzano, R. J., Marzano, J. S., & Pickering, D. (2003). *Classroom management that works: Research-based strategies for every teacher.* Association for Supervision and Curriculum Development.

McCallie, M., Blum, C., & Hood, C. (2006). Progressive muscle relaxation. *Journal of Human Behavior in the Social Environment, 13*(3), 51–66.

McClelland, M. M., Ponitz, C. C., Messersmith, E., & Tominey, S. (2010). Self-regulation: The integration of cognition and emotion. In R. M. Lerner & W. F. Overton (Eds.), *The handbook of life-span development (1)*(509–553). Wiley.

Miller, C. F., Kochel, K. P., Wheeler, L. A., Updegraff, K. A., Fabes, R. A., Martin, C. L., & Hanish, L. D. (2017). The efficacy of a relationship building intervention in 5th grade. *Journal of School Psychology, 61*, 75–88. https://doi.org/10.1016/j.jsp.2017.01.002

Modecki, K., Zimmer-Gembeck, M., & Guerra, N. (2017). Emotion regulation, coping, and decision-making: Three linked skills for preventing externalizing problems in adolescence. *Child Development, 88*(2), 417–426. https://doi.org/10.1111/cdev.12734

Moeller, J., Brackett, M. A., Ivcevic, Z., & White, A. E. (2020). High school students' feelings: Discoveries from a large national survey and an experience sampling study. *Learning and Instruction, 66*. https://doi.org/10.1016/j.learninstruc.2019.101301

Moffitt, T., Arseneault, L., Belsky, D., Dickson, N., Hancox, R., Harrington, H., Houts, R., Poulton, R., Roberts, B., Ross, S., Sears, M., Thomson, W. M., & Caspi, A. (2011). A gradient of childhood self-control predicts health, wealth, and public safety. *Proceedings of the National Academy of Sciences of the United States of America, 108*(7), 2693–2698.

Moore, S. A., Varra, A. A., Michael, S. T., Simpson, T. L. (2010). Stress-related growth, positive reframing, and emotional processing in the prediction of post-trauma functioning among veterans in mental health treatment. *Psychological Trauma: Theory, Research, Practice, and Policy, 2*, 93–96. https://doi.org/10.1037/a0018975

Morisano, D., Hirsh, J., Peterson, J., Pihl, R., & Shore, B. (2010). Setting, elaborating, and reflecting on personal goals improves academic performance. *Journal of Applied Psychology, 95*(2), 255–264. https://doi.org/10.1037/a0018478

Nadinloyi, K., Hajloo, N., Garamaleki, N., & Sadeghi, H. (2013). The study efficacy of time management training on increase academic time management of students. *Procedia - Social and Behavioral Sciences, 84*, 134–138. https://doi.org/10.1016/j.sbspro.2013.06.523

The National Institute of Mental Health. (n.d.). *5 Things You Should Know About Stress.* National Institute of Mental Health. https://www.nimh.nih.gov/sites/default/files/documents/health/publications/stress/19-mh-8109-5-things-stress.pdf

Nelson, R. M., & DeBacker, T. K. (2008). Achievement motivation in adolescents: The role of peer climate and best friends. *Journal of Experimental Education, 76*(2), 170–189. https://doi.org/10.3200/JEXE.76.2.170-190

Newman Kingery, J., Erdley, C. A., & Marshall, K. C. (2011). Peer acceptance and friendship as predictors of early adolescents' adjustment across the middle school transition. *Merrill-Palmer Quarterly, 57*, 215–243.

Ng-Knight, T., Shelton, K. H., Riglin, L., Frederickson, N., McManus, I. C., & Rice, F. (2019). 'Best friends forever'? Friendship stability across school transition and associations with mental health and educational attainment. *British Journal of Educational Psychology, 89*(4), 585–599. https://doi.org/10.1111/bjep.12246

Nicol, D., Thomson, A., & Breslin, C. (2013). Rethinking feedback practices in higher education: a peer review perspective. *Assessment & Evaluation in Higher Education, 39*(1), 102–122. https://doi.org/10.1080/02602938.2013.795518

Oblinger, D. (2004). The next generation of educational engagement. *Journal of Interactive Media in Education, 8*(1), 1–18.

Ozbay, F., Johnson, D. C., Dimoulas, E., Morgan, C. A., Charney, D., & Southwick, S. (2007). Social support and resilience to stress: From neurobiology to clinical practice. *Psychiatry (Edgmont), 4*(5), 35–40.

Palmer, V. J., Dowrick, C., & Gunn, J. M. (2014). Mandalas as a visual research method for understanding primary care for depression. *International Journal of Social Research Methodology, 17*, 527–541. https://doi.org/10.1080/13645579.2013.796764

Patel, S. (2017). *Breathing for Life: The Mind-Body Healing Benefits of Pranayama.* Chopra. http://www.chopra.com/articles/breathing-for-life-the-mind-body-healing-benefits-of-pranayama

Payer, D. E., Baicy, K., Lieberman, M. D., London, E. D. (2012). Overlapping neural substrates between intentional and incidental down-regulation of negative emotions. *Emotion, 12*(2), 229–235. https://doi.org/10.1037/a0027421

Perrotta, C., Featherstone, G., Aston, H. and Houghton, E. (2013). Game-based Learning: Latest Evidence and Future Directions (NFER Research Programme: Innovation in Education). Slough: NFER.

Pezzino, M. (2018). Online assessment, adaptive feedback and the importance of visual learning for students. The advantages, with a few caveats, of using MapleTA. *International Review of Economic Education, 28*, 11–28. https://doi.org/10.1016/j.iree.2018.03.002

Pintrich, P. R. (2000). The role of goal orientation in self-regulated learning. In M. Boekaerts, P. R. Pintrich, & M. Zeidner (Eds.), *Handbook of self-regulation* (452–502). Academic Press.

Porges, S. (2019). Survivors are blamed because they don't fight;" The psychiatry professor on the polyvagal theory he developed to understand our reactions to trauma. *The Observer.* https://www.theguardian.com/society/2019/jun/02/stephen-porges-interview-survivors-are-blamed-polyvagal-theory-fight-flight-psychiatry-ace.

Poteat, V. P., Scheer, J. R., Chong, E. S. K. (2015). Sexual orientation-based disparities in school and juvenile justice discipline: A multiple group comparison of contributing factors. *Journal of Educational Psychology, 108*, 229–241.

Ramnani, N., & Owen, A. M. (2004). Anterior prefrontal cortex: insights into function from anatomy and neuroimaging. *Nature Reviews Neuroscience, 5*(3), 184–194. https://doi.org/10.1038/nrn1343

Rigby, M., & Taubert, M. (2016). Colouring books for adults on the cancer ward. *BMJ, 352.* https://doi.org/10.1136/bmj.h6795

Robson, M., & Cook, P. (1995). Helping children manage stress. *British Educational Research Journal, 21*(2), 165. https://doi.org/10.1080/0141192950210203

Rothbart, M. K., Ahadi, S. A., & Evans, D. E. (2000). Temperament and personality: origins and outcomes. *Journal of Personality and Social Psychology, 78*, 122–135.

Salovey, P., & Mayer, J. D. (1990). Emotional Intelligence. *Imagination, Cognition, and Personality, 9*, 185–211.

Sarine, L. (2012). Regulating the social pollution of systemic discrimination caused by implicit bias. *California Law Review, 100*(5), 1359–1399. https://doi.org/10.15779/Z387221

Schulze, R., & Roberts, R. D. (2005). *Emotional intelligence: an international handbook.* Cambridge: Hogrefe.

Shih, M., Wang, E., Trahan Bucher, A., & Stotzer, R. (2009). Perspective taking: reducing prejudice towards general outgroups and specific individuals. *Group Processes & Intergroup Relations, 12*(5), 565–577. https://doi.org/10.1177/1368430209337463

Sinclair, L., & Kunda, Z. (1999). Reactions to a black professional: Motivated inhibition and activation of conflicting stereotypes. *Journal of Personality and Social Psychology, 77*(5), 885–904. https://doi.org/10.1037/0022-3514.77.5.885

Siqueira, C., Valiengo, L., Carvalho, A., Santos-Silva, P., Missio, G., De Sousa, R., Di Natale, G., Wanger, G., Moreno, R., Machado-Vieira, R., Buchowski, M. (2016). Antidepressant efficacy of adjunctive aerobic activity and associated biomarkers in major depression: A 4-week, randomized, single-blind, controlled clinical trial. *PloS One, 11*(5). https://doi.org/10.1371/journal.pone.0154195

Smit, J. (2017). The role of empathy in the knowledge building of eighth grade girls as they reflect on their experiences with literature. *Scientific Study Of Literature, 6*(1), 59. https://doi.org/10.1075/ssol.6.1.05smi

Stanton-Chapman, T. S., & Snell, M. E. (2011). Promoting turn-taking skills in preschool children with disabilities: The effects of a peer-based social communication intervention. *Early Childhood Research Quarterly, 26*(3), 303–319.

Taylor, R. D., Oberle, E., Durlak, J. A., & Weissberg, R. P. (2017). Promoting positive youth development through school-based social and emotional learning interventions: A meta-analysis of follow-up effects. *Child Development, 88*(4), 1156–1171. https://doi.org/10.1111/cdev.12864

Thornberg, R. (2008). 'It's not fair!'—Voicing pupils' criticisms of school rules. *Children & Society, 22,* 418–428. https://doi.org/10.1111/j.1099-0860.2007.00121.x

Thornberg, R. (2008). School children's reasoning about school rules. *Research Papers in Education, 23*(1), 37–52. https://doi.org/10.1080/02671520701651029

Tone, E., & Tully, E. (2014). Empathy as a "risky strength": a multilevel examination of empathy and risk for internalizing disorders. *Development and Psychopathology, 26*(4 Pt 2), 1547–1565. https://doi.org/10.1017/S0954579414001199

Trivedi, M. H. (2004). The link between depression and physical symptoms. *Primary care companion to the Journal of clinical psychiatry, 6* (Suppl 1), 12–16.

Uchino, B. N. (2006). Social support and health: A review of physiological processes potentially underlying links to disease outcomes. *Journal of Behavioral Medicine, 29*(4), 377–387. https://doi.org/10.1007/s10865-006-9056-5

Van Der Vennet, R., & Serice, S. (2012) Can Coloring Mandalas Reduce Anxiety? A Replication Study. *Art Therapy, 29,* 87–92.

Véronneau, M. H., Vitaro, F., Brendgen, M., Dishion, T. J., & Tremblay, R. E. (2010). Transactional analysis of the reciprocal links between peer experiences and academic achievement from middle childhood to early adolescence. *Developmental Psychology, 46,* 773–790.

Walters, G., & Espelage, D. (2018). Resurrecting the empathy–bullying relationship with a pro-bullying attitudes mediator: The lazarus effect in mediation research. *Journal of Abnormal Child Psychology, 46*(6), 1229–1239. https://doi.org/10.1007/s10802-017-0355-9

Wang, M., & Eccles, J. (2012). Social support matters: Longitudinal effects of social support on three dimensions of school engagement from middle to high school. *Child Development, 83*(3), 877. https://doi.org/10.1111/j.1467-8624.2012.01745.x

Wentel, K. (1977). Student motivation in middle school: the role of perceived pedagogical caring. *Journal of Educational Psychology, 89*(3), 411–419.

Wentzel, K. R. (2009). Peers and academic functioning at school. In K. H. Rubin, W. M. Bukowski, & B. Laursen (Eds.), *Handbook of peer interactions, relationships, and groups* (531–547). Guilford Press.

Wilder, D., & Shapiro, P. (1989). Role of competition-induced anxiety in limiting the beneficial impact of positive behavior by an out-group member. *Journal of Personality and Social Psychology, 56*(1), 60–69. https://doi.org/10.1037/0022-3514.56.1.60

Yazdi, N., Bigdeli, S., Arabshani, S., & Ghaffarifar, S. (2019). The influence of role-modeling on clinical empathy of medical interns: A qualitative study. *Journal of Advances in Medical Education and Professionalism, 1,* 35.

About the Author

JAIME DOMBROWSKI, PhD, holds degrees in educational psychology and counseling. She is also a licensed mental health counselor, registered play therapist, and a certified school counselor. In addition to serving as a school counselor, she has worked with children and adolescents in community mental health. Dr. Dombrowski currently serves as an SEL Specialist for Florida Virtual School and enjoys researching the most effective strategies to support students in their social-emotional learning journey, as well as grant writing to fund and support SEL efforts.